M000223440

Hell-Bent for Music

Pee Wee King on Boots

Hell-Bent for Music

The Life of Pee Wee King

Wade Hall

THE UNIVERSITY PRESS OF KENTUCKY

Copyright © 1996 by The University Press of Kentucky

Scholarly publisher for the Commonwealth,
serving Bellarmine College, Berea College, Centre
College of Kentucky, Eastern Kentucky University,
The Filson Club, Georgetown College, Kentucky
Historical Society, Kentucky State University,
Morehead State University, Murray State University,
Northern Kentucky University, Transylvania University,
University of Kentucky, University of Louisville,
and Western Kentucky University.

Editorial and Sales Offices: The University Press of Kentucky
663 South Limestone Street, Lexington, KY 40508-4008

Library of Congress Cataloging-in-Publication Data

Hall, Wade H.
    Hell-bent for music : the life of Pee Wee King / Wade Hall.
        p.   cm.
    Includes bibliographical references and index.
    ISBN 0-8131-1959-6 (alk. paper)
        1. King, Pee Wee, 1914-   . 2. Country musicians—United States—
Biography. I. Title.
    ML422.K57H35   1996
    781.642'092—dc20
        [B]   95-41294
                                                                        MN

This book is printed on acid-free recycled paper meeting
the requirements of the American National Standard
for Permanence of Paper for Printed Library Materials.

Manufactured in the United States of America

In Memory of
Joe L. Frank
and the other unsung pioneers
of American country music

Contents

Illustrations follow pages 52 and 164

Preface

PEE WEE KING'S birth on February 18, 1914, into a Milwaukee working-class Polish family named Kuczynski was hardly an indicator that he would grow up to become a pioneer and superstar of country and western music. No one could have foreseen his influence on the direction of American popular music, from country to "crossover" to rock 'n' roll. Who could have predicted that he would help brush off the clods from country music and make it acceptable to a broad spectrum of musical tastes? Surely no one in the Polish-German community of his youth could have dreamed that he would bring to the crude backwoods hillbilly music of the South a professionalism, sophistication, and showmanship that would help pave the way for making it today the most popular form of music in the United States. Who could have envisioned the central role that Frank Kuczynski would play in the American revolution in music that led to the more than 2,200 radio stations that now feature country music and to the annual sales of country recordings approaching two billion dollars? Even Pee Wee King himself is incredulous at the unlikely twists and turns of his remarkable career.

When Pee Wee entered the country music field in the mid-1930s, literally by accident, country was considered hick music that appealed mostly to rural whites in the backcountry of the South. The few educated urban fans of Lulu Belle and Scotty, Gene Autry, Vernon Dahlhart, the Carter Family, and Jimmie Rodgers were secretive and apologetic. As much as any other musician, Pee Wee King made it respectable to like country music.

Pee Wee took the polka and waltz rhythms of his own background, mixed them with the sounds of the big bands of the 1930s and 1940s and flavored it all with the balladry and mood of the western cowboy. Then he brought this amalgam to the hillbilly and folk traditions rooted in places like Louisville, Knoxville, and Nashville.

The result was more than a sum of its ingredients. It was a smooth, listenable, danceable, understandable, up-to-date music with roots and soul. Indeed, the changes that he helped to facilitate have led to a melting pot of waltzes, polkas, ballads, two-steps, and other sounds from Old World traditions with such homegrown strains as blues, jazz, western swing, cowboy songs, and gospel. As this new country music spreads its net ever wider, it has continued to assimilate elements as varied as spicy Cajun sounds and street-smart rap. Moreover, Pee Wee has helped to open up the country stage to a medley of new instruments, including, in the early days, the accordion, the trumpet, and drums.

The backwater country music of my own youth is now American mainstream. In an era when so much music tends to be deafeningly loud and dissonant, with unsingable and incoherent lyrics, country music, with fidelity to its origins, with words that can be understood and tunes that can be sung and remembered, and with content that speaks to common pains and pleasures, has indeed become "the music of America."

For more than sixty years Pee Wee King has been a prime mover in these new and broader dimensions of country music. Unfortunately, he has received but little recognition for the historic contributions he has made. It is time he is acknowledged for his major influence and achievements in breaking new ground in American music as bandleader, performer, and composer. Furthermore, he has served in numerous other capacities, as promoter, manager, booking agent, comedian, emcee, movie performer and producer, merchandiser, as well as a family man and a friend to almost every significant country and western musician of his time. Indeed, if there is one leitmotif that runs through Pee Wee's career, it is his decency, his generosity, and his eagerness to help others in his profession. You will never meet a man more dedicated to his vocation, to his family, or to his country. Pee Wee himself has summed up his attitude toward his profession: "I always tried to get along with everybody. I never meant to hurt anyone. If I did, it was not my intention. I never felt I was competing with anyone. I always thought we were all working in the same profession as coworkers and friends."

Memory is the raw material of art. A book based in large part upon memory, however, requires the verifying and shaping of memory pieces into a coherent whole. That has been my job in putting together this oral biography based principally upon more than thirty hours of taped conversation with Pee Wee King in his home on

Country Lane in Louisville, Kentucky, where he lives with Lydia, his wife of more than fifty years. I wish to thank the Kentucky Oral History Commission for help in getting the interview tapes transcribed, and I wish to express my gratitude to Greg Swem for his painstaking care in the transcription.

In addition, I have read widely in the literature of country music, ranging from recent encyclopedic tomes to vintage souvenir programs. Some of the books that I have found especially rewarding are Chet Hagan's *Grand Ole Opry* (1989), Bob Millard's *Country Music* (1993), Jack Hurst's *Nashville's Grand Ole Opry* (1989), the Country Music Foundation's *Country: The Music and the Musicians* (1988), Paul Hemphill's *The Nashville Sound: Bright Lights and Country Music* (1970), Frye Gaillard's *Watermelon Wine: The Spirit of Country Music* (1978), and Irwin Stambler and Grelun Landon's *Golden Guitars: The Story of Country Music* (1971). I have also read a number of biographies, ranging from Ralph Emery's *Memories* (1991) to Minnie Pearl's *Autobiography* (1980) and Tammy Wynette's *Stand By Your Man* (1979). Furthermore, I have examined hundreds of pieces of sheet music, songbooks, keepsakes, advertisements, trade magazines, fan newsletters, and clippings. From my own collection of country music memorabilia, I have drawn on materials ranging from George D. Hay's thin but seminal *Story of the Grand Ole Opry* (1945) to Minnie Pearl's *Diary* (1953), a collection of her down-home humor that still awakens memories and produces laughs in anyone over fifty with rural roots. Pee Wee also opened up his own extensive professional files to me. Finally, I have spent many, many enjoyable hours listening to vintage and contemporary country music and reliving years long past.

Somewhat like today's country music, therefore, this book is a combination of many materials and sources. Perhaps most important, however, is the fact that I have been listening to country music all my life. Growing up on a farm near Montgomery, Alabama, I was exposed to live country music at nearby school shindigs, political gatherings, church homecomings, and "fiddlers' conventions." On the radio I listened with my family to country music from Montgomery's WSFA and WCOV. If I had been old enough at the time, I could have heard Hank Williams in person as he played in our community schools and honky-tonks in the 1940s. I can still recall the plaintive sounds of "Cold, Cold Heart" and "Lovesick Blues" and the joyful "Jambalaya" played on jukeboxes at local dance halls and cafés. I was a senior at Troy State Teachers College in 1953

when Hank died at twenty-nine, and well do I remember the out-
pouring of grief at his funeral in the city auditorium in Montgomery. I never met Hank Williams or heard him in person. I don't
even recall clearly his radio broadcasts from Montgomery. But I do
recall very vividly his lonesome ballads that came into our backwoods farmhouse from WSM's Grand Ole Opry on Saturday nights.
On our battery-powered radio we could hear Hank, the Solemn Old
Judge, the Duke of Paducah, Roy Acuff, Eddy Arnold, Bill Monroe, Ernest Tubb, and the man and band with the most exotic name
of all, Pee Wee King and His Golden West Cowboys. I never ques-
tioned Pee Wee's credentials as a country musician, but somehow
his music was different from all the others. And I liked it.

Many years later I met Pee Wee in Louisville, where I have
lived for more than thirty years, and where Pee Wee has lived most
of his life since leaving his native state of Wisconsin in 1934. I was
impressed with Pee Wee's honesty and openness and, most of all,
with his memory of and friendships with almost everybody in country
and western music, from Gene Autry to the bright and shining stars
of today. I was surprised to learn that there is no full-length biography of this important pioneer of country music, and I asked him to
work with me on a book about his life and career. He agreed. We
met periodically at his home on Country Lane between February
and May of 1992. Since then I have kept in close contact with him
and Lydia, and they have given me updates on their activities and
the inevitable events of old age, including the deaths of his brother
Gene and his friends Roy Acuff and Ernest Tubb and the incapaci-
tating stroke suffered by Minnie Pearl. Then in the early summer
of 1994 while I was out of town, Pee Wee suffered his second mild
stroke. We agreed that it was therefore urgent that I complete work
on his book. It is finally ready. I hope that Pee Wee is as pleased
with the book I have made out of his life as I am pleased with what
he made of his life by living it. Such good and productive people
seldom pass this way.

Go with me now to a comfortable but unpretentious ranch-
style brick house at 501 Country Lane in Louisville, Kentucky, where
Frank Kuczynski is waiting to welcome and tell you about a remarkable
life and career. He will take you back to a time when "the King"
referred not to a swivel-hipped singer from Tupelo but to a Polish
musician from Milwaukee who came south and became Pee Wee
King.

The View from 501 Country Lane

We want to say Hello
Right through your radio.
We want to say, "How do you do"—
We are happy and hope you are too.
You are the good folks who listen in
Always smilin,' so keep up your chin.
We are the Log Cabin Boys—
Hello, hello, hello.

HELLO, HELLO, HELLO. Friends and neighbors, I'm Pee Wee King, and that used to be our theme song way back in 1935, when I was one of the Log Cabin Boys and we sang on WHAS radio right here in Louisville, Kentucky. But a lot of time has passed since then—some sixty years, in fact—and I'm in the basement study of my home on Country Lane, within arm's reach of my books, sheet music, recordings, songbooks, souvenir programs, old copies of *Variety*, and all the other bits and pieces of my life and career as a country and western musician.

Through the years I've kept scrapbooks and files about my career and personal life. I have dozens of photographs squirreled away. I am surrounded by pictures—in my memory and in these albums and on the walls. Here is a picture of me in 1917 when I was three years old and got my first bicycle. It was taken at our home in Milwaukee at Sixth and Beecher Streets next to a tavern. And here is the concertina I first played. On the walls are photographs of me

1

with Loretta Lynn, Eddy Arnold, Minnie Pearl, Roy Acuff, Marty
Robbins, Hank Williams, and someone I must never forget, Patti
Page, whose recording of "The Tennessee Waltz" made it one of
the most popular songs of all time. I also have pictures of people in
other fields that I've known and worked with, from Mickey Mantle
and Colonel Harlan Sanders of Kentucky Fried Chicken to Eddie
Cantor, Bob Hope, Perry Como, and Spike Jones. Here is even a
picture of me with Elvis himself. Dr. Wade Hall of Bellarmine College
believes that we'll have enough—if my memory proves good enough—
to make a book. He's taking down my reminiscences as I talk. My
wife Lydia is close by and she will correct me—boy, will she correct
me!—if I make a mistake. When my memory fails me, as it's beginning to do now with some regularity, I'll jog it with these souvenirs
as I ramble through the past. I'm always writing myself notes so I
won't forget things, and I'll have them to guide me. I sometimes
forget my hat at Shoney's and leave my coat at church, but I don't
believe I'll ever forget my life as a country musician.

First, let me complete our tour of my office. Over here is the
exercise bicycle I had to get after my first stroke in July of 1978.
On the wall above my desk is the swordfish I caught many years
ago in Florida and had mounted. On the right wall is the set of guns
I used as props for one of my television shows back in the 1950s.
All of these memorabilia are constant reminders of who I am and
where I've been.

Now, I'll make a confession. I'm not what you'd expect of a
country musician. I'm not from Anglo-Scotch-Irish stock. I'm not
from the South. I don't play the fiddle professionally. When the Golden
West Cowboys was selected as the nation's number one western band
in the 1950s, Bob Wills, who was from Texas and played the fiddle,
said to me, "Pee Wee, how in the hell can a Polish boy from Wisconsin play the accordion, write 'The Tennessee Waltz,' be a star
on the Grand Ole Opry, and lead the country's most popular western swing band? It just doesn't add up." I said, "Bob, all you got to
do is please the people and sell records."

I've never tried to hide my background or make up some story
about being born in a shack in the middle of a cotton field. I've
always been up front about having grown up in Milwaukee and in
the Polish communities around the frigid shores of Green Bay about

as far from the Smokey Mountains and the Suwannee River as you can get. I was never ashamed of my birth name. I changed it for convenience. I've always been proud of my Polish and Austrian ancestry and the fact that I was baptized Frank Julius Anthony Kuczynski. Polish sausage may not be as American as apple pie, but don't forget that there are millions of Americans of Polish descent in this country. We have dozens of towns and counties named Pulaski after a Polish general who died in the American Revolution. Poles have done their share in the building of this country.

I've tried to make my own contribution as a productive citizen. I don't believe I have anything to hide. I've never been arrested. I've never gotten into trouble with the law. I'm just an ordinary family man who happened to make his living as a country and western musician.

In order to become a popular musician, I simply had to remold myself when I came south as a country entertainer. That's show business. I came from Wisconsin, but so did a lot of other people who went on to make a name for themselves in entertainment—people like Liberace, Fred MacMurray, Alfred Lunt, Pat O'Brien, Spencer Tracy, Hildegarde, Woody Herman, and even Wayne King, whose real name, by the way, was Krolikowski.

By the time was I was twenty, I knew I was hell-bent for music. There wasn't anything else that I wanted to do. Nothing else even came close. When I had the opportunity to come south and play in a country music band, I took it. Most of the music I played in Wisconsin was polkas and waltzes because that's what the people wanted, but I was certainly no stranger to country music. It was already popular in many parts of the Midwest when I was a boy. I had even performed on the "Badger State Barn Dance" in Milwaukee; then when I came down to Kentucky and Tennessee, I realized that I was close to the center of country music, and so I adapted to it.

I learned when I was starting out as a high school bandleader that you have to please the people or you'll have no audience and no income. I have always thought of myself first and foremost as an entertainer who could change moods, tempos, styles, costumes, jokes, and anything else when it was necessary to entertain an audience. I have tried to be versatile. I'm known for being an accordionist, but that's just one side of me. Someone said to me recently, "Pee Wee, you're a classic entertainer. You've been a bandleader, a songwriter, a movie star, a television personality. You have a lot of talents. You can do anything." Well, I can't do *anything*, but I do know that in order to survive in the music business you have to wear a lot of different hats.

The other day I was talking with a young disc jockey on a country music radio station, and I mentioned some of my old music buddies long departed like Cowboy Copas and Hawkshaw Hawkins. He said, "I never heard of them. They must have been before my time. I am of the Garth Brooks and Clint Black generation." He was new on the job, so maybe we can forgive his ignorance. He should, however, learn about the people of my generation and before who paved the way for the people of his generation. Maybe he'll realize that in order to understand and appreciate Clint Black and Garth Brooks, he'll have to go back to Cowboy Copas and Hawkshaw Hawkins. They made the way easier for country music stars today. I've lived through most of that history, and I can tell you it was a rough way to make a living. Some people still can't understand why I chose a profession without any kind of guaranteed salary or job security. It never bothered me, not even after I got married and had a family. I never worried about starving.

Physically, I'm a fairly small man, not quite five feet and seven inches tall. When I was in good shape, I tried to keep my weight to around 135 pounds. I have blue eyes. and when I was younger my hair was brown. It has now turned completely silver. I had a second mild stroke in the summer of 1994, but when I follow my doctor's orders and do what Lydia tells me, I feel all right. I've had a long life already, and it's been a good life. I have no complaints at all. The Good Lord has been good to me. He's let me do what I wanted to do. I wanted to be a musician who could make people feel good with my music. I wanted to find what I thought was the top of my career. When I believed I had found it, I stopped striving and searching and enjoyed it. That doesn't mean I have retired from life itself. I'll never do that. I'm now busy in ways that don't put too much stress on me.

Not long ago I sat on my glasses and broke them. I went to my eye doctor, and he said, "What the hell, Pee Wee? You don't wear glasses on your rear end, do you?" I said, "Yeah, I do. I want to see what I'm backing into!" What I'm now proposing to do is to back into my life with my glasses on and see what I can remember—the good times, the not-so-good times, the highlights, the low lights. I will try to recall the people and the events that have given my life shape and meaning. I will try to remember them accurately but compassionately.

I don't have a lot of formal education, and I know I don't always speak very good English. Sometimes the scripts we used on radio and television would have words for me to speak that weren't in my vocabulary, and I'd scratch them out. It would have been awkward and funny if I'd tried to use words I didn't know. Dr. Hall will have to do some tinkering with the "script" for this book to make it readable, but he has assured me that this book we are making will be in my voice and in my words. Yes, I want the glasses that I wear in this memoir to be clear and straight because I don't want to distort and falsify. If I make errors, I hope you will forgive them as the mistakes of an old but well-intentioned man.

The Country
of the North

IN MANY WAYS, MY LIFE has been a good example of the American Dream. I'll tell you why. To begin, I was born on February 18, 1914, when my parents were living on South Fifth Street on the southside of Milwaukee. It's an area that is now almost completely commercial. Like most children of my generation, I was born at home, though I think my mother had a doctor with her. I was the oldest of four children born to John and Helen (Mielczarek) Kuczynski in a home where Polish was the common language. My parents were both born in this country, but all four of my grandparents came from Europe, three of them from Poland and my dad's father from Austria. My father wasn't much interested in genealogy, and when I would ask any of my grandparents about their lives in the old country, they would never say much. I do remember that one of them said, "Frankie, be glad you were born in the United States. We're glad we had the opportunity to come here." About all I could learn was that they were poor, landless people who came to America willing to exchange hard work for a better life.

My parents met when they were all living in northern Wisconsin on farms that their families had homesteaded. Years before they had heard that the government was giving away land up north in the Green Bay area to people who would move there and work it. Grandpa Mielczarek moved his family from Chicago, where Mom was born, up near Sobieski and homesteaded 87 acres. My dad's people moved his family from Reading, Pennsylvania, where Pop was born, to Little Suamico, named after a river that flows nearby. They already had relatives from their little Polish village in the old country that had settled there. The whole area was filled with Polish immigrants set down in the Wisconsin wilderness. Grandpa Kuczynski homesteaded 120 acres, then added another 80. He must have felt like a landed aristocrat with all that land. It was probably the first time that anyone on either side of the family had ever been a landowner, and you know it must have made them feel proud. At last, they were true Americans with land to prove it!

My dad's parents raised seven children and lived out their lives on the farm. Like me, Pop was the oldest child. Then came Walter, followed by a girl named Helen who died young. Helen was also my mother's name, and I was shocked as a boy when I saw her name, Helen Kuczynski, on my dead aunt's tombstone. "My mother's not dead," I screamed. "She's still living. Why is her name on this grave?" After Helen came Uncle Tony and Aunt Pearl and Aunt Anna. I had an Aunt Anna on both sides of the family. The last member of Pop's family was Carrie, the seventh one and the baby.

Mom's parents had five girls and two boys. She was the oldest, followed by Anna, Marie, Lottie, and Stella. Her brothers were Tony and Vic. One day after the oldest children got up some size, Grandpa Mielczarek abandoned the family, and my grandmother had to take over the farm and support the children. She used to say that he was a stubborn, ill-natured man, especially in the winter when he couldn't get outside to work. I think he must have run away in the dead of winter, though he didn't seem to be a bad man. He had a good reputation in the community and once served as a school trustee. All I know is that one day after an argument with my grandmother, he packed his bags and disappeared. Nobody knew where he had gone for a long time. Finally, he notified them that he had bought a bean farm near Dunkirk, New York, and the family went up to see him on the train. He never returned to my grandmother, at least not while they were alive. They were finally united in death and are buried next to each other in the church cemetery in Sobieski.

After Mom got grown she moved to Chicago and worked for a while as a seamstress, then moved back to Sobieski. She and Pop met at St. John's Catholic Church, and they hit it off right away. He was tall, looked a bit like John Wayne, had a good sense of humor, and he played in a polka band. He operated a taxi service and would meet people at the train station and drive them by horse and buggy to the hotel or their home. If there was snow and ice on the ground, he would take them on his sled. Mom was working as a maid and waitress in the little hotel, and she could see Pop whenever he made a delivery there. They courted for a few months, then got married and moved to Milwaukee.

In Milwaukee Pop worked in a tanning factory where they took raw hides and processed them into leather pieces that could be made into shoes and gloves. Two of my aunts, Marie and Anna, worked in the Friedosterman Glove Factory about a block away. Pop and his men didn't do any killing at the tannery. They bought all their hides from the slaughterhouses. As a farm boy, Pop had grown up learning a lot about hides and how they should be treated and processed and baled for leather working. He was a steady, dependable worker and was soon made a supervisor. Several Mexicans worked under him. Pop also had another job. He kept bar in a tavern in exchange for free rent in the apartment on the second floor. After we moved to a house on another street, I'd walk by the tavern with my school chums and brag, "Here is where we used to live, right above that bar." I thought living above a tavern would impress my little friends, and I think it did.

Pop didn't make much money at any of his jobs, but he had one luxury that he took a lot of pride in. That was his old Chrysler, which was as big as a small bus and was the most comfortable car I ever rode in. He made a little extra money by organizing a car pool and transporting other tannery workers to the factory. Pop kept his car clean and sparkling. He would wash it out on the street, and I'd sit on the front porch and guard it to keep anybody from smearing or scratching it. That was one classy car! And to this day, the Chrysler is my car of choice. I have one parked outside in the driveway now. I've spent a lot of my life on the road, and the Chrysler is especially good on long trips. It's comfortable, dependable, and easy to drive. Weary show business people appreciate those qualities when they have to drive hundreds of miles between performances.

Mom was a little woman about a half foot shorter than Pop. You could never catch her idle. She was always busy doing something. She loved to knit, and she mended all the family clothes. When we had girl boarders, she'd mend their dresses too. If she wasn't repairing somebody's clothing or cleaning the house, she was cooking something to eat. As the oldest girl in her family, it had been her responsibility to put food on the table. She learned to be a good cook long before she married. Man, I can still taste in memory all those good Polish dishes she fixed for us: veal chops, stuffed fish, cabbage rolls, sauerkraut, beet relish, mushrooms in sour cream, pickled pickerel, buckwheat and raisin pudding. It makes my mouth water just to think of that good food. She even taught me how to make homemade noodles, the big thick ones for Polish chicken soup. That was a meal by itself!

One of her specialties was a Polish dumpling called pierogas. She started with a flat piece of dough, which she filled with cabbage or with some kind of fruit and then folded over and sealed. Then she dipped them in hot water and cooked them for several minutes and dropped them in hot grease to brown. The last step was to bake them in the oven for a few minutes. Man oh man, they were something else! One time she was on a radio program with one of my disc jockey friends in Wisconsin, and he said, "Folks, I want to tell you something about this lady. Helen Kuczynski invited me to supper at her home last Sunday night, and I mean this woman should get a blue ribbon for making the best pierogas I ever ate." While they were still on the air, he began getting a ton of calls from people wanting her recipe, so he said, "Well, Helen, what do we do?" She said, "I guess I'll just have to give out my recipe right now." So she told her recipe, and for months she heard from people all over Wisconsin complimenting her on her pierogas. I'll bet there are still people up there using her recipe.

Even though my parents didn't have much formal schooling—not more than two or three grades—they could read and write very well. Mom wrote me letters all her life, but you couldn't get Pop to write if his life had depended on it. I have the last letter Mom wrote me shortly before she died in 1967. Polish was their first language, but they spoke some broken English. We used Polish at home, and it was the language we used in speaking with all my grandparents. Speaking Polish was as natural to me when I was a boy as speaking English. I've lost most of my Polish now, but I was bilingual until I left home. I can still read it pretty well. When I first moved to Louisville, I subscribed to a Polish newspaper from Milwaukee. I've not had many people to speak Polish with since I left Wisconsin. As the young people began leaving the rural Polish communities and moving to the city, they left behind a lot of their culture, including their language.

Many of my uncles and aunts and cousins from the country came to stay with us in Milwaukee until they could find good jobs and get on their feet. One time we had living with us Mom's sister Anna, Pop's sisters Pearl, Anna, and Carrie, and a cousin, Adam Drobeck. I don't know how we fitted so many people into our small house. The air was filled with the jabber of English and Polish words, but most of us younger people thought Polish was old-fashioned and backward, and we used it only when we had to.

At the same time, our neighborhoods in Milwaukee tended to be tightly knit around ethnic churches, schools, and taverns. Everybody knew everybody else, and we didn't have much crime. It was unusual when we had an act of violence or a theft or a robbery. But one of my first memories is tied to a crime. I was three and my parents had bought me my first tricycle. I have a photograph of my Uncle Kelly in his military uniform with Mom standing next to him and me on my tricycle. He and Mom's sister Aunt Anna got married a few days after the picture was taken. We were living at that time above the tavern, and the tricycle was my birthday present. I loved that tricycle. It was hard for Mom to get me to come in and leave it parked under the steps that led to our apartment. It seemed to be a safe place because it was where Pop stored all his tools and yard equipment. For a week or two, everything was fine. It was always waiting there for me when I went down every morning to go for a ride on the sidewalk. I couldn't imagine anything in this world any prettier or more valuable than that bike. In another photograph that I still have, Mom is teaching me how to ride it on the sidewalk in front of our tavern apartment. It was the first real possession I ever had.

Then one day I went down to take my bike out, and it was gone! Somebody had stolen it! I couldn't believe it! We searched all up and down the streets and alleys and yards and garages, but we never found it. I was heartsick. To think that my parents who had so little money had spent so much and bought me that beautiful bike, and now it was gone forever. Stolen! I didn't think I would ever get over that great loss. I know I was too young then to understand fully what it meant. But I think that deep down in my instincts I was crushed not only because I had lost my cherished bike but because I knew for the first time that there were people in the world who would stoop low enough to steal a poor kid's only toy.

Fortunately, the pains of youth don't last forever, and I eventually recovered. I had a little baby sister named Irene to help look after. She was born two years after me, and four years later Irvin, who was called Max by the family, was born. Then brother Gene, who died in 1994, was born in 1926.

Our little apartment had become too small for us; and when I was about eight, we moved to 901 Windlake Avenue. The street was named after a nearby lake that the city had filled in. We lived in an ordinary frame house—one that you would see in any blue-collar neighborhood—but for the first time in my life I was living in a whole house and not just the top floor of a tavern. The house was built on a little rise with concrete steps leading from the sidewalk up the yard to a set of wooden steps that went up to the front porch. The house is still standing and looks about the same as it did when we lived there, except there's an auto body shop a couple of doors down. About a block away now is the Kosciusko Middle School, which was named for another Polish patriot who fought in the American Revolution. We had three bedrooms, one downstairs and two on the second floor. Later on, Pop added a bedroom for Mom's sister Anna, who lived with us until she married Uncle Kelly. Downstairs we had a dining room that we used like a den. Pop called it his music room because it was where he played his concertina. We also had a big basement where we'd have parties and family get-togethers. Relatives would visit for Sunday dinner and afterwards Pop would get out his concertina and play. Soon everybody would be dancing and having a good time. That's a tradition I've continued here in my basement, where I've had many, many parties for my family and for members of my band.

Our house was comfortable, but with a family of six plus an extended family, our living space was at a premium. At one time I was sleeping on a small homemade bed about the size of a cot. We didn't have room for pets either, and we never had a dog or cat. We didn't really have a garden, but Mom usually found room somewhere for a few peppers and herbs, which she used for seasoning. Her special pride was her flowers. In a very small area she managed to grow the most beautiful flowers in the neighborhood. She could plant a broomstick in the ground and it would grow. Women would walk by our house just to see her flowers. They'd say, "Now Helen, what kind of flower is this one? And that beautiful red bush? Where did you get such a pretty red rose?" Mom grew tulips, lilacs, jonquils, and many other kinds of flowers, but roses were her favorite. She had rose bushes all over the place. Her little yard was a blaze of reds and pinks and yellows when they were all in bloom.

Just about everything we needed was available in our neighborhood or close by. Milwaukee was a big city in the 1920s when I was growing up, more than 200,000 people, but we didn't need to go out much into the larger city. As I got older we'd sometimes go to a movie downtown, but most of our life was lived close to Windlake Avenue. It was an exciting place and time to grow up. We were within a mile of Lake Michigan, and I would wake up in the morning to the sound of foghorns.

We seldom left town except to see relatives in Chicago or to visit my four grandparents who still lived on their farms near Green Bay. We tried to see them several times a year. I especially liked the early spring trips to the farms, when most of the snow and ice had melted and it was easier to get around. I knew we'd have fresh yard-raised chicken when we got there. Grandmother Kuczynski would select one of her spring fryers, hold its head down on the chopping block, go whack! with a little chop-ax, and dip it in boiling water to get the feathers off. Then she'd cut it open, clean out the insides, cut it up, and fry the pieces in a deep skillet of oil. I always looked forward to her plates full of fried spring chicken. Sometimes, Mom would help by twisting off their necks, but I always found it easier to chop off their heads like my grandmother.

I also tried to help my grandfather slaughter his hogs. He showed me how to hit the hog's heart with a long dagger from the side. Then we put him in boiling water and scraped off the hair from the hide. We cut the insides out and saved the intestines to use in making Polish sausage. I thought the intestine was the secret ingredient that made them taste so good. Many years later when I told Pop I was moving to the South, he laughed and said, "Frankie, you'll have to learn to eat hog guts they call chitlins, but I don't believe you can ever eat that stuff." I laughed and said, "Pop, I think I've had pretty good practice with Polish sausage. I think I can eat chitlins too." Boy, was I wrong!

One time we were doing a show in Paris, Tennessee, and next door to the theater was a restaurant that advertised chitlins. I said to my manager, Mr. Joe L. Frank, "Now what exactly are chitlins?" He was from Alabama and knew all about them. "Chitlins," he said, "are pieces of a pig's small intestines that have been cleaned, soaked for a few hours, then boiled for a few minutes, dipped in batter, and fried in deep fat. And they're a lot better than Polish sausage! I'll get you some if you'll try them." I said, "Sure, I will. When you're in Rome you should eat like the Romans. If they're better than Polish sausage, I know I'll like them." So during the break in our show, he brought over a plate of some white-looking meat. It didn't look very appetizing, but I know looks can be deceiving, so I cut off a piece and chewed on it for a while. Then I chewed on it for another while. And another while. Finally, I said, "I'm sorry, Mr. Frank. These chitlins just don't seem to want to cooperate. I've done all I can, but if I try to swallow them, I know I'll choke." So I deposited my mouthful of chitlins in a napkin as properly as I could and gave up on that Southern delicacy. I'm sure I'm missing a rare treat, but I've not tried chitlins since. It must be a taste you have to acquire with your mother's milk. I'll take a piece of my grandfather's Polish sausage any day!

As I got older I began to spend a part of each summer with my grandparents. I loved all my country relatives, but I idolized Pop's brother, Uncle Tony. Every morning after milking we'd take the milk to the creamery on his wagon and on the way home we'd stop by the grocery and buy a nickel's worth of candy for me. I remember a big old stone boundary marker on the corner just before we turned into town. A farm family named Wedgewood lived there. Many years later after I got on the Grand Ole Opry, Mr. Wedgewood would round up groups of neighbors and bring them down to Nashville to see me. That stone was always a pleasant sight because when I saw it, I knew we were close to town. The last time I checked, that stone was still there.

During those summers on the family farms, I did a number of different chores—cutting and bailing the hay, harvesting the oats, shucking the corn. When I got to be about fourteen, I made a dollar a day working with an itinerant threshing crew as the blower boy on the threshing machine. The blower is the pipe that sticks out over the machine to guide it so the straw comes out evenly and not in one big pile. The machine was owned by the farmers' co-operative, but the crew boss was a man named Peters. We worked the area between Suamico and Sobieski about twenty-five miles from Green Bay. If we were on a big job that lasted several days, we'd sleep on the hay in the farmer's barn. Then we'd move on to another farm. I stayed with Mr. Peters for two summers. We didn't make a lot of money, but we got good food and lots of it. Different farms meant different nationalities and different food—usually German, Polish, or Swedish. The tables they laid for us were loaded with delicious food. From a German farm we might have goose liver sausage and rye bread. The Poles would feed us their good Polish sausage, of course, which was made of beef and pork and a lot of garlic. The Swedes served us bowls of spicy meatballs. Everywhere

we went we got all the fresh milk and coffee and cheese we wanted—
that tasty Wisconsin cheese. There were always many kinds of cakes
and pies—blackberry and apple pies, cheese tortes, homemade doughnuts.
All the women baked bread three days a week, white and wheat. I don't
remember a bad meal anywhere. The food alone was worth our hard
labor at the threshing machine.

Each barn had a threshing floor, and in the evenings after supper
we would have music and dancing. Mr. Peters would have me play my
concertina, and somebody else might have a fiddle he could play. Another guy might beat on a block of wood like he was playing a drum.
Our makeshift band could produce some pretty good music, and we
had many lively jamborees on those threshing floors.

I was a very active young fellow, but I didn't get into a lot of trouble.
When I did something wrong, it was usually Mom who disciplined
me. When I saw her coming toward me with a stick, I knew I was in
for a whipping. One time in Milwaukee I made a slingshot and acci-
dentally broke out a window in the tavern down the street. Somebody
went up to our house and told Mom, and she was waiting for me when
I got home. She said, "You're going to get it, so come here." I said,
"Oh, I don't think so. It was an accident." And I ran out in the yard
and crawled under Pop's car. "Wait until your dad gets home," she
said. "He'll catch you and then you'll get it. You've got to come out
sometime to eat." I said, "I ain't going to come out and eat with you
and Pop ever again. I'm going to eat with Aunt Anna." About that
time Aunt Anna, who had married and moved next door, came out on
her porch and said, "What's wrong with Frankie, Helen? What do you
want to whip him for?" When Mom told her, she said, "Well, make
him pay for it. Take it out of his money." Suddenly I felt like I'd lost
my last friend in the world. Aunt Anna wasn't going to take me in. So
I crawled out and got my whipping, and then I had to pay for the broken window as well. It didn't seem right that I was paying for that
window twice—with money and a whipping.

The only time Pop ever whipped me was when I hit my sister
Irene near her eye with a spitball. I was in the bathroom right off the
kitchen. Irene, who was washing the dishes, stuck her head around
the corner and said, "Frankie, come on in here. You're supposed to
dry these dishes." I said, "Stick your head around here one more time
bothering me, and I'll let you have it." When she did, I was ready and
shot off a spitball that hit her smack in the face. She started scream-

ing, and Pop came in and jerked me out of the bathroom and put me over his lap and paddled as hard as he could with his hand. When he finished, he said, "Is that enough, or do you want me to go get my razor strap? Do you know never to hit your sister again?" I said, through my tears, "Yes sir." Fortunately, Irene wasn't hurt, but I soon realized that if I had hit her square in an eye, I could have put it out. When I shot her, I wasn't thinking about what I might hit. If she had stuck her rear end out, I would have shot it. Whatever she stuck out was my target. It just happened to be her head.

All in all, I think we behaved like decent children, and our parents treated us with love and understanding. They treated us kindly because they treated each other right. I never saw them abuse each other. Milwaukee is beer country, and Pop would drink beer or schnapps or what he called a boilermaker, which is a small glass of whiskey followed by a beer chaser. We had our neighborhood drunks, but I don't remember a lot of drunkenness. Just about all the men drank, but they didn't get drunk very often. When Pop had a party in our basement, he was always the bartender and measured out the drinks so nobody got more than he could hold. One night we were having a wedding dance that lasted until five o'clock in the morning. It was still going when the milkman arrived, so he came in for a drink, leaving his horse and wagon parked outside. Pop said, "Now John, you still have a long way to go, so be careful how much you drink. You may never find your way home." The milkman said, "Don't worry about me getting home. My horse knows the route a lot better than I do, drunk or sober. He'll take me home. Why, my horse is so smart that if I let him, he'd reach around and carry the milk in for me."

We were a healthy family, by and large. Maybe it's because we drank so much milk, whether we lived on the farm or in the city. None of us children had any serious illnesses or accidents. The big health scares in those days were tuberculosis—we called it consumption—and flu. None of us ever came down with consumption, and we never had any bad cases of flu. In addition to all that milk, I think my mother's good cooking and my father's beer helped keep the family healthy. The Poles and Germans were used to recreational drinking in the old countries, and they brought their drinking customs to America. Alcoholic beverages were served almost everywhere adults got together—at home, at picnics and parties, at church socials, neighborhood carnivals, street dances—everywhere.

When Prohibition came, it hit our way of life pretty hard, but we had our own ways of getting around the new law of the land. Pop made his own home brew in the basement. The process involved mixing malt and hops in boiling water and putting it in kegs to ferment. One night we were all upstairs when we heard a noise like a cannon shot in the basement. We ran down and all Pop's beer was foaming out of the keg on the floor. The pressure built up inside the keg had popped the plug out of the bunghole. When the process worked right and the beer fermented properly, Pop took a dipper and poured it into bottles and corked them. I can still smell the strong odor that came up from the basement and filled the house when the beer was fermenting. Pop made good beer, and everybody loved to drink it. He also made good root beer for us kids until we got big enough to drink the real thing. Pop made beer all his life, Prohibition or no Prohibition. During the Prohibition days of the 1920s people would bring their homemade beer to church socials, and we never had any trouble with the law. The beer seemed to loosen people up so they could enjoy the food and the dancing in the church recreation hall. Not only did Pop bring the crowd's favorite home brew, his band provided music for the entertainment.

We children were usually present at these adult parties, but we knew to keep in the background. We were told to keep quiet and not bother the grown-ups. We played our own games and ate our refreshments and had a good time. Sometimes, of course, we got bruised and scratched when we played a little too rough on the streets and playgrounds, but it was usually something our moms could handle with a homemade remedy. The only time I ever had anything serious to happen to me was when I was run over by a hit-and-run driver. That was the first time I ever had my name in the paper. Mom had sent me to the bakery to get a birthday cake. We didn't live far from the bakery, but I was in a hurry and jaywalked across the street without looking. About that time a guy came racing out of the alley, ran into me, and knocked me down. A crowd gathered quickly, somebody called an ambulance, and I was soon at the hospital. I was pretty well banged up, black and blue, but I came out of it all right. Pop was very upset and brought a judge friend of his to see me in the hospital. The judge said, "Frankie, your dad wants to find the guy that hit you and sue him for your injuries and suffering. What do you say?" I said, "Oh, I don't think so. I'll be all right. Anyway, it was partly my fault. I should have been looking."

Pop never got to sue anybody because we never found out who hit me. For years I carried around a clipping from the newspaper in my billfold. The little headline read: "Frank Kuczynski Run Over by Car, 6th and Mitchell Street." I thought I was a celebrity because my name was in the paper, and everybody would know me. My dad's friend, the judge, later came up to Sobieski to my sister's wedding, but we had so many relatives at the house he had to sleep in the barn on a strawstack.

I may not have been a model student, but I did finish grade school and high school in Milwaukee. My first school was St. Cyril, which was attached to the parish church we attended. Everything went smoothly until I got disciplined by one of the nuns. I was caught sneaking out during recess to go down to the corner store to buy some penny licorice sticks. The windows of the school were a couple of feet above the playground sidewalk, and some of us boys would crawl through the opening. One time I happened to be the last one out the window, and the sister saw me, jerked me back inside, and took me to her room. "Hold out your hand, Frank Kuczynski," she said. I went, "Oh, oh." She took a leather strap from her desk drawer, bent my hand back, and whacked me as hard as she could. Then she looked straight at me and said, "I don't think that was good enough. I'll have to do it again." And she did a better job the second time. It was good enough to make me cry. In addition, I had to take a note home to my mother. Mom didn't want me to violate school rules, but she didn't want me whipped with a strap that could draw blood. So she yanked me from St. Cyril's and put me in a more humane but less disciplined public school, Windlake Avenue School. My first public school teacher, Miss Schott, was so pretty all us boys had crushes on her. I got along very well in the public schools and stayed with them until I graduated from high school.

My first girlfriend was in my class at school. She was the daughter of one of the Mexicans who worked under Pop at the tanning factory. She was my school chum, and I carried her books when we walked home together. I was so in love I thought I would never forget her, but now I can't even remember her name. Actually, I never had any serious girlfriends until I met Lydia Frank years later. One of my female acquaintances was Sylvia Machinski, who lived on our street a few doors from our house. She finally married a musician in a polka band. Up on the farm I liked Mary Drobeck, who was a cousin by marriage, but she married a policeman. I only danced with her one time. No wonder I didn't have any serious girlfriends. I was not much of a ladies' man!

I did, however, have a number of boy chums. I remember two that stand out even to this day. Angelo Giardoni was an Italian boy I met through basketball. We palled around for a long time. He'd come to our house for Mom's good Polish cooking, and I'd go to his house and have Italian spaghetti. Angelo was taller and bigger than I was, and he stuck up for me when I needed him.

My best friend was Alfred Kallas, who was Uncle Kelly's brother. When we were in school together, we were inseparable. We'd play a short two-inning baseball game at lunch period. After school we'd play basketball. If it was winter, we'd go skate in the park. His dad had a team of horses and delivered coal for a large coal company. Sometimes Alfred and I would go to the livery stable and help him harness his team. Even after Alfred's parents took him out of public school and enrolled him in a Catholic school to prepare him for confirmation, we still saw each other regularly because we sold newspapers together.

I remember very well the man in charge of us paperboys. He had eight or so sheds where we would go pulling our sleds about four o'clock in the morning to pick up our papers for our regular customers. If something big happened—like a Jack Dempsey fight or a big explosion or a fire or a train wreck—and the newspaper put out a special edition, we'd go out at midnight and hawk them on the streets: "Extra! Extra! Dempsey knocked out by Tunney!" Or: "Whole city block goes up in flames in Chicago! Fifty people burned to death! Five firemen injured!" We paid two cents for each paper and sold them for three cents, though nearly everybody gave us a nickel.

On Sundays Alfred and I would put the papers on our sleds and go out to where the ocean liners docked near the lake shore. In the wintertime when the boats would freeze up on the lake, we'd be the first paperboys to get out to them. The Sunday *Milwaukee Journal* sold for a dime, but several sailors would usually chip in to buy one and pay us a quarter. We thought we were getting rich fast. After I began making pretty good money selling my papers, I started paying my mother eight dollars a week for my room and board. I continued doing it as long as I lived at home. I wanted to be independent and support myself.

Of course, Milwaukee was a major inland seaport, and ships docked there from all over the world, but we felt especially close to the merchant seamen from Wisconsin and Michigan. They always fascinated me. They had a hard life, but it was a life they loved. "Once you get saltwater in your blood," they told us, "you won't be satisfied doing anything else." It wasn't long before I understood what they meant because I was getting music in my blood. We also got to know the crews of the boats that took garbage out to a little island in the lake, where they turned it into fertilizer. Milwaukee was one of the first cities in the country to recycle garbage, and this was back in the mid-1920s.

One of the best things about growing up in Milwaukee was that it was a city of sports—amateur and professional. We had the Brewers in baseball, and we had some of the best ice skating facilities in the world. Every kid learned to ice skate—right after he learned to walk. In wintertime the rivers and lakes, even the playgrounds and school yards, were frozen over, and we skated everywhere. There were fiercely fought competitions in all the grade schools and high schools. Sometimes Alfred and I would go down to Kosciusko Park and skate all day long. People don't skate as much as they used to, and I don't think they have as much fun as we did. I was good enough at skating and other sports to enjoy myself. I was good enough to play basketball on our high school and church teams. My hero was Bud Foster, the coach at the University of Wisconsin, and whenever I'd see his picture in the paper, I'd say, "I want to be like him when I grow up." But I soon learned that I would never be good enough to play on a college or professional team or to coach one.

My problem was that I was a little guy, and there are not many sports for guys my size; but I did the best with what I had. One winter day when my sister and I were walking home from school, some big guys started throwing snowballs at her. I ran up to them and said, "That's my sister. You stop that." Well, they did stop, but they turned and beat the hell out of me—all three of them—and I went home bruised and bloody. I did feel good, though, because I'd done what any older brother should do. I had protected my sister's honor.

Despite my size, I decided one time to take up amateur boxing. I was fourteen, weighed about 112 pounds, but I thought I could make up in speed what I lacked in power. I was boxing as a flyweight for a fraternal organization called the Eagles. I kept it a secret from Mom, but Pop knew and even took me to Green Bay for the Golden Gloves Tournament. He told Mom we were driving up there to pick up a part for his car. My opponent was an Italian kid, and I took one look at him and his physique and knew I was a goner. Sure enough, it didn't take him long to beat me to a pulp. After a couple of rounds, he knocked me out, and I came to in the dressing room, with Pop bending over me and saying, "Well, kid, what do you think?" I said, "Pop, I think I've learned my lesson. No more boxing for me." I retired from boxing without a single win. It was left to sister Irene's husband Bruno Cetnarowski to win family fame in the ring. He was once lightweight champion of Wisconsin, but he got to hurting from all the training and punching, and Irene made him quit.

I think my growing-up years in Milwaukee were ordinary for that time and place. By the time I got to high school, my parents were living with my grandmother Mielczarek on the farm. I was going to Bayview High School and started my first band. For a while, I worked as an apprentice mechanical draftsman for my Uncle Lawrence. He suggested that I quit high school and go to vocational school to learn a trade. So I tried a course at the Milwaukee Vocational School just to please him. It was pure drudgery, making all those diagrams and drawings and calculations. I stuck it out and finished the course, but I knew I wasn't cut out to be a draftsman.

Even then, I knew I wanted to be a professional musician, but people were always asking, "What's your trade? If you don't have a trade, you'd better go to pre-vo and learn one." Pre-vo was a program of pre-vocational training that helped you decide what trade to choose and gave you some of the basic training in it. I never learned anything that seemed important to me. About all I learned was how to build simple things for my mother, like a bread board or a book rack. I did learn how to take a car apart and put it back together, but I learned that by watching a mechanic. In my drafting classes we read about how to do things, but I was more interested in actually doing them. I had long before decided I didn't want to go to college. I didn't need a college degree to be a musician. I never thought I'd get rich on music, but I thought I could at least make a fair living doing something I liked.

A lot of people think I was born and grew up in Abrams because

Mom and Pop lived there permanently after they moved from Milwaukee around 1940. They had grown tired of the city and bought the farm from some friends. I used to call it home because that's where they lived, and after I moved south that's where I visited them many times. If my band was playing close to Abrams, the boys would say, "Are we going to stay with Mom and Pop tonight?" They loved to visit there because Mom put on such a big spread for them. So during most of my professional career, people have identified me with Abrams. The people of Abrams have claimed me as a native son, and I appreciate it. In July of 1974 they honored me with a parade and a plaque that proclaimed Abrams the "Home Town of Pee Wee King."

Of course, I had spent a lot of time during my boyhood with my grandparents on their farms. They grew oats and all kinds of vegetables, but their main source of cash was the dairy. I learned to milk cows as soon as I got big enough to squeeze a cow's tit. On Grandfather Kuczynski's farm we milked a couple of dozen cows every day by hand and took the milk to the Abrams creamery in large milk cans. At one point around 1932 I was milking a dozen cows every morning and a dozen cows every night and playing music whenever I had the chance. My band was called the Farm Hands and included two of my uncles, Uncle Tony and Uncle Vic, both on the guitar. One summer when I was fifteen and my parents were living on Grandmother Mielczarek's farm, I had an argument with Mom about the work I was doing and ran away from home to live with my Aunt Marie. I hadn't been there but a few days when Uncle Walter and Uncle Stanley came and said, "Frankie, your mother is sick in bed. You'd better go home and see her." A fellow I knew with a motorcycle and a sidecar drove me home. I went into my mother's room and said, "Mom, I'm sorry I ran away. I heard you were sick, and I've come home to see you." She started crying, and then I started crying. I knew, though, that once I finished high school I would be able to make my own decisions about what work I did.

Despite the hard work, I enjoyed farm life as a youngster. One reason I liked the farm was that it was safe. We didn't have to lock anything up. Our watchdog Shep would have chewed up anybody who tried to break in. We didn't have a dog in the city, but Shep was our faithful companion on the farm. He would follow Mom when she went to the pasture or to the woods to pick blackberries. If she saw a snake, she'd pick him up with a stick, hang him on the barbed wire fence, and Shep would chew him up.

I also liked farm life because it is a natural way of life. Take sex, for instance. On the farm we learned about sex in a natural way. It wasn't something hidden and ugly. We saw bulls and cows and stallions and mares coming together. We saw kittens and pups and farm animals being born. Living on the farm was learning about life in a natural, wholesome way.

On the farm we learned the value of honest work, even if we didn't always like it. One time many years later, I took my daughter Marietta and her husband Dean Wuchterl with Lydia and me up to visit my parents in Abrams. Pop was threshing oats and filling sixty-pound bags. My son-in-law said, "Grandpa, I'd like to help you," and he hoisted a bag onto each shoulder. Well, that impressed me. He started to walk toward the storage area, and Pop said, "Son, that's too heavy. You'll never make it with both sacks." But Dean said, "Just let me try. I think I can make it." He was a husky fellow and walked straight up those steps with two sixty-pound sacks. I've always admired a man who is not afraid to do physical labor, whether or not he was raised on a farm. If they worked even briefly on a farm, young people today would learn a lot of good lessons, such as the value of work and an appreciation of the folks who grow their food. I would say to them, "You must do something worthwhile. If you don't work at something, then you don't eat." That's the way it was when I was a boy on the farm, and I think it's still a good lesson for young people.

I am so thankful for the many wonderful legacies my parents and grandparents left me, especially my love of music. When I was a boy I was always surrounded by music and musicians. We had an old wind-up phonograph player and stacks of 78-rpm records on such labels as Okeh and Blue Bird. Uncle Tony had a huge collection of polka records, which I used to listen to for hours at a time. I also listened to music on the radio, but it was live music that set my feet to tapping. Wisconsin was filled with polka and waltz bands that played good German music, except, of course, during World War I, when German music went out of style.

The best music was what I heard at home. Pop played the violin and concertina and entertained the family and anybody else who happened to pop in. My godfather lived close by, and when he would come over he and Pop would play the concertina and fiddle and we kids would play the harmonica. That was the first instrument I learned to play, and I taught myself. When I was eight I won three dollars in an amateur contest at a little shotgun theater in Milwaukee. The theater had a regular amateur night, and one day some of my buddies came by and said, "Come on, Frankie. Let's go and see if we can't win us something." So I entered the contest with my harmonica rendition of "Ain't She Sweet?" and won second prize. First prize was five dollars. Following the contest, there was a silent movie, which was accompanied by a theater piano. But I was so excited about my prize, I don't remember anything about the movie. "Oh boy," I said, "I've found an easy way to make money."

After the harmonica, I learned to play the violin, which was a much more difficult instrument. Or so I found out. I thought all I had to do was scrape the bow across the strings. Pop said, "Kid, it's not that easy. I'll show you." He could read music, so he brought out a piece of music and played a Polish dance. I looked at the notes and said, "Wow, that sounds like classical music. It looks hard." I knew then I had to take lessons to learn the violin. A bar owner my dad knew said, "John, why don't you send Frankie to my daughter? She's a good violinist and will teach him." I took lessons on Pop's violin from her for several months; then he bought me my own.

Next, I learned to play the concertina. One night Mom and Pop went out to a movie, and to give me something to do, Pop brought out his concertina and some sheet music. While they were gone, I figured how to read the notes and numbers, and when they returned, I played "Over the Waves" for them. It was a simple beginner's tune, but they couldn't believe I had learned so fast. As time went on, I learned to strum the guitar, and many years later, after I formed the Golden West Cowboys, I learned the cordovox, which looks like an electrified accordion. It's sort of like a portable organ that you plug in. It's a versatile instrument and came in handy when I was doing a lot of sports shows in the 1970s.

All of the children in our family learned to play some kind of instrument. Irene took piano lessons and a few accordion lessons. Soon after she started the accordion, her breasts began to develop and it became uncomfortable for her to hold the instrument, so she told Pop she didn't want to play it anymore. I was about fifteen and Pop had thought Irene and I would make a good duo on the violin and accordion. When she gave it up, he said, "Frankie, Irene's got six lessons left. You can take them." So I took the rest of her lessons, saved my money from my paper route, and bought my own accordion. Irene was a good musician, and I think she always wanted to be in show business; but she married a fine man and they lived a good life together until he died a few years ago.

My brother Irvin—the one we called Max—learned to be a champion concertina player. One time a famous concertina player from France gave a concert in Milwaukee, and Max took his concertina and went backstage to meet him. He asked Max to play for him, and afterwards he said, "Boy, you're good. You've got too much jazz in you to be a Polish boy." He was right about Max being good. He was good enough to be inducted later into the Concertina Hall of Fame. At one time he played with my band in Louisville; then he went down to Nashville to work with a band called Slim Smith and the Oklahoma Cowboys. Max didn't stay with them long. They thought they wanted a concertina player and advertised for one, but Max said they didn't even know what one looked like till he showed them and then didn't know how to fit it into their band.

You can see, then, that I come from a musical family. Mom encouraged our musical development, but it was Pop who had the most influence on me. He played music most of his life. He got his talent and encouragement from his dad, who was an old-time fiddle player, and I got mine from him. Pop had a band called the Midnight Four, which became the Midnight Four Plus One when I was fourteen and joined it to play the concertina. With me, the band had six members, and I asked Pop if he counted correctly. He said, "Yes, I did. Our sixth player plays bass and he drinks a lot, so I don't know how long he will be with us. But there's another reason I named the band the Midnight Four Plus One. People will see that there are six of us and say, 'Why is the band called the Midnight Four Plus One when there are six players?' If they ask the question, they will remember us."

From Pop, I was learning not only music but a thing or two about show business. Take crowd control, for instance. Pop knew how to keep the audience under his thumb. Usually he'd play three tunes to a set, including perhaps two serious love songs, and the couples would be close dancing and getting all worked up. Then he'd say to the fellows, "Boys, now that you've made love and whispered sweet words in her ear, we're going to change the tempo," and he'd play a loud oomph-pah, oomph-pah for about five minutes. It cooled things off, and everybody was happy. Pop also knew how to handle drunks and other people who might have caused trouble. He never needed a bouncer because he never had any fights or arguments. He was a master bandleader and showman. After playing in his band and observing him up close for several months, I said, "Yes. This is what I want to do." Even before I organized my first band, I knew that I was hell-bent for music.

I also knew that Pop would back me up if I went into show business, though not even Mom tried to discourage me. I think she knew it was in my blood from both sides of the family. After all, when she first knew my dad he was playing in a band in Sobieski. In fact, I think she was at least partly attracted to him because he was a musician. It added some glamour to their relationship. After they started courting, Pop would see her after church. He would visit her at her home, and sometimes he would take her to hear his band play. But Pop didn't want any competition. He was so jealous of her he'd make her sit on his concertina case and not let her dance with any of the other guys.

In 1929, when I was fifteen and still in high school, I organized my first band. There were four of us: Lenny Shaw on the guitar and banjo, Fat Mike on drums, and Ted Fabian on clarinet and tenor sax. I played the accordion. We were very conscious of our appearance and either wore tuxedos or attractive street clothes, depending on the audience. We looked real spiffy. Ted was a big fellow, about 250 pounds. He was a good comedian—a natural fall guy—and we'd play jokes on him during our shows. Fat Mike had one of those big drums with a hula dancer painted on it, with a light inside. We'd put him out front so the audience could see the dancer do the hula.

Ours was a pop and novelty band, and we did a lot of parodies of popular and children's songs. Audiences expected comedy, and we tried to make them laugh. We'd make up funny lyrics to popular songs like "When the Moon Comes Over the Mountain" or "I Met Kansas City Kitty." We'd see guys like Freddie Schnikelfritz and his band in a movie and try to copy their styles. It was the sort of stuff that Spike Jones came out with later. Ted Fabian used to tease me after our band broke up. "Pee Wee," he said, "if we'd kept on, we could have been Spike Jones." Of course, we did songs straight and serious as well.

Our typical show would open with "Sentimental Journey," which was our signature song. We'd do a set of three songs, take a short break, then do another set. After several sets we'd have an intermission of thirty minutes. Then we'd have a floor show, with jokes and audience participation. Sometimes we'd have a stump-the-band contest. We kept up with the newest popular songs, and when somebody asked us to play a song, we usually knew it. We played dance music and background music, and we did a lot of requests and dedications. As the emcee, I'd say, "Here's a song we want to play for Mr. and Mrs. Korzeniowski, who got married three days ago: 'It Only Hurts for a Little While.'" Then I'd say, "And they brought their twenty-two-year-old son with them tonight." People loved corny jokes like that, and I'd tell a string of them. The audience liked for me to poke fun at our band members too, with just a slight hint of sexual misconduct. I'd say, "Lenny Shaw's wife is the proud mother of a bouncing baby boy," and Lenny would sit there and make believe he didn't know anything about it. Then I'd say, "Will the proud father please stand up and take a bow?" And all the boys would stand up and bow and say, "Thank you. Thank you." It would crack the audience up, especially since they could see that we were all too young to be married anyway. I used variations of that joke with all my later bands, and it never failed to get a good response.

Our floor shows were sometimes as long as our dance sets. We tried to please a lot of different tastes, so we played Italian and German and Polish music. A show would last from about nine to one, and during the last hour we played romantic dance music without a break. We'd carry Eight Brothers Tobacco cans with us for spotlights. We cut the ends off and put cellophane on one end and a bulb in back. Fat Mike would switch them on when we played mood music. I had a painter fix up cardboard fronts for all the band members, and we put that sparkling stuff on our name that said, "Frankie King and the King's Jesters." There were no microphones in those days, so we had to play and sing over the crowd.

We played in a variety of places, from formal dances in clubs to picnics and fish fries and taverns. The taverns were especially noisy, but even if they drowned us out, we went on playing. We got paid whether or not they could hear us. It wasn't much because when we began the band it was at the start of the Depression, and that was starvation time. It was tough. I mean tough! When we played a big dance hall, we could get as much as sixty dollars or as little as twenty-five dollars, depending on how much the sponsors took in at the gate. For a dance or picnic at the lakes, we might get thirty-five dollars. For a wedding party we'd ask fifty dollars, but we would take a lot less. We'd also try to get the sponsors to pay us eight cents a mile for gas money. At the taverns we got very little, maybe three dollars for each of the boys and five dollars for me as the bandleader. If there was a big crowd, we might get a bonus, and we'd always get a good feed, especially on Friday fishdays. One of the classiest taverns on the southside was owned by a Mr. Stark, who would take us every Friday night we were open. In those Depression days, the crowds were thin everywhere, and my aunts would help us out by getting their boyfriends to take them where we were playing.

But even during those lean days, I never regretted my career choice. I was never tempted to go into another line of work. While I was still in high school, I worked every day after school for my Aunt Frances's husband, Uncle Lawrence, who was an optician. I'd spend about two hours cleaning and straightening up his work rooms, and he paid me five dollars a week. With my little band we could play three or four hours, and I might make fifteen dollars. So I said to myself, "Why am I working for Uncle Lawrence?" I went to him one day and said, "I don't think I want to spend my life cleaning up your office and wiping your pens. I can do better with my music."

Pop wasn't the only musician I was around when I was growing up. I was crazy about the big bands and always tried to hear them when they came to Milwaukee. I would also try to get backstage and meet leaders like Jan Garber, Tommy Dorsey, Sammy Kaye, Kay Kyser, Guy Lombardo, Tommy Tucker, and my favorite, Wayne King. I used to listen to Wayne King's radio program, "The Lady Esther Serenade," every Sunday from WBBM in Chicago. Then in 1930, when he was playing the lakes in Milwaukee, I got to meet him. There are about twenty different lakes around the city, and my band was playing one evening to an empty ballroom and the manager said, "Don't worry about it, Frank. Wayne King's over in the Eagles Ballroom, and he's got the crowd. Why don't you boys sack up and go over there and hear him?" So that's what we did.

At the intermission we went back to his dressing room, and a member of my band, Ted Fabian, introduced me to him. Ted, of course, didn't know Mr. King any more than I did, but he said, "Mr. King, excuse me, I've got a boy here I want you to meet. It's Frank Kuczynski." We shook hands, and Mr. King was very cordial. When it came time for his band to go back on stage, he said to them, "You fellows go ahead and do one set without me. I want to stay here and talk to this guy. He's on the wrong track, and I want to set him straight." After the band left, he turned to me and said, "If you're going to play pop and novelty music, you need a catchy name. Are you on radio?" I said,

"No sir, we don't have a radio show yet, but we will." He said, "That's the spirit. Now remember: K-I-N-G. Nobody can misspell it. Nobody can mispronounce it. That's your hook. You say your name is Frank. Call yourself Frankie. It has a better ring. Frankie King. That's a name nobody will forget." That's when I began to use King as my professional name, and I made it my legal name after Lydia and I got married. My high school band became Frankie King and the King's Jesters. The boys in the band loved the name and said, "Well, we're hot stuff now." That name change may not seem like much, but it was one of the smartest professional moves I ever made. We immediately began getting better dates and bigger dances and ballrooms all over southern Wisconsin. Of course, I'm still proud of my birth name and my Polish heritage, but who can spell and pronounce and remember Frank Kuczynski?

Every musician wanted to get on the radio in the 1920s and 1930s. My first radio appearance was on station WTMJ in Milwaukee in 1929. Then in 1933, when I was nineteen, I played on the "Badger State Barn Dance," which was a lot like the "WLS Barn Dance" in Chicago. Mr. Quartermont, who ran the barn dance, had singers, guitar players, fiddlers, accordion players, comics—every kind of instrument and act other barn dances had. He also had star performers and headliners. I have a poster here in my files advertising the show. It says, "Come one. Come all. Hear the Stars of the Original WIS Barn Dance" (which referred to the Wisconsin Barn Dance), and underneath it said, "The Badger State Barn Dance." I played it several times, and I made friends that came in handy when I needed players for the Golden West Cowboys, which I would organize a few years later in Knoxville.

The Wide Open Country of Gene Autry

BY 1933 MY BAND AND I were playing dates all around Milwaukee and southern Wisconsin and over as far west as Madison and up to Oshkosh, Appleton, and Green Bay. But we were one of many bands like us, and I was just one of many bandleaders. Then my lucky break came. A politician in Racine heard one of our shows and liked us. He contacted me and said he wanted to help us get on their local radio station WJRN. "You are Polish boys," he said, "and there are a lot of Polish department stores and grocery stores and butcher shops between Racine and Milwaukee, and they will advertise on your show in Polish." So he talked to the station manager, who said, "Okay, we'll give the boys a try, but they must play all kinds of music and promise not to tell any jokes. Just play music." So we had our first radio show, which didn't pay us one red cent. But we got something better than money. We got publicity. We could announce where we'd be playing and everybody would know our name. That was good preparation for the ten years we later played on the Grand Ole Opry, which didn't pay us anything either.

We were on the Racine station for about six months. We'd do a Polish song, then a song in English. The announcer would do commercials in both Polish and English. There's no telling how many rolls of toilet paper we sold, advertised at six rolls for a dollar. We thought we were on top of the world. We had a radio show, and we were making good money playing dates all around Wisconsin. What more could I ask for? But my lucky star was still shining over me. One day we were doing our radio show when my path crossed two men who would change my life, Gene Autry and Joe Frank.

First, I'll tell you about Gene Autry and how he got me started in country and western music. Gene didn't stay around long. Within a few months after I met him, he had left for Hollywood to make movies. During the short time we worked together, however, he helped me change my musical direction. It was in early spring of 1934, and my band and I were playing our Polish-American Hour on WJRN in Racine. Gene Autry was touring southern Wisconsin with his manager, Joe Frank, and his band called the Range Riders. In Milwaukee a car sideswiped them and caused a fender to rub into one of the tires. When they got near Racine, the tire blew out and caused the car to crash into a ditch, injuring three members of the band. They managed to pull into a service station to get the tire tubed and the bent fender pulled off the tire and straightened.

As they were waiting for the car to be repaired, the mechanic happened to be listening to our radio show, and Mr. Frank said, "I like the sound of that band. I wonder if I could borrow several of those fellows to fill in for my injured players. Who are these boys?" The mechanic told him that we were a popular local band and played the Milwaukee area. Mr. Frank said, "I think I'll call the station and see if I can hire a couple of them." We had just finished our show and I had sacked up my accordion when the phone rang. I picked it up and for the first time I heard the voice of the man who would soon become my manager and my father-in-law. He said, "This is Joe Frank. I'd like to speak to the leader of the band that has just been playing." I said, "You got him." He said, "I need to hire a couple of players for this afternoon. Have you got a bass fiddle?" I said, "No, but we've got a fellow who can play the tuba. We use it to set the beat for the polkas we play." He said, "What the hell is a tuba? Have you got a guitar player?" I said, "Yes. And he sings too." He said, "I don't need a guitar player who sings because I've already got Gene Autry." I said, "Who in the hell is Gene Autry?" He said, "Well, he's the singing cowboy on the 'WLS Barn Dance,' and he's already made some recordings. We're finishing up a tour before he leaves for Hollywood to make movies." I said, "Oh yes, I believe I've heard of him, but I've never heard him play or sing." He said, "We've had a little accident and I need someone to play the accordion." I said, "That's me. And I used to play a pretty good violin." He said, "I thought I heard a saxophone in your band, and I also need a drummer." I said, "We have a boy who doubles on the clarinet and the sax, and we have a drummer." So before he hung up, four of us had agreed to meet him at the theater in Port Washington about twenty miles north of Milwaukee that afternoon for a three o'clock matinee. We got there just in time to do the show.

My boys played just that one engagement because his regular musicians returned, but Mr. Frank asked me to complete the tour with Gene and the Range Riders. He said he liked having an accordion in the band because it added a different sound to the music. The other instruments in Gene's band were a fiddle, a bass fiddle, a guitar, and a steel guitar. I wasn't with the group long before I got my nickname. There were too many Franks in the band, so Mr. Frank said we had to have nicknames to tell us apart. He first wanted to call me Shorty, but I didn't like that one, so we settled on Pee Wee.

We were on the road about two weeks. It was during Lent, and in southern Wisconsin people didn't go to dances at that time of the year. So I was free to play with Gene's band. We played a park in southern Illinois, then went up to Iowa around Des Moines and back through Illinois to Chicago. I wasn't able to play with Gene on the "WLS National Barn Dance" at the end of the tour because my band was already booked for that Saturday night. When I left Gene and his band, I realized I had been working with a very talented and versatile performer, but I certainly didn't dream that he would soon become one of the legends of American entertainment history. And I didn't realize that I had just had the big break of my life. I thought Gene would go to California, Mr. Frank would go back to Chicago, and I would return to Milwaukee and never see either man again. As I left to return home, however, Mr. Frank said, "Pee Wee, I'm planning to move to Louisville, Kentucky, and I want you to come down and join me and a new band. I'll see you soon." I thanked him but said to myself, "I'll bet you will. This is the last time I'll ever see you."

After several weeks, Gene left for California and the Range Riders disbanded. When I met him, Gene already had his movie contract, but Mr. Frank wanted him to get as much exposure as he could before he left. That's why they played WLS in Chicago and then WHAS in Louisville. Both were 50,000-watt clear channel stations and covered half the country after dark. Appearing on such powerful stations was good advance publicity for Gene before he left to make his movies. Mr. Frank had gotten Gene the movie contract, but he decided not to go out there himself. He said he had too many projects going on in Illinois and the Midwest, and he had already planned the move to Louisville to set up shop. He said, "I have no interest in Hollywood." It was a risk he didn't want to take. Gene, on the other hand, already had his career mapped out. He knew what he wanted to do, and he knew he was going to succeed in the movies as a singing cowboy. And he did. He took only two members of his band with him to Hollywood, Frankie Marvin and Smiley Burnette, who became his comic sidekick in his movies. Later that year he made his first film. It was with Ken Maynard and was called *In Old Santa Fe*. Four years later we went out to Hollywood and made a movie with him and Smiley, but more about that later.

When you think about Gene's background, you realize that he was a natural for a career as a western singer and movie star. He was born on a ranch near Tioga, Texas, and grew up in Texas and Oklahoma riding horses and doing ranch work. He didn't have a horse on our midwestern tour, but I'm sure he already had plans to make Champion a part of his film career. He was working as a railroad telegrapher when Will Rogers heard him sing on the radio and encouraged him to enter show business. One of his grandfathers was a Baptist preacher, and Gene grew up singing in church. His mother played the piano, and his father was a horse trader. As his career developed, it showed he owed something to both sides of the family. Unlike most of us who played on the radio in those days, Gene got paid for his radio appearances. He's always been a shrewd businessman who knew how to turn his talents into a lot of money.

Gene was a likable guy when I met him in 1934, and he still is. He knew what to do to make himself popular. In 1934 he was already calling himself "The Oklahoma Singing Cowboy" and dressing in a fancy western outfit. Back then, you could buy denim trousers and cowboy shirts in a few dry goods stores, but nothing classy. Several stores in Texas made regular western wear for regular cowboys and bronco riders, but I don't know of any place where stage costumes could be bought. In fact, Mrs. Frank was responsible for his first dressy costume. She took his Panama suit and cut the legs down to fit his boots and then sewed a few decorations on his suit coat. When she finished it, Gene tried it on and came out to show it to Mrs. Frank's daughter Lydia. "What do you think of your mom's work?" he asked. "How do you like me in my cowboy suit?" Lydia said, "Gene, Mom is a good seamstress, but you look like a sack of oats tied in the middle." Gene kept in touch with the Franks until they both died, and sent Lydia condolences each time.

In 1937 Gene was offered a spot on the Grand Ole Opry about the same time we were, but he turned it down. By then, he was a big success in the movies. He was also afraid his cowboy music wouldn't fit in too well with the hillbilly style of music that was mostly played on the Opry then. Mr. Frank did talk Gene into doing an Opry show with us in 1940, and Gene did the show as one stop on a national tour with his horse Champion. Gene's cousin, Ray Purdy, had quit his job as a Texas Ranger to join Gene, and he was driving the van that carried Champion. Ray hired a black man as his helper, and they rode together in the van. The two men were on a dream trip, riding with Champion all across the United States. Finally, they reached Nashville and pulled up to the hotel, which happened to be on one of the hills in the downtown area. Ray left his assistant with Champion while he went inside the hotel to check on his reservations. Just after he left, the brakes on the van slipped. The van rolled backward into a floral shop across the street and finally hung up on a downspout. Luckily, no one was injured—not even Champion—but it could have been a disaster. Ray's assistant was sweating and shaking when they got to him. Gene came out and offered to pay for any injuries or property damages. The lady in the shop said not to worry. She was so thrilled to meet Gene Autry in person she didn't care about the broken glass and damaged flowers.

I've stayed in touch with Gene through the years. During World War II Gene joined the army and became a sergeant and then a flight officer and spent a lot of time entertaining servicemen on his "Melody Ranch" radio program. I appeared with him several times during the war and afterwards. In October of 1987 I went to Knoxville to tape a special edition of The Nashville Network's *Melody Ranch Theater* with Gene and Pat Buttram. Earlier, in 1945, Minnie Pearl and I and all the Golden West Cowboys went to the dedication of the town Gene Autry, Oklahoma, which had changed from its old name of Berwyn. In the mid-1940s I did a number of shows with Gene's brother Doug, who played with us on the Opry several times. I even named my son after Gene. One time Gene said to him, "Now son, tell me who is your favorite cowboy." Gene King said, "Roy Rogers." Gene Autry said to me, "Pee Wee, you better talk to that boy and tell him who he's named after."

While Gene was becoming a fabulous success himself, he always had time to help younger performers. When Jimmy Wakely was making himself into a cowboy star, he copied Gene to the letter. Gene knew it, but it didn't bother him at all. "Let him copy," he said. "It can't hurt me. I got it made, and he's just starting out. I'll even try to help him if I can." That was Gene's attitude. He wasn't jealous of other performers. He did his own work and didn't look over his shoulder to see if anyone was gaining on him. One New Year's Day Gene was supposed to be the grand marshal for the Rose Bowl parade, but he became ill and couldn't do it. He called Wakely and said, "Hey kid, how'd you like to take my place in the parade? I'm in the hospital. Now you can't say no because I've already got it fixed up for you, you little lucky son of a gun. This is your big break, so take it." Now, you know it takes a big man to help someone like that.

I don't mean to say that Gene let people run over him. He was a savvy businessman and took no prisoners when it came to business decisions. He was a financial genius and built an empire of oil, hotels, and radio and TV stations. He even owns the California Angels baseball team. When Gene started making movies, he hired bands like mine from cities that had 50,000-watt radio stations. The local bands were good tie-ins to the movies when they were released. Fans of every musical group wanted to see the movies they were in. It increased the audience for each movie. Gene would also take a hit song and turn it into a motion picture. That's what he did when he made *South of the Border* and the movie we were in, *Gold Mine in the Sky*. Gene may not have been the first singing cowboy in the movies, but he was the first one that became a big star; and he was the first one to make music as much a part of the movie as the action. It just seemed that everything that Gene touched turned to gold, from records to real estate to oil. He was a top movie star when he realized that television was the coming thing, and he plunged right into it right after he got out of the army and became a TV performer and producer.

In 1989, when I was in Nashville for a meeting of the board of the Country Music Association, Gene was there for a baseball owners conference. We were all staying at the huge Opryland Hotel—he and his new wife Jackie and Lydia and I—and Gene said, "Damn it, this hotel is so big they ought to give us roller skates to get around." As soon as he saw me, he said, "Kid, how in the hell do you look so good at your age, especially since you've had a stroke?" But Gene is the one who looks good for his age. He looked great and hadn't even had any face-lifts at that time, though Jackie may have talked him into it by now. I'm sure his pictures have been face-lifted—airbrushed, they call it—but most entertainers have their photos retouched.

Gene was married to his first wife Ina Mae for almost fifty years; and after her death he married Jackie, who's in her early fifties, which is about thirty years younger than Gene. Gene was never divorced. Jackie was the president of his bank, and they got to know each other over business lunches. All his friends were glad they married. It kept those Las Vegas showgirls from getting to him and his money. It was a smart business move too. He said, "You can tell everybody I married the president of my bank, but it's a woman." Gene doesn't have any children. At first, when he and Ina Mae were struggling to get established, they were childless by choice, but later they were unable to have children. Now he doesn't have a choice, I'm sad to say.

Yes sir, Gene Autry is the oldest friend I have. Our friendship goes back to when we were both starting out, a time when we were both five-dollar-a-day acts. He was several years older than me and taught me a lot about business and showmanship and the business of showmanship. He gave me many good pieces of practical advice. "Memorize people's names," he said, "especially the names of booking agents and show managers. They are the ones who can give you an audience, and without an audience you can never be a star." Who would have thought that Gene Autry would become an American hero and superstar? Certainly not the people who booked him and his Range Riders that spring of 1934 in little towns in Illinois and Iowa. But he did. He knew where he wanted to go. And he knew what it took to get there. You have to admire a man like that.

The Country
to the South

GENE AUTRY HELPED GIVE ME a sense of what I wanted to do musically, but Joe Frank showed me how to do it. After I left the tour with Gene, I never expected to hear from any of them again. But I did. A few weeks after Mr. Frank brought Gene down to Louisville to sing on WHAS radio and to wait for his Hollywood contract to come through, Mr. Frank called me and said, "How about you and the drummer coming down here? I can put you both to work." I said, "I don't think the drummer can come, but Ted Fabian is available." Mr. Frank said, "All right, I think I can get a drummer from Chicago. Gene Autry is leaving us now, so I'm dissolving his band and putting together another one with the Log Cabin Boys. You and Fabian come on down." That sounded good to me, so Ted, the drummer Al Mee (who had decided he was available after all), and I came down to Louisville.

When we arrived, Gene Autry had already left for Hollywood. He had gotten the exposure he wanted in Louisville over WHAS and was gone. So Ted, who played the sax and clarinet, Al, and I, plus a local trumpet player named Buddy Brock, joined the Log Cabin Boys that already included Chuck Hurta on fiddle, Frankie Moore on guitar, and Freddie Owen as vocalist. Later we were joined by Lydia Frank and her sister Marie, who were billed as the Little Hoosier Maids. Another featured player was Cousin Emma, who was from Lamb, Kentucky. She was a national champion fiddler and one of the first girls to play the five-string banjo professionally. She also played the guitar, the mandolin, and the harmonica. Ted's saxophone didn't fit very well with country music, so he played his clarinet. Frankie and Freddie, the original Log Cabin Boys, had started out in Chicago singing duets on the "WLS Barn Dance." They sang mostly ballads and folk songs like "The Big Rock Candy Mountain." The band members changed from year to year—sometimes from week to week—but at one time we were billed as "radio's funniest band," featuring Bashful Freddie and Frankie; Uncle Ozzie, radio's hottest fiddler; Al Mee, radio's funniest drummer; Tater Ted; plus Little Pee Wee, and other entertainers.

We opened WHAS every morning at 5:45 and played live until 7:00. After our program came Asher and Little Jimmie Sizemore, followed by Clayton McMichen and two comedians named Monk and Sam. We also did a daily show at 12:30. Foster Brooks, who later became famous as the "Lovable Lush," was the staff announcer for most of our programs. Our show was more of a variety show than a straight country music program. In fact, at that time we didn't really consider ourselves country musicians, since we were doing mostly popular and novelty songs. Also playing in Louisville at that time was the Atcher Family from out in the country near West Point, Kentucky. They were closer to a mainline country show. Many of our instruments—the clarinet, the saxophone, the accordion, and the drums—weren't considered country music instruments. Our stage costumes were about what country musicians wore—shirts and trousers with bandanas around our necks, nothing western-looking at all. The hayseed comedians might have on overalls with one gallus undone or a slouchy pair of denim pants, with a tooth blacked out and hair pasted down the middle of their heads.

Gradually, we began to play more country songs, many of them written by Asher Sizemore. In 1936 Mr. Frank compiled a songbook called *Log Cabin Songs*, which was published by Sizemore and featured mostly songs by him. On the cover is a photograph of me with my accordion along with six other Log Cabin Boys. Inside are pictures of Mr. Frank, our manager, Frankie Moore, our announcer, the Little Hoosier Maids, and Cousin Emma. Most of our songs were sentimental and nostalgic and are syrupy by today's standards. They were the kinds of songs we used both on our radio shows and

our road shows: "Horse and Buggy Days," "Memories of Old Kentucky," "My Old Coon Dog," "Shake Hands with Mother Again,"
and "Two Little Orphans." Every show had to have a gospel song,
such as "When We Kneel with Our Savior in Prayer," "How Beautiful Heaven Must Be," and one of the favorites with our audiences,
"The Royal Telephone." We also sang traditional songs of the West,
like "Cowboy Jack," "I Ride an Old Paint," and "The Cowboy's Dream."
One of the songs we used was written by Mr. Frank, with lyrics like
this:

> *My memory leads back to a tumble down shack*
> *Down by the lonesome pine.*
> *I'm leaving today headin' that way*
> *To that old fashioned mother of mine.*
>
> *There's an old fashioned lady with old fashioned ways,*
> *And a smile that says "Welcome to all"—*
> *An old fashioned bed where she kneels to pray,*
> *When the toil of the long day is through.*
>
> *Tho she wears no fine clothes or rich silken hose,*
> *There is something that makes her divine—*
> *Only God up above knows how I love*
> *That old fashioned mother of mine.*

Such songs may not win any awards for originality, but our
audiences loved them. We also did comic and novelty songs for a
change of mood. We tried to have something on every program for
everyone.

Soon after I joined the Log Cabin Boys, Mr. Frank was booking us in high schools and grade schools around Louisville. He'd
write to the graduating classes and say, "You sponsor us at your school,
and we'll give you 30 percent of what we take in." The students
would work hard to get a big crowd because that meant more money
for them. Before long, thanks to our radio shows, we had become
well-known and were doing shows all over Kentucky and Indiana
in towns like Brandenburg, Owensboro, Bowling Green, and
Georgetown, Kentucky, and Austin, Pekin, Madison, Columbus, and
Scottsburg, Indiana. We played not only in schoolhouses but opera
houses, amusement parks like the Fontaine Ferry Dance Casino in

Louisville, Knights of Columbus halls, courthouses, fraternal clubs like the Elks and the Moose, movie theaters, and even barns. Our theater shows would be advertised as half of a two-part billing, called "On Stage" and "On Screen." Many a time we shared the billing with Claudette Colbert, Joan Crawford, Gary Cooper, and Fred MacMurray. When we played a good-sized town like Owensboro on Fridays and Saturdays, we'd do three shows, a matinee at two o'clock and evening performances at seven and nine o'clock.

Soon we were signed to do a big Saturday night show on WHAS called "The Crazy Water Barn Dance." Our sponsor was a health tonic called Crazy Water Crystals, which was like a popular tonic called Hadacol that swept the country some ten years later. They both contained mostly alcohol. Crazy Water Crystals was a patent medicine that might not have cured anything, but it certainly made you think you were feeling better. The show was a combination of three or four acts that Mr. Frank put together, featuring Freddie and Frankie, the Callahan Brothers, Bob Atcher and the Atcher Family, and Bob Drake and his animal puppets, which he called the Jackson Family. Mr. Drake would have a screen and dangle the puppets in front of it. He did all the voices for the animal characters. The alligator was the bad guy. Drake got so popular Mr. Frank hired him to go on the road with us and gave him a ten-minute solo act on the show. His act was added to give variety to the playing and singing, and everybody liked variety.

We began to bill our shows as barn dances. In fact, one of our favorite locations was an actual barn out near Shelbyville, Kentucky, where a farmer named Ralph Strange stored his hay and tobacco. He had built a dance floor in the middle of the barn, and there were haylofts on both sides. There were some rows of benches along the sides if you wanted to sit down and listen. Mr. Strange had washtubs full of soft drinks and beer to sell. Crowds would range from forty to sixty, mostly farm people in their thirties. The Saturday night dances would last from about seven to ten o'clock because people had to leave early to get up the next morning for church. Our dance music was mostly for square dancing and round dancing, which were like waltzes and two-steps. Square dancing is, of course, a form of group dancing with a caller who directs traffic and tells the dancers when to make certain movements and figures. Mr. Strange was one of the best callers I ever heard.

Several years ago Lydia and I were guests at an auto dealers banquet and awards night, and a man came up, put his arms around me and said, "Look at me close and see if you remember me." I looked at him and said, "Are you sure you know me?" He said, "Sure, everybody knows you, Pee Wee, and I've known you since I was a little boy." I said, "Well, tell me your name and I'll probably remember." He said, "Does the name Strange mean anything to you?" I said, "Oh my Lord, it sure does. We used to get to your father's barn early in the evening so we could eat dinner and rest before we played for the dance in your barn." That was another important lesson I was learning from Mr. Frank. We had to get on friendly terms with our sponsors and our fans. We got to know so many of them as real people with names when we sat down to eat with them.

Louisville was an ideal city for a country and western band in the thirties not only because it had popular and powerful radio stations like WHAS and WAVE but because it was so well located. It was a hustling, bustling town, much more progressive I thought than cities like Knoxville and Nashville, which seemed to me more laid-back and old-timey. It was a commercial and manufacturing center, a sort of crossroads for the North and South and the East and West. It was located on a major river, and river commerce was still an important part of the city's economy. It was cleaner than most cities—except for the waterbugs, which I think were really roaches, that covered the downtown. The dampness from the river must have made the city a good breeding ground for all kinds of bugs.

In those days Louisville looked more promising as a music center than any other city in the South or Midwest. WHAS with its 50,000 watts of power was a main reason, and a lot of musicians came here to be on the radio, many of them managed by Mr. Frank. The Callahan Brothers had come here from Black Mountain, North Carolina. They renamed themselves the Town and Country Boys and were like a 1930s version of the Everly Brothers. WAVE wasn't as powerful as WHAS, but it attracted a number of good performers. After we spent a year in Knoxville, we came back to Louisville and did two shows on WAVE radio, one at six o'clock in the morning and one at noon. The morning show, which appealed to early-rising farmers, was sponsored by Patterson Fruit Trees. "Order six apple trees for $2.98 and you get fourteen other assorted trees absolutely free. But this is a limited offer, so act today." So went one of our commercials. So what if your bundle of trees arrived and they were little switches. If you waited long enough and the trees lived, you would eventually have apples or peaches or whatever.

Country and western stars who didn't live in Louisville performed here frequently, as they still do. If you want to sell out a show in Louisville even today, whether it's at a local club or the state fair, just book Reba McEntire or George Strait or Alan Jackson. After Gene Autry started touring with Champion, he seldom missed a chance to play Louisville. I have a snapshot of Gene playing the old Savoy Theater on Jefferson Street with the Golden West Cowboys. A funny incident occurred while he was performing there. His road show featured Champion and another horse, which he brought to the theater in a great big truck. He parked the truck behind the theater in the alley and blocked it completely. Somebody reported the blockage and a fireman arrived and said to Gene, "You've got to get rid of that damn van that's blocking the alley." Gene said, "Where am I going to put my horses?" The fireman said, "Hell, put them on the stage." Gene said, "Yeah, that's where I use them, but they can't stay on the stage all the time. They don't perform the whole show. They got to go somewhere to rest." So they stayed in the alley.

My first home in Louisville was a room in the Chelsea Hotel, which was next to the Salvation Army. Several of us Log Cabin Boys lived there. One day I was talking to one of the players for the Louisville Colonels baseball team, and he said, "Why don't you fellows get yourself a permanent room? It's a lot cheaper if you don't just rent a room for a night or two at the time." So that's what we did. Several of us band members got rooms in a rooming house for seven dollars a week at Third and Chestnut. Like so much of downtown Louisville, it's a parking lot now. We all had separate rooms and we ate in a restaurant next door that was run by an Italian guy. He had pinball machines in the back where we'd relax and kill time. We didn't have anything to do when we weren't playing or rehearsing. We rehearsed every day at Mr. Frank's house at Third and St. Catherine, right across from Walnut Street Baptist Church.

Clayton McMichen lived around the corner from Mr. Frank. Lydia and her sister worked for him for a while. He had come to

Louisville to play on WHAS. He was a champion old-time fiddler and had a group called the Georgia Wildcats. He set the style for square dance fiddle music. His shows featured a lot of animal imitations and hee-haws. In addition to Louisville, during the 1930s and 1940s he broadcast over radio stations in Pittsburgh, Chicago, New York, and the NBC network. He wrote dozens of novelty songs like "My Carolina Home," "Corn Licker Still in Georgia," "Back in Tennessee," "Peach Picking Time in Georgia," "Riding on a Humpback Mule," and "Sweet Bunch of Daisies," which was his theme song he named after his wife. When he lived in Louisville, he owned the town. Everybody loved him and his music. When I didn't have anything to do, I'd pal around with him. Later on, I roomed with several of his Georgia Wildcats—Slim and Loppy, who were brothers, and Jumping Joe, a buck-and-wing dancer—and we took turns making beds, buying groceries, and cleaning up, such as it was.

After a while, we moved to the Dawkins Rooming House at Third and St. Catherine, next door to Mr. Frank, which made it convenient for rehearsals. That's near where Lydia and I were living a couple of years later during the big 1937 flood. We didn't have to evacuate because we were on high ground, but the water eventually rose up even with the kitchen floor. You could put a broom handle in a knothole in the floor and touch the water. Lydia's brother came over and turned off our gas so we wouldn't have an explosion. We could see boats going up and down the streets all the time. Sometimes they brought us water and beer in five- and ten-gallon milk cans. It was much deeper up closer to the river around Broadway, but where we lived on St. Catherine it was plenty deep for boats to go through. We could look out our windows and see cars under water. We stayed in our apartment and didn't go out except to get food. We were comfortable but felt like prisoners.

We were booked to play the Elks Theater across the river from Louisville in New Albany when the flood hit, but we couldn't get out to play that date or anywhere else. Mr. Frank had promoted our appearance for weeks with posters and ads and radio spots. The very day we were supposed to open, the water reached the stage of the theater. The stage was wet. The seats were soaking. Everything was wet. So we stayed in our rooms and spent most of our time rehearsing shows we couldn't play until the water went down. Lydia and I were just married, and times were hard even before the flood. I had never managed to save any money since I had come south. I was usually broke between paydays. A few times I had to swallow my pride and borrow money from Mom and Pop. If he had it, Mr. Frank would advance us a few dollars; but times were hard on everybody. People paid a dime or quarter to see our shows, and we never took in much, plus a big percentage of the gate always went to the sponsoring group. After we started printing and selling our own songbooks and souvenir programs and pictures, we were able to add a lot to our income.

Yes sir, in the mid-1930s with so many good musical acts based in Louisville, it looked as if it was going to become the regional musical capital. Another act I should mention is Salt and Peanuts, a vaudeville act that played WHAS in the late 1930s. Salt was Frank Salt, who grew up on a ranch in Kansas, and Peanuts, the only name she ever gave out, was from Joplin, Missouri. They were veterans of the Keith Vaudeville Circuit and had done radio shows from WLW in Cincinnati, KDKA in Pittsburgh, and then finally WHAS. They wrote a lot of the songs they used in their act, including "Down the Old Ohio River Valley," "My Heart's in the Hills of Old Kentucky," and a song that reflected the hard times, "Can I Sleep in Your Barn Tonight, Mister?" Another popular entertainer based in Louisville was Jimmie Osborne, a Kentucky native who had a show on WKLO called the "Osborne Opry." He played the guitar and sang and later recorded for King Records. But perhaps the most important musical asset that Louisville had in those days was Mr. Joe Frank, who had become one of the best promoters and booking agents in the South and Midwest.

So why did Nashville and not Louisville become Music City USA? I think it was for a combination of reasons. First, the radio stations that were affiliated with the networks weren't interested in developing recording studios. It was a business complication they didn't want to bother with. Next, there was no large company in Louisville like the National Life and Accident Insurance Company in Nashville that was interested in supporting music of any kind, country or otherwise. There may also have been the feeling among the power people in

Louisville that country music was low-class, and they didn't want that image for the city.

WHAS had a number of good country and popular acts, and it had the same 50,000 watts that WSM had in Nashville. It reached huge audiences at night. Asher Sizemore and Little Jimmie and Clayton McMichen and all the others were immensely popular. So were the Log Cabin Boys and, later, the Golden West Cowboys. All of us got tremendous responses to our songbook and picture offers on the radio. The Bingham family, who owned WHAS and two local newspapers, could have been an important influence in the development of Louisville as a popular music center, but they were more interested in the fine arts of opera, ballet, plays, and classical music. So there was no one person or family or company with money and power to get behind Louisville, even though the potential was here. Louisville may also have been a little too far north to be the capital of what was basically, in those days, a southern music form. Nevertheless, Louisville has been good to me, and I have been happy to live here most of my life, except for ten years in Nashville, when I was a regular on the Grand Ole Opry, and except for one year in Knoxville, when we played on the "Mid-Day-Merry-Go-Round."

In the
Hillbilly Country

WE WENT DOWN TO KNOXVILLE because Mr. Frank got a phone call from Joe Pearson, the station manager for WNOX, a new CBS station, inviting us to come. "There's room down here for a guy like Pee Wee King and the Log Cabin Boys," he said. "I've got the perfect setup for all of you. Come on down." It was perfect timing. The Log Cabin Boys were splitting up. Frankie Moore had left for Wheeling and organized a new band with Cousin Emmy, who was a big barn dance star at that time. Freddie was going to California to become an FBI agent. Nobody was making any money at WHAS, not the players or Mr. Frank, who was paying all the bills and worrying about the payroll all the time. Mrs. Frank said, "Joe, you're not making enough money here to keep us alive. Maybe you'd better consider that job. Find out what they pay." So Mr. Frank called back and they offered us a guaranteed salary of one hundred dollars a week in script money for seven people. That was for six shows a week, including Saturday. That seemed like a lot of money for us in 1935, and we accepted it.

It turned out to be a lucky move, even though it only lasted for a little over a year. The new job provided us with a steady income. It made it possible for Lydia and me to marry. It was where we organized the Golden West Cowboys, and it was where we began to develop a national reputation. I also began to meet country musicians from Tennessee like Roy Acuff, Archie Campbell, and Homer and Jethro, all of whom would soon become big stars.

My first impression of Knoxville and the new job, however, wasn't very positive. When we arrived at the new studios of WNOX, I was shocked at what I saw. I'll never forget the way it looked. The walls and curtains and furniture were all done in different shades of purple and black. When you switched on the lights, it looked like a funeral parlor. I turned to Mr. Frank and said, "Well, what have you got us into now? I don't see how you got talked into coming down here to work in a place like this." He said, "Joe Pearson likes it here and thinks we will too. It's worth a hard try." Indeed, it was.

Our show was called the "Mid-Day-Merry-Go-Round," and it was on daily from noon to one o'clock. It was a kind of variety show, with a lot of different acts, including Roy Acuff, the Carlisle Brothers, Homer and Jethro, Archie Campbell, and a four-piece combo called Albany Musco and His Modern Band. Lowell Blanchard was our announcer. The Log Cabin Boys did at least one number a day, and we tried to make it a signature piece that people could identify us with. We also wanted to create an image with words so that the radio listeners could imagine what we looked like. Sometimes they imagined wrong. Archie used to tease me: "Pee Wee, do people mistake you for somebody else?" I said, "Sure, from the radio they think I'm a big, heavy-set guy. When they see me, they think I'm somebody else named Tiny who used to be on a barn dance program around here."

The show was divided into four fifteen-minute segments. One portion was sponsored by the Red Ash Charcoal Company that sold Red Ash Coal. Archie would say, "Get your Red *Ash* Coals. Get 'em while they're hot." He would hesitate and stumble before he said "Ash," suggesting that he might be about to say "Ass": "Get your Red—Ah, Uh, Ah—Ash! Coals." If he'd actually said "ass," he'd have been kicked off the air in those days. But Archie knew exactly what he was doing, and he knew what people would imagine. Another of our sponsors was a big Knoxville grocer named Cas Walker. Planters Peanuts was also a sponsor for a time.

Our broadcast studio had benches that could seat about four hundred people, and it would be filled every day. Most of the studio audience were townspeople who came in for the free show on their lunch break, but most of our radio audience were people out in the country. Sometimes farmers in town on business would come to the show, but they usually heard us on their home radios when they came in from the fields at noon for dinner. That was the best time for a country show. It wouldn't have worked in the afternoons because they were back in the fields hoeing and plowing and picking. It wouldn't have worked as well at suppertime either because they were out tending to animals in the barn and doing other night chores. Then they went to bed. Many of the farmers were listening to us on battery radios, and they didn't turn them on much at night because they didn't want to run their batteries down. They would listen to us on Saturday nights, when we had our big three-hour jamboree and the studio would be overflowing.

The radio show was a good promotion for our road shows. Like WHAS, WNOX was a 50,000-watt station, the strongest the government allowed, and the stronger the radio signal the more territory it would cover and the farther we could take our live shows. The big stations were reputation and audience builders for us. Each week we'd announce where we were going to play; then we'd put up posters that featured our radio connection: "Pee Wee King and Other Stars of WNOX's Mid-Day-Merry-Go-Round. Maryville High School. October 22, 7 P.M." That was the major benefit we would have a couple of years later when we joined the Grand Ole Opry on WSM. The Opry paid us nothing, but at least in Knoxville we got a basic salary. What we made on the road was extra.

Many of our road shows were at schoolhouses, where we would try to schedule a ten-cent matinee at three o'clock for the kids and then a night show, with admission at, say, fifteen and twenty-five cents. Mr. Frank was making all the arrangements, and he tried to book several schools in the same area. We'd send someone out to put up our posters two or three days in advance at the schools, in grocery stores, hardware stores, and filling stations. We used generic posters with a blank spot where we could print in the place and date. Regardless of where we were playing, we knew we had to get back to Knoxville for the daily and Saturday night shows.

We were in Knoxville for the last part of 1935 and all of 1936. Before we came back to Louisville, I made two important decisions that affected the rest of my life. I married Lydia Frank and, with

Mr. Joe Frank's help, I formed the Golden West Cowboys. First, the most important event in my life was marrying Lydia in December of 1936. I had known her since I started working with Mr. Frank. He was her stepfather, but she always called him her father because he was the only one she ever knew. Her blood father was August Winkler, an Austrian-born concert pianist, but he died when Lydia was only three years old. Her older brother and sister were born in Shreveport, Louisiana, where he was an orchestra conductor at a local theater. He was very young when he died and left his widow with five children. Lydia was born in Chicago, where they moved shortly before her father's death. That's where her mother met Mr. Frank about a year later and married him when Lydia was about six. A few years later Mr. Frank started out in the music promotion business. Lydia, therefore, had been born into and lived in a musical family all her life. She was pretty and talented and knew the music business better than I did. In other words, she was the ideal wife for me. I thought my love for her was mutual, and so it turned out to be.

She and her sister Marie were twelve and fourteen when they started singing on WLS in Chicago on a noontime show. They were also singing for funerals, political rallies, store openings—any occasion where they might be hired. When Lydia was about seventeen, Mr. Frank got them a job at WJJD in Chicago with one of Gene Autry's sisters, Veda, and they became a trio. On the six o'clock morning show they were called the Sunrise Girls, and on the evening program at six they were called the Sunset Girls. They earned fifteen dollars a week each and car fare. Later she and Marie performed as the Little Hoosier Maids and also with Clayton McMichen as the Georgia Peaches.

I began to get interested in Lydia soon after I moved to Louisville and met her. One day her mother invited two of us single Log Cabin Boys, Ted Fabian and me, to come up to their apartment for a quick lunch of creamettes, which was a kind of macaroni dish; and we got to know each other better. We started out as mainly friends and fellow performers. Lydia and Marie were very close, and when I'd see one I'd see the other. I was always teasing Marie, so when I finally called Lydia for a date, Lydia answered the phone and said, "Oh hello, Pee Wee, you must want Marie." I said, "No

Lydia, I want you." On our first date we went over to New Albany, Indiana, to a theater to see the Siamese Twins, and we had a flat tire on the bridge coming home. After I changed the tire, I said, "I know where we can get the biggest drink in town," and we went to a malted milk shop on Third Street and got a huge malted milk with two straws.

We continued to date occasionally in Louisville, but we didn't get engaged until we were in Knoxville. Marie got married, and Lydia got a new partner and they called themselves Sally and Sue. After Sue decided to go home to Pittsburgh to get married, Lydia and I began to get serious. We weren't dating anyone else because neither one of us had time for boyfriends or girlfriends. We worked together every day, and when we weren't performing we were rehearsing for the next show.

As our time in Knoxville was drawing to a close, we were both ready to commit to each other. I'm afraid I wasn't a very romantic suitor. On dates we'd go to the movies or out to dinner. When I asked her to marry me, I didn't get down on my knees. We knew we liked each other from the beginning, and that fondness developed gradually into a genuine and deep love. We got formally engaged when I hocked my tuxedo for six dollars and bought her a ring. Then on December 23, 1936, we ran away to Sevierville about twenty-five miles southeast of Knoxville to be married. I was twenty-two, and she was nineteen.

I had made arrangements through a radio fan to be married by a preacher named Fox. I don't remember his first name or the name of his church. Sevierville is Dolly Parton's hometown, but she wasn't born until 1946. One time I told Dolly that Lydia and I were married in her hometown by a preacher named Fox, and she said, "Oh, I know him. He's still living. I'll look him up and give him your best wishes." She told me later that she had, indeed, seen him and, she said, "Pee Wee, he's ninety-four and wants you to stop by to see him sometime when you're on your way to my place at Pigeon Forge." The next time we drove through Sevierville we stopped and asked directions to his house but were told he lived way out in the country, and we didn't have time to go searching for him. I tried to call him, but no one answered. So I never did see again the man who married Lydia and me. I wanted to tell him he did a very good job.

We didn't have a formal church ceremony with all the trimmings, but we did get married in a church. It was a little white church and was still standing the last time I was down there. When we got to town we called Preacher Fox at his home, and he said he'd meet us at the church. He arrived, began to fumble in his pockets, and said, "My Lord, I forgot to bring the key. I'll have to go home and get it." We were in a big hurry, and I said, "Isn't there some other way to get in?" Abner Sims, my fiddle player who had come down with his wife Alice to be our witnesses, looked up at the church and said, "If I can find an unlocked window, I can crawl through." Abner was a tall, skinny fellow, and he found an open window, slipped through, and went around and opened the front door and let us all in. Our wedding party consisted of Lydia and me, Abner Sims and his wife, Mr. Frank, two ardent fans, and a woman who later became Dolly's grade school teacher. We all went into the sanctuary, where the preacher performed a two-ring ceremony—the first one he said he'd ever done.

By the time we'd said our final "I do's" and the preacher had pronounced the benediction, we were exhausted. It had been a full day for us all. We had done our show on the "Mid-Day-Merry-Go-Round" from noon to one o'clock, then driven the twenty-five miles over a rough, two-lane highway to get to Sevierville. We got back to Knoxville just as it was getting dark and spent our wedding night in one of the guest cottages where the band was living on the north side of town. A week later we went back to Sevierville and had our honeymoon—such as it was—at the city hotel. It was Sunday, and we had no radio show or barn dance to do that day.

Near the end of our stay in Knoxville, we formed the Golden West Cowboys but waited until we were resettled back in Louisville to have our official debut as a new band. Before we left, we spent several days talking with Roy Acuff and his Crazy Tennesseeans about merging our two bands, but both of us wanted to be the head man, and it didn't work out. Mr. Frank had already gone back to Louisville, and Lydia went to stay there with her parents until I could finish several obligations in Knoxville.

Our last big show in December 1936 was a private function for a Knoxville politician. It was one of those swanky parties with uniformed waiters serving little finger sandwiches and drinks. It was the Christmas season, and a waiter brought the band five or six glasses of eggnog. Abner Sims took a sip, put it down, turned up his nose, and said, "Hell, I don't like this stuff. Take the whiskey out and you're drinking melted ice cream. I don't drink my whiskey like that. I'll take mine straight with water." Saying that, he went over to the bar and got himself a shot of bourbon and was happy.

In fact, we were all happy because we would soon be returning to Louisville. We had decided that Knoxville was no longer good for us professionally. We had burned out the territory. WAVE had offered us a good job back in Louisville, and we accepted gladly. We would be getting an attractive salary and a new sponsor, a patent medicine called Peruna. The Golden West Cowboys were ready to make our mark in the world of music, whatever it might be. By the middle of January 1937 we were again settled in Louisville and ready for our grand debut as the Golden West Cowboys. Except for occasional shows and "Merry-Go-Round" reunions, we would never again be in Knoxville. Our last reunion was held September 13, 1992, at David's Music Barn six miles north of town on Highway 25-W. By then there weren't many of us old-timers left.

Palmyra, Indiana
HIGH SCHOOL AUDITORIUM
Wednesday Nite, Nov. 6

Hello! Hello! Hello!
HERE COMES THE
LOG CABIN
= BOYS =

Radio Stars From

W
H
A
S
Louisville

Music Songs and Laffs

TUNE IN

WHAS

7:15 to 7:30 A. M. Daily

SEE AND HEAR
RADIO'S FUNNIEST FELLOWS
- IN PERSON -
ADMISSION:

Children under (15)
15c

Adults
30c

A flyer for a Log Cabin Boys performance at an Indiana high school.

Early portrait of Pee Wee King.

Pee Wee King poses with his accordian in 1932.

Left, Pee Wee playing accordian for the Log Cabin Boys. *Above*, Pee Wee with band of friends. *Below*, Pee Wee and his wife, Lydia Frank King.

Above, The Golden West Cowboys joined the family of the WSM Grand Ole Opry, which is still aired every Saturday night in Nashville, Tenn. *Below,* The Golden West Cowboys pose in front of an ad for an upcoming show.

Standing, Left to Right—CURLY RHODES, COWBOY JACK, ABNER SIMMS.
Sitting, Left to Right—PEE WEE KING, TEXAS DAISY, MILTON ESTES.

Above, The Golden West Cowboys (left to right): (standing) Curly Rhodes, Cowboy Jack, Abner Simms, (sitting) Pee Wee King, Texas Daisy, Milton Estes. *Right*, Pee Wee King and Gene Autry, who performed with him on radio, stage, and screen. *Below*, Pee Wee King, Judge Hay, and Ernest Tubb are featured on a Royal Crown Broadcast in 1945.

Pee Wee King and the Golden West Cowboys, along with Minnie Pearl, stop in Silver Springs, Florida, while on a Camel Caravan Tour.

Left, Pee Wee King with his daughter, Marietta Jo, son, Frankie Pee Wee Jr., and wife, Lydia. *Below*, Pee Wee and six-year-old Marietta Jo practice the accordian together.

Above, Singer/songwriter Redd Stewart, folk songwriter Fred Rose, and Pee Wee King rehearse for a session at the RCA Victor Recording Studio in December 1946. *Right*, Pee Wee King and Roy Acuff. *Below*, a scene from the Autry movie "Gold Mine in the Sky," with Pee Wee King.

The Billboard

JANUARY 18, 1947
25 CENTS

THE WORLD'S FOREMOST AMUSEMENT WEEKLY

Hep Hillbillies Make Music Biz Talk Turkey
—Music

Video Goes Pubserv With a Verve
—Television

•

PEE WEE KING
"Chanter in Chaps"
(See Music) ▷

Pee Wee King, featured on the cover of *The Billboard* in January 1947.

The Country of the Golden West Cowboys

IN THE FALL OF 1936 while we were still in Knoxville, Mr. Frank decided to disband the Log Cabin Boys. He said, "Pee Wee, I want to organize a new band, and I want you to lead it. You keep saying you want your own band again, and here's your chance." I said, "Yes sir, it sounds good to me. I want my own band." He said, "Get some of your friends to come down from Wisconsin to join you, but make sure they don't talk like you, with 'deeses' and 'dems' and 'doses.'" I said, "Don't worry. I know some fellows with the "Badger State Barn Dance," and they don't talk or sing with that big city brogue. Their English is a lot better than mine." So I went to Milwaukee and contacted Curley Rhodes, his sister Texas Daisy, and Jack Skaggs and brought them down to Knoxville. We got the idea for the name of the new band from Millie and Dolly Good, a popular cowgirl duet that sang with Gene Autry on WLS and called themselves the Girls of the Golden West. We got the Cowboy part from our own "Cowboy" Jack Skaggs. We put it all together and came up with the Golden West Cowboys.

There were six members of the original band. Abner Sims from Corydon, Indiana, was billed as "the fastest fiddler in the world." Oral "Curley" Rhodes, also known as Cicero Sneezeweed, was a comedian. Curley's sister, Texas Daisy, was a guitarist and ballad singer and a hell of a good yodeler. Curley and Texas Daisy sang as a duet and did a rube comedy routine as Odie and Jodie. Sometimes I would do a comic dialogue with them. I would say, "Curley, do you love to sing with Texas Daisy?" He'd say, "I sure do." Then I'd say, "Well, do you love Texas Daisy?" He'd say, "I sure do. She's my sister. Why shouldn't I?"

Other original band members were Jack Skaggs, vocalist, guitar, and bass player from Brownsville, Kentucky, and Milton Estes, another guitarist and our emcee from Middlesboro, Kentucky. Milt had one of those heavy Georgia-Alabama country accents, and that's what we needed. I certainly couldn't have done it. It was natural for him to say "Sure 'nough" and "Y'all come." I was still saying "tirdy-tird" and "fordy-ford," and this southern country talk was strange to me. It took me a long time to get used to it and understand it. I was the sixth member of the band, and I played the accordion. Out of the six members of the band, then, three were from Wisconsin, two from Kentucky, and one from Indiana. We didn't have anybody from the "Golden West" because we didn't know anybody west of the Mississippi River. At that time I'd never been west of the Mississippi River myself. While we were playing on WHAS and doing shows out of Louisville, the farthest west we ever got was Paducah, Kentucky. The first time most of us ever saw the Golden West was in 1938, when we went to California to make a movie with Gene Autry.

In November 1936, just before we planned to leave Knoxville, WNOX exercised an option and extended our contract for about eight weeks, so Mr. Frank said, "Just sweat it out, and then you can come back to Louisville, and we'll have a grand debut of the Golden West Cowboys in January." So the band played out the extension; then we moved back to Louisville and began preparing for our opening. Unfortunately, our grand debut coincided with the biggest flood in Louisville history. The result was that the newly minted Golden West Cowboys spent eleven days huddled together with little food, no lights, and no heat on the second floor of a rooming house barely above the flooded streets below. We were all broke by the time the waters receded. Luckily, we got billed into a Louisville theater for a one-day engagement that stretched to thirty-three and got us an invitation to appear on the Grand Ole Opry.

I kept the band together in one form or another for more than thirty years. During that time we had a lot of performers to come and go. I'll recall a few of the dozens that played with the band over the years: Lost John Miller, guitar; Harry Adams, guitar; Becky Barfield, vocalist and master yodeler; Red Penn, vocalist and bass player; Homer Haynes, guitar; Jethro Burns, comedy; Eva Nichols, known as San Antonio Rose, guitarist and vocalist; Shorty Hayes, fiddler and vocalist; Gene Engle, pianist; Donnie Hale, saxophonist; Jimmy Widener, bass; Shorty Boyd, violinist; Gene Schuler, banjo; and Tommy Sosebee, vocalist. In 1947 Don Davis, who played steel guitar, left us to join Tex Ritter's Western Caravan in Hollywood and was replaced by Roy Ayres, who was later replaced by Doug Oldham. Sticks McDonald, who had worked with such western bands as Spade Cooley and Bob Wills, joined us in the mid-1940s. The list goes on and on. . . .

There are a few players I want to single out for special mention. Cowboy Copas was a singer from Oklahoma and was a popular recording star for King Records. He was the second artist to record "Tennessee Waltz." One day he told me he was leaving my band to form his own group. I tried to get him to stay with us, but he was determined to go out on his own; so I wished him good luck. About eight weeks later he was killed in the plane crash that also killed Patsy Cline and another of my former band members, Hawkshaw Hawkins. There's no telling how popular Copas would have become had he lived. He was selling records like crazy when he died. He was the one who suggested that I hire Grandpa Jones to work as a comedian with Minnie Pearl, who worked with me off and on for most of her career. Eddy Arnold and Ernest Tubb and Roy Acuff also performed with the Golden West Cowboys at various times. More about all of them later. They have special places in my memories. I must not forget Chuck Wiggins, a guitarist and comedian who was my right-hand man for a long time. Neither can I omit Fiddlin' Hal Smith, who hailed from Alabama.

In 1953 and '54 our band was fortunate to have a talented young man named Neal Burris, who called himself the Shuffling Cowboy. Neal was doing gyrations several years before Elvis came along, though we never let Neal shuffle his whole body like Elvis. We didn't consider it wholesome enough for a country music show. Neal also wrote a number of songs, which we published in our songbooks. He later formed his own group called the Melody Ramblers and recorded such songs as "Put a Little Sweetnin' in Your Love" and "Bonita, Chiquita" for Columbia. His big break came when we signed a girl singer named Bonnie Sloan from California. She was recording for Capitol Records, and her manager wanted her to get some Midwest exposure. She and Neal hit it off and their voices blended just right, so we had a popular duet for a good while.

Redd Stewart and his brother Gene were very popular members of the band for a long time. Redd joined us in 1940, then spent about four years in the army during the war, and returned to help create the golden age for the Golden West Cowboys. While Redd was away, we had several good male singers, including Eddy Arnold, but no one seemed to have the voice that represented our sound as well as Redd's did. After Eddy left us, Redd became our featured male singer. Although Redd comes from a very musical family, he is mostly self-taught. He plays the bass fiddle, guitar, fiddle, and piano.

Mr. Frank hired Redd after he saw him one day headed toward his job at WGRC radio in Louisville with his fiddle in a gunnysack. Mr. Frank said, "What's your name and what do you do?" He said, "My name's Henry Stewart, and I play in a little country band called the Kentucky Wildcats." Mr. Frank said, "How would you like to work with Pee Wee King?" Redd said, "I wouldn't mind it." So Mr. Frank said, "Well, when you finish your present job and want to go into business with Mr. King, we'll work it out." That's how Redd became a member of the Golden West Cowboys. Within months he was a principal member of the band, and we were beginning to write songs together. Later he became a partner with Mr. Frank, Charlie Adams, and me in a publishing company. After a year or two he sold his share of the company and went into business for himself. He became a big recording star for King Records in Cincinnati. Whenever our band ran big promotional ads in trade publications like *Billboard* or *Cashbox* or *Record World* or in newspapers, we always featured Redd and called him a King recording star and listed his new releases.

Redd was with the band during the twenty-year period between about 1947 and 1967, when we were in top shape. Redd was on violin, Chuck Wiggins on guitar, Shorty Boyd on violin, Gene Schuler on banjo, Gene Stewart on bass, Sticks McDonald on drums, Roy Ayres on steel guitar, Gene Engle on piano, and Terry Tichy on electric guitar. I emceed and played the accordion. On our Louisville radio and television shows the announcer was my good friend Bob Kay, who often traveled with us. The boys in the band liked each other personally, and their music blended to perfection.

We had a low but steady turnover in the band. Some fellows like Eddy Arnold and Ernest Tubb wanted to try the big time on their own—and made it. Others were not so successful. Hal Smith, who played the fiddle, left to become a big star. He finally became successful, but not as a performer. He started a publishing company in Nashville, Pamper Music, and made a lot of money publishing songs like Hank Cochran's "Don't Touch Me."

My steel guitar player, Don Davis, left me to become Waylon Jennings's Nashville office manager. He was an Alabama boy only eighteen when I hired him, but he looked a lot older. He was working a radio show in Jackson, Mississippi, when he wrote me a letter saying his work there was a drag and he wanted to get out. I called him and said one of our boys was being drafted and we were looking for a replacement. "We'll be playing in Mississippi soon, and you can join us in Jackson for a tryout," I said. After the audition, I offered him a job. He was excited and said, "Oh boy, I got it made now. I got the tiger by the tail." But it wasn't true. He began to feel that something was still missing in his life. His music got stagnant, and eventually he left for better things. His star began to rise. He worked for Tex Ritter and Waylon Jennings and married one of the Carter sisters. His star in the Alabama Music Hall of Fame is next to Mr. Frank's.

I've tried to give talented newcomers a break and an opportunity when I could. I tried to hire people who liked to work, but I tried to avoid the temperamental artist who thinks he's already a star. Unfortunately, we've had a few like that too. One time Mr. Frank found a blond-headed boy named Royce Sprayberry down in Greenville, South Carolina, and he thought he could make another Gene Autry out of him. At that time things were tight and we couldn't really afford anybody else on the payroll, especially a man with a wife and three kids. But we liked him and gave him a job. When he wanted to move his wife and family to Nashville, where we were living then, I tried to discourage him. "We're gone a hell of a lot of the time," I told him, "and wives don't like to raise the kids by themselves, especially in a strange city. Your wife will have to understand that your new job means that you will be away from home a lot of the time." He said, "Oh, that won't be a problem." But it was, as I knew it would be. She moved to Nashville and didn't like the setup at all. Finally, Royce came to Mr. Frank and said, "My wife's not happy here. I'm not as big a star as I was in South Carolina. Nobody knows me here. So I think I'll just take my family and go back home and be a star there." He went back home, changed his name to Roy Spray, and nothing happened. He wasn't even able to get his old job back. He got angry with me because he thought I didn't do enough to make him a big star on the Opry. It's hard to do much for youngsters who already think they are superstars.

We had another bad experience with a big artist from Philadelphia named Jesse Rodgers. He and his wife were the hottest western acts in that part of the country, but he wanted to be a star on the Opry. He talked Mr. Frank into bringing him to Nashville, although his wife decided she was too big a star to leave Philadelphia for a town like Nashville. Rodgers had bad luck from the start. Right after he arrived, somebody broke into his car and stole all his wardrobe. He appeared on our Opry show several times and got zero response. Finally, he packed up what clothes he had left, went back to Philadelphia, and before long I heard he had died.

So I've seen them come and I've seen them leave. Luckily, nobody ever crippled the band severely by leaving. We always managed to fill in or find someone else to close the gap. The closest we ever came to being really damaged was when Redd Stewart left us, but we survived. It was a difficult period for us. I was trying to adjust to the new rock 'n' roll music and hired a boy named Dick Glasser from Cleveland. He was a very good rock 'n' roll singer and appeared on my television show in Cleveland one time. He came to me after the show and said, "I'd like to go to work for you. I can even write songs for your publishing company." So we hired him, and he fit into our group like the missing piece of a jigsaw puzzle. The first two recordings we did with him were a smash. The people at RCA Victor thought I was going nuts with our new sound. I said, "No. I'm an entertainer and we have to change with the times. Rock 'n' roll is changing American music, and that includes country music." That's exactly what happened, and even the Opry was eventually influenced by what came to be called rockabilly.

I think I was always able to judge realistically what our band could and couldn't do. I knew what our strengths and weaknesses were. I knew from the beginning of my own career, for example, that I would never be successful as a singer. I just didn't have the voice. I did sing solos occasionally and even some recordings, but more often I sang with groups in the band. My most successful voice performances were recitations, and I did them during live performances and on records. My most popular recitations included a political takeoff called "History Repeats Itself," "A Soldier's Deck of Cards," and "Hillbilly Heaven."

I wasn't a good vocalist, but I was smart enough to know that a successful band has to have good singers. In fact, we emphasized vocals more than most western swing bands, and we always had good male and female singers on our shows. At different times we had such singers as Cowboy Copas, Tommy Sosebee, Eddy Arnold, Roy Acuff, Ernest Tubb, Redd Stewart, Gene Stewart, and Hawkshaw Hawkins. The female singers ranged from the Collins Sisters, a song and dance team that dressed in skimpy cowgirl outfits and wore six-shooters and holsters, to San Antonio Rose and Little Becky Barfield, whom we billed as "the Singing Sweetheart of the Cowboys." The Collins Sisters worked for me for the better part of twenty years and often during intermissions would teach the kids how to clog and tap dance. They wore dazzling, sequin-filled costumes that would put some Las Vegas shows in the shade.

We tried to make the Golden West Cowboys a unique band. We were a dance band and more. Since most of the players came from the South and played in the country tradition, we put our western dance and swing sounds together with country sounds and came up with a smooth blend of several influences. By the time we got to the Grand Old Opry, we were a well-rehearsed, versatile band. We could play just about anything—a violin playing a single note, an accordion doing two-part harmony, waltzes, two-steps, polkas, ballads—just about any kind of popular music you could name. One of the reasons our boys were more versatile than other country and western bands is that they could all read music. Many good folk musicians play and sing by ear and can't read a note of music, but I decided in the late 1940s that as professionals everyone in the band would have to read music. There was some resistance. Some band members and fans thought the band might lose its homey, folk touch; but that didn't happen. The band sounded just as genuine after everyone began reading music as it did before.

Another reason that we were different—at least for a country and western band—is that we were all members of the musicians union in Louisville. When we went down to Nashville and tried to transfer our membership to that local, they didn't want to accept us. They said country musicians weren't professionals and many of them couldn't read music; but I convinced them that we were professionals and could read music. They would have had to accept us anyway because we were already members of another local of the American Federation of Musicians. After that, other Opry members joined the Nashville local, and within a few years the Opry itself was unionized.

Our band, therefore, was a melding of many sounds and traditions, but I always thought of the Golden West Cowboys as basically a modern western swing band. I simply took ideas and hints from everywhere and put them together to give our band its sound. When I heard Bob Wills, I liked his sound and borrowed some of it; but I didn't intend to make our band a carbon copy of his or any other band. Bob, for example, didn't use an accordion; but the leader of our band was a fellow named Pee Wee King who played the accordion, so we featured that instrument. When I heard Spade Cooley, I liked his smoothness and class. When I came south, I began to pick up more country sounds by reading the songbooks put out by Jimmie Rodgers, Carson Robinson, and others, and listening to their recordings. It all came together in our music. We played dance songs, tragic songs, novelty songs, love songs in a variety of styles and tempos. We played whatever people wanted to hear. We wanted to make people feel good and want to dance.

In order to survive, we knew we had to adapt to what the people wanted. Sometimes that meant not just bringing in new sounds but even adjusting the makeup of the band. When I played in the Upper Midwest—Minnesota, the Dakotas, for example—I'd use musicians from that area for a band with some pick-up members that had a regional appeal. I'd even tamper with our core band if I needed to. If I was doing a recording and thought a certain singer or musician was not quite right for the session, I'd get somebody else. The band knew that I was doing what was necessary to maintain our popularity on the road and to sell records, and they got used to being shifted around. They knew I made changes that would benefit the whole group. Fortunately, we usually had eight or nine regular band members who were so talented and versatile they could do almost anything— solos, duets, trios, quartets as vocals or instrumentals. I convinced them that in my band everybody was a star. If you don't believe me, just ask them.

For a specialty or small band, we played a wide range of music. With at most twelve people in our group, we thought we were a big band, but we weren't. The Big Bands of the time like those of Tommy Dorsey and Glenn Miller had as many as fifty players and performers. A band like ours had fewer players and a tighter focus, but our small size made it easier for us to respond to very specific demands. We could always shrink our band or enlarge it, as occasion required. Let me give an example of how we adapted to one of the most successful dates we ever played. In 1985 a convention manager called to ask if I could play Lawrence Welk or Wayne King style music for a national meeting of McDonald's franchise holders in Atlanta. I said, without any hesitation, "Of course we can."

At that time I had only six permanent members of the band, so I hired two saxophones, one trombone, one trumpet, and a few other instruments to remake it into an orchestra. My band became Pee Wee King and His Orchestra for that event, and we played in the big ballroom at the Hyatt Regency. It was a spectacular setting, with ice carved into golden arches at the entrance. We tailor-made our program for the audience. We started out with our usual "Sentimental Journey," then began to play faster and faster dance tunes. Finally, when I felt the timing was right, I said, "As you know, I love to play polkas. Are you ready for a polka now?" Their response was deafening, and pretty soon we had five thousand people dancing the polka—some of them for the first time—and having a wonderful time. The convention manager said our band sounded as good as any big orchestra they ever had at triple the price. "Last year," he said, "the Big Band we had couldn't play diddly-squat. The people didn't like it, and not many of them even tried to dance. Now, look at all these people having the time of their lives. Pee Wee, you know how to please your audience."

Pleasing our audience was exactly what we wanted to do. We played a variety of music, but we knew we couldn't be all things to all audiences. We couldn't have a Big Band sound no matter how hard we played. After we'd been on the Opry for a few months, I realized we weren't going to attract a strictly country crowd like Roy Acuff or Eddy Arnold. We found that when we did shows with Roy or Eddy, they would be featured and we'd get second billing. So we didn't try to compete directly with either extreme. It was Mr. Frank who said we had to find our own niche and change our strategy. He started, for example, booking us into five-day runs at big hotels like the Baker in Dallas or the Thunderbird in Gulfport, and we played smooth dance music like the two-step, which the people liked. It was a setting that we were perfectly suited for.

Even though we played a lot of dance music, we put on a complete show. I always had a girl singer and a boy singer with the band, plus various combinations like trios and quartets. At one point, we had a trio called the Bardstown Bucklebusters and a comic duo called Spike and Spud. Between sets of dance music, we also did about twenty minutes of a floor show when the people would sit and listen.

A successful band had to be on the move. We couldn't stay in one place and hope to gain a national reputation and sell records. But getting from one place to another was sometimes hazardous to our health. I used to kid the boys about all the driving we had to do. "To work for me," I said, "you don't have to be a good musician, just a good driver." We were very lucky that we had good drivers and no serious accidents when we sometimes had to drive long distances over narrow, winding roads, through blinding rainstorms and icestorms in pitch blackness. But we did have a few mishaps, and two of the most serious involved Eddy Arnold, who joined the band in 1938. One wreck happened on a steep, winding road in the mountains outside of Asheville, North Carolina. He was with Mr. Frank and was driving up a mountainside behind a slow-moving truck. Eddy got impatient and said, "By God, I'm going to pass that truck if it's the last thing I do." Joe said, "If you're not careful, Eddy, it might be the last thing either of us will do." Just as Eddy pulled around to pass the truck, he saw a car coming right toward him head-on, and in swerving to miss it, he drove the car into the side of the mountain. He fell against the steering wheel and it slammed into his body and knocked him to the floor unconscious. Mr. Frank shook him and said, "Oh my God, Eddy. Oh my God, you're dead!" After a few seconds, Eddy opened one eye and moved. When he came to, he said, "I knew how to protect myself. I just scrunched up against the floorboard." He wasn't seriously injured.

In 1940, when we were again living in Louisville and working on WAVE radio, Eddy fell asleep driving from Vincennes, Indiana, back to Louisville. We had played a late show in a Vincennes theater and couldn't get away until after midnight. Eddy said, "I don't feel like any of you guys are in any condition to drive, so I'll take over at least until we get to Greenville." That's a little town thirty or so miles west of Louisville, where we might switch drivers for the last leg of the trip home. I said, "It's okay with me if you think you're up to it." So the rest of us dozed as Eddy drove through the night. Just as he approached Greenville, I heard him say, "I don't think I can make it all the way, but I see the light in Greenville up ahead. I'll get to that light and then give somebody else the wheel." Texas Daisy and I were sitting in the back seat, and Milton Estes was in the front seat with Eddy. All at once the car went wowhhhhhh! wommmmmpppppp! and down a bank of the road, into a basement wall, and we all flew out of the car. Milton said later I was so stunned I grabbed an ear of corn and said, "Hello operator, give me Mr. Joe Frank in Louisville. We've had an accident." Somebody did say, "Pee Wee, go wipe the blood off your face." I said, "Oh my God, why have I got blood on my face?" We all got some bruises and scratches, but it was a miracle that we weren't seriously injured or killed. Daisy slipped under me, and wasn't hurt much, and Milt went straight through the corner of the windshield and got his nose cut up. Eddy was hardly injured at all.

Two days after the accident, we had a date in another little southern Indiana town—Warsaw, I think it was—and Mr. Frank said, "I want to change the name on the marquee from 'Pee Wee King and the Golden West Cowboys' to 'Pee Wee King and the London Refugees.'" Milt came hobbling on the stage on crutches. Daisy had a Band-Aid on her forehead, and I had bandages all over my head.

We did indeed look like the walking wounded from the London air raids. But the shows had to go on, and we played that date and several others right afterwards without missing a beat. Each time, we all hobbled out on stage and said, "Here we are, folks—what's left of us."

The show had to go on because we needed the income. In the 1930s and early 1940s we frequently ran out of money. It was especially tough when we didn't have adequate funds on the road. I used to ask our sponsors for an advance of fifty or a hundred dollars, with the rest due after the performance. We'd use the advance to pay for gasoline and other travel expenses in getting there. It worried me to know that I was responsible for the band, but I accepted it. I used to get a funny feeling when I counted up how many people were dependent on me. At one time, including my partner in Hollywood in the publishing business, my booking agent, my office staff, my brother Gene and his family, my family, and the members of the band and their families, it came to fifty-seven mouths to feed. It was a big responsibility, but I couldn't afford to lose sleep over it. It was a situation that came with the job, and I'd been used to it most of my career. Now that I look back on it, I can see how much weight was on my shoulders. Just think! Our little cowboy band could feed fifty-seven people. With all that pressure, I guess it's a miracle I didn't have my stroke long before I did.

As we became more successful and our income increased, I tried to keep a little cash reserve to meet emergencies. But none of us had any capital to back us up. Most of us were from poor or modest backgrounds and didn't have any resources to tap. The boys in the band expected their checks to be ready every Friday in my Louisville office. If they were on the road, their wives or parents could pick up their checks. They trusted me to be good for their salaries, and I'm proud to say I never failed them. Our whole business relationship was based on trust. Except for a short contract I had with Redd Stewart, I never gave contracts to my band members. They stayed with the band as long as it was mutually satisfactory.

For several years we had a Golden West Christmas Club, and all the boys contributed a few dollars a week, which they would draw out in December for Christmas money. It was sort of like a Christmas Club account, except we handled it through my office. One time two of the boys got into a tight spot and wanted to borrow from the fund like it was a credit union, but I said no. To me the fund was a sacred trust, and I didn't want to risk everybody's Christmas money with bad debts. In addition, it could have soured all our relationships. You don't lend money to friends.

What is the recipe for a successful band? For me, it was good management, good promotion, and most of all, a good bunch of talented guys and gals that got along with each other. I never had much trouble with any of them. To my knowledge, we never had any serious jealousy in the band, not among the boys. And we couldn't have had any jealousy among the girls because I usually had only one girl at the time. Everybody knew that a band can have only one boss. And everybody knew who that was. If somebody didn't like me or the way I ran the band, he knew where the door was.

Naturally, there's some jealousy in a profession like ours so filled with egos, especially among the superstars—or those who think they are. I'm speaking now about people outside my band. When we played on the Opry, we were on the road most of the time, maybe 250 days a year, so I didn't have the time or the desire to be a part of the backbiting and backstabbing that I heard about. I have heard, for example, that several girl singers on the Opry wanted to get Loretta Lynn bumped from the Opry lineup when she was getting started and beginning to rise to stardom. I was never a part of anything like that. I believed—and still do—that a real professional should respect and honor the work of other professionals. When we worked package shows—that is, shows with several important performers on the same billing—I knew we had to have one headliner, one star. Who was the star? He was the main draw, the one that attracted the most people, the one who sold the most records. He was the one who headlined the show and closed it. There's always a pecking order in the business, beginning at the top with the superstar, followed by performers who are talented but need a break or don't quite have the charisma to reach the top, and finally, the newcomers who are learning the ropes and are sharpening their talents and image. Everybody can't be a headliner at the same time.

In a profession that is as unstable, demanding, and irregular as music, there is bound to be some strain on family relationships. The wives sometimes resented the fact that their husbands had to be gone on the road so much of the time. Lydia tried to serve as mediator and pacifier for the wives. She had a lot of social events for them at our house when we were on the road. When the band was at home, we had dinners and dances here in our basement. Sticks McDonald and Dorothy were married in our living room, and still are married. We had a party for Shorty Boyd and Glenna at our home. Occasionally, the wives would get a little jealous of each other, especially when one would get a diamond ring or a fur coat or a new car. One of the boys said his wife was complaining because she didn't have an expensive ring like so-and-so's wife. I said, "You boys all get the same salary. You and your wife have two children. The other couple have no children, and they obviously can afford to buy a bigger diamond. Tell your wife she's got children, and the other woman has a ring. You make your own choices about how you spend your money." Indeed, I always paid the band members the same salary, regardless of how long they had been with the band. They got a regular salary, and they all got part of the income from souvenir items and songbooks. I paid them all the same because they were all equally important to the success of the Golden West Cowboys. One of the reasons we got along so well is that I never played favorites with anyone.

The boys and their families all worked to build a good image for the band. Country music has always been family entertainment. Look at a photograph of country music audiences at the Opry in Nashville or at a theater in Tupelo, and you'll see a mixed group of people, men and women, boys and girls. I tried to present the Golden West Cowboys as a wholesome band with a family image. When Minnie Pearl was performing regularly with us, she used to say, "Pee Wee, you've not only got the best-dressed boys I've ever worked with, but they always behave like gentlemen. Why, when I go out on the stage and tell my jokes, they still laugh—even after they've heard them a hundred times! That's dedication and showmanship and good manners."

Such a spic-and-span image was not always the full picture. We didn't air any dirty linen we might have, and we didn't talk about everything we did. On stage, we might be a bit off-color with our humor, but we told no jokes that would embarrass a family group. Backstage, the boys were a little more earthy. Men will be men, and back there or on the bus the fellows sometimes shot craps or played poker and took a swig of liquor, but we were careful not to allow any photographs of us doing any of those things. It would have been bad publicity. Hank Williams couldn't hide his drinking near the end of his life, but he was such a genius that people loved him in spite of his bad habits. Most of us couldn't have gotten away with such public behavior. Hank was an exception.

Alcohol and drugs have ruined many an entertainer. Fortunately, we never had any serious problems with our band members. A few of them slid down the bar stool after they left us. A few years ago I heard from the wife of one my former pianists who said her husband was in a nursing home in Missouri. We started corresponding, and he wrote that he was still playing the piano and enjoyed entertaining the old people at the home. The head nurse wrote me a note to say that he was one of the best loved people there. His problem, she said, was alcoholism. He had sunk so low from where he was when he played in my band. He had been like the glue that held us together. Then he left us, and his drinking began to get out of hand. Finally, his drinking destroyed his talent, his career, and his marriage.

I had another talented musician who ruined his life with alcohol. After he left us, I tried to use him for recording sessions, but he began to come to the studio drunk as a skunk. The last time it happened I tried to sober him up, but he pushed us away and said, "I don't need you. I'm a big star already." I never called him for another session. I couldn't run the risk of working with someone who was not dependable. In recent years drugs have become a curse of the music business, and almost all performing groups have been affected. I let my band members know that I would not tolerate drug abuse. I know how stressful the entertainment business is. It's one of the most high-pressured ways to earn a living. But alcohol and drugs are not the solution. If you take them too far, they will lead you to a dead end. I said to my boys: "You can have a good career and a good time and not become an addict to anything. If you absolutely have to unwind and feel you need to get high, then go ahead and do it. Just make sure when you come to work for me, you're sober. Just make sure you don't get a reputation as a drunk or drughead. The public won't take it for long. And I'll tolerate it even less." It usually worked. Even with our best efforts to keep our image clean and to keep band members and their wives together, we had a few divorces. Nobody bats a thousand.

Minnie was right about my boys being well-dressed gentlemen. I've always believed that clothes help to make the man, and I insisted that my band look good. If I had allowed the boys to go on stage in cheap, sloppy, dirty suits, it would have reflected on us as professionals. If you look at photographs of the Opry cast or the "WLS Barn Dance" performers in the 1930s, you'll see that most of the men dressed in denim trousers and flannel shirts or in overalls, and the women wore gingham dresses. To me, they didn't look classy or professional. I bought the best costumes for myself, and I required that the rest of the band do the same. When I started my first band up in Wisconsin, the players usually wore tuxedos. When I came south and formed the Golden West Cowboys, I decided that we should wear cowboy costumes more in keeping with our music and our name. Our first costumes were fairly simple outfits that looked like the trim-fitting costumes used in cowboy movies. Then we began to get a bit more glittery, and we had our costumes custom-made in Hollywood by a rodeo tailor named Nudie. He made the costumes for all the big cowboy stars like Rex Allen, John Wayne, Tex Williams, and Roy Rogers. At first, our outfits raised a number of eyebrows, especially at the Opry, because we were wearing satin shirts and fancy leather boots when the other performers were still in bib overalls and checked shirts. An exception was Hank Williams, whose Drifting Cowboys band wore western clothes and boots. When he was a teenager Hank went to Texas and worked in a rodeo, but he never really played western music. His music is about as country and hillbilly as it can get. I guess he just liked the glamour of the western image. Another, later exception to the rule was Patsy Cline, who often wore fancy cowgirl outfits.

As the leader of the Golden West Cowboys, I wanted my own outfit to stand out. It had to be not just bright and shiny, but flashy, with gold and red and green embroidery. Even in the 1950s my shirts would cost as much as sixty-five dollars each. My boots cost even more. Redd Stewart said that the first time he saw me performing at the old Savoy Theater in Louisville in my sparkling cowboy costume and shiny cowboy boots, I looked larger than life. But, he said,

I still sounded more like a Yankee than a cowboy! The best costume I ever had was made for me in the late 1960s and cost about six hundred dollars. Not long ago, I gave it to the Music Valley Wax Museum in Nashville. Even though the figure itself is not the right size and doesn't look much like me, I recognized myself right off. It was the costume that made the figure.

Not all country performers adopted western dress, of course. Bill Monroe and his Blue Grass Boys never wore western outfits. In addition to their bluegrass music, they did more traditional ballads and sacred music and preferred dressing to look like Kentucky plantation owners with white hats, plaid shirts, riding pants, and boots. Those rhinestone cowboy costumes are still worn by older performers like Porter Wagoner and Little Jimmie Dickens, but a lot of the younger generation like Garth Brooks and Alan Jackson have reduced the glitter and wear regular street clothes with maybe a cowboy hat and boots.

In addition to music, my band had another bond that held us together. That bond was Masonry. At one time, in 1952, every band member was a Mason. That bond gave us a common cause and a strong camaraderie that saw us through thick and thin. I think it made us better musicians. I never selected band members because they were Masons, but I invited them to become Masons after they joined the band. Mr. Frank was a Mason, and he was the one who sponsored me. Then I sponsored Redd Stewart and others. Masonry is a bond with a lot of country musicians. Most of the big guys I know are Masons—Roy Acuff, Gene Autry, Eddy Arnold. I'm a 32nd degree and Eddy is a 33rd degree, which is as high as you can go. My home lodge is in Nashville, but when I moved back to Louisville I transferred to the Kosair Temple. I got my fifty-year pin several years ago, and I still attend meetings. I enjoy getting together with the guys, and I heartily support the Masons' two major objectives, fellowship and good works.

Luck, of course, plays a role in becoming a successful band. So does timing. You have to get to the right place at the right time and perform for the right people with the right material. You have to have something to offer when the opportunity comes. You have to be prepared to take advantage of breaks. One time we had a chance to audition to take over the "Midwest Hayride" radio show on WLW.

Jack Soebel had arranged the spot if the Wiedemann Beer people would buy it. So we went up to Cincinnati, set up our instruments in the studio, and did a show for about fifteen people in the audience. When we finished, the executives said, "When can you start?" I said, "We already have. You just saw the first show." You see, we were waiting and ready. We had tried to anticipate what they wanted. We had the right material. The door was open, and we walked right in.

It takes time to find your niche and to create your image. A musical group has to pull together. They have to have a spirit that makes them one. The leader is responsible for creating and nourishing that spirit. He has to lead the band in setting goals and then achieving them. One of our goals, for example, was making hit recordings. Without them, we couldn't consider ourselves successful. Once such goals are met, what you get is a Vaughn Monroe and His Orchestra, a Guy Lombardo and His Orchestra, and a Pee Wee King and His Golden West Cowboys. I managed to get to the public with our best talent and performances. The reason my band was picked as the number one country and western band so many times was that we all stuck together and strived for the same objectives. The awards we won made me a happy man because they certified that we were what we thought we were, the best band of its kind in the country. When I look back now and realize how many hits we had, I am truly amazed. I am amazed at how popular we were. I am amazed at the awards and honors we won. I am amazed that so many of our songs have become standards.

But all good things must come to an end, even a good band like the Golden West Cowboys. In 1958 I was working myself to death with television and radio shows, private parties, road shows, recordings, and our publishing company. I was tired. Our television contracts in Chicago and Cleveland were ending, and it seemed like a good time to take a break. The boys were tired and wanted a rest too. Some of their families were under heavy stress and on the verge of breaking up. Bill King, who was my manager at the time, said, "Pee Wee, why don't you pull back and put together a little group that can play dates close enough to Louisville so you can get home every night? You still have your television show on WAVE. A few road shows in Kentucky and the nearby states and your TV show—that's enough to keep you busy." That's what we did for a while.

It wasn't long before I formed another group called Pee Wee King and His Band for a road show with Minnie Pearl. We did a lot of tent shows and state fairs, and I continued to adjust the band as needed. One time we played with the Collins Sisters in Ohio, where they were teaching dancing. Minnie said, "Those girls would add a lot to our show. We ought to invite them to join us." I agreed. She liked their singing and dancing act, but she also liked their company. They usually traveled with Minnie and her husband Henry Cannon in their plane, and the rest of us used our regular touring cars. Minnie left that show in 1963, but I continued the band playing military bases with package shows for five more years with Redd Stewart and the Collins Sisters as the headliners. Then in 1969 I disbanded the Golden West Cowboys for good and used pickup musicians when I did shows. I certainly didn't intend to give up show business just because I didn't have the Golden West Cowboys any more.

Music Country
USA

WHEN I WAS GETTING STARTED in the 1920s and 1930s, barn dances were the rage in country and western music. They were usually Saturday night country shows that were not only called barn dances but sported names like hayrides, jamborees, shindigs, and fiddlers' conventions. One of the biggest and best known was the "National Barn Dance" on Chicago's WLS, which originated in the "hayloft" of the Eighth Street Theatre. It started around 1924 and by the mid-1930s had featured some of the best early country music talents, including Pat Buttram, from Winston County, Alabama, who did backwoods humor; Kentucky's Lily May Ledford, who played the five-string banjo and was billed as "the fiddlinest girl to ever come out of the mountains"; Georgie Gobel, "the littlest cowboy" who dressed in a cowboy costume and played the ukelele; Lulu Belle and Skyland Scotty, a North Carolina duo who performed and also composed or arranged such novelty songs as "Chewing Chawing Gum" and "How Many Biscuits Can You Eat?" as well as the popular love song, "Have I Told You Lately That I Love You?"; the Prairie Ramblers and Patsy Montana, who sang mountain and cowboy songs. The "National Barn Dance" also provided a stage for other well-known performers of the day like Clyde Julian "Red" Foley of Kentucky, a comic hayseed named Uncle Ezra, and the best-known one of all, Gene Autry, who was a regular on the show when I met him in 1934.

The "National Barn Dance" played to overflow crowds from

their hayloft studio and to huge throngs at state fairs. At the 1933 Chicago World's Fair, more than thirty thousand people attended the barn dance show. WLS was owned by a rural newspaper called the *Prairie Farmer* and published a popular weekly radio magazine called *Stand By*, which had articles and news about their country music stars. Chicago remained an important country music center until after World War II.

Another popular barn dance was "Renfro Valley," a folk music show that started in 1937 on WLW in Cincinnati, then moved about two years later to a log cabin settlement in the Kentucky hills of Rockcastle County about eighty miles south of Lexington. It was started by a native of that area, John Lair, who had worked at WLS as their music librarian, with help from performers like Red Foley, the Duke of Paducah, and Homer and Jethro. John's idea was to present the actual residents of the Kentucky hills and mountains and their culture as they lived it, including the clothes they wore, the instruments they played, the songs they sang, the dances they danced. He wrote a beautiful ballad called "Take Me Back to Renfro Valley," which became his theme song.

He wanted his barn dance to be a genuine folk show, and I think he did a great job. He had a big following on network radio, especially for his Sunday morning "gathering," which featured church songs. His main weakness was lack of money. He had very little capital backing him. It was hard to get rich Kentuckians to back a barn dance. They'd say, "If I let you have $100,000, will I get back at least half of that within a year?" Well, it couldn't be done—not with their small seating capacity and small admission charge and the fact that they were so far away from a big urban area. They had to depend mainly on tourists who stopped by on their way to and from Florida. Since John's death a few years ago, a number of improvements have been made. The management books Opry acts on Saturday nights. Like John, they are desperately trying to upgrade the facilities and attract new audiences. They have a new barn and programs to draw young people. I have performed a number of times on the Saturday night show and had a wonderful time. On our way to Tennessee when John Lair was still alive, Lydia and I always stopped to eat at the Renfro Valley restaurant. They had excellent home cooking.

There were many other barn dances scattered all over the country.

The "Louisiana Hayride" on KWKH from Shreveport's Municipal Auditorium had many of the superstars of country music, including Faron Young, Webb Pierce, Johnny Horton, Floyd Cramer, Johnny Cash, Hank Williams, and Elvis Presley. Springfield, Missouri, had a very popular show called the "Ozark Jubilee." KNX's "Hollywood Barn Dance," hosted by Cottonseed Clark, was just one of the many barn dances on the West Coast. In the 1950s Jimmy Wakely starred in a Saturday night program on CBS radio called "Hollywood Hay Ride." Barn dances were dotted all over the map. Cincinnati had its "Midwestern Hayride." Danville had its "Virginia Barn Dance," which aired over WDVA and went national in 1953 over the Mutual radio network. Wheeling had its "World's Original Jamboree" on WWVA, which began in 1933. WBT in Charlotte had its "Carolina Hayride." Kansas City had its "Brush Creek Follies" on KMBC.

Many smaller towns had their own versions of the big barn dances. The "Old Kentucky Barn Dance," for example, was started in a livestock auction barn in Lexington in 1949. It was broadcast on Saturday nights over WKLX and sponsored by Eureka Flour Company of Beaver Dam, Kentucky. Entertainers included Earl Scruggs and Lester Flatt and the Foggy Mountain Boys, Randall Parker, who sang mountain ballads, and a comedian named Oscar Goobertooth Shagnasty. The list goes on and on and reaches all corners of the country. It was a combination of luck and planning that put Nashville's "Grand Ole Opry" ahead of all the others.

The Golden West Cowboys were poised and ready for the big time when our break came in 1937. With so many barn dances and country music hubs all over the South and Midwest, Mr. Frank knew there would be a shakeout before long, and he predicted correctly that Nashville would be the main survivor. The biggest hub was Chicago and WLS, but it was too far north. All the other cities—Cincinnati, Pittsburgh, Shreveport, Atlanta, Charlotte, St. Louis, Louisville, Kansas City, and others—had problems in location or local support and interest. Nashville is centrally located in the middle of the traditional country music territory. It speaks the language of the South, which is the language of country music. There weren't many competing barn dances close by. It had a 50,000-watt radio station, WSM, a smart general manager named Harry Stone, and a program manager named George D. Hay, who knew what his resources were and how to use them to the best advantage. Finally, it had the National Life and Accident Insurance Company. By 1937, when we moved to Nashville to be on the Grand Ole Opry, it was already the capital of country music. Not many people knew that, but Mr. Joe Frank did.

One of Mr. Frank's main goals was to get one of his acts on the Opry, and we were the first one to make it. We had put together a good band and were ready when we went down to audition on Easter weekend of 1937. We were asked to stay for the Saturday night show, but we had a commitment at Horse Cave, Kentucky, and returned instead the following Saturday to begin what would become a ten-year hitch on the Opry. Mr. Frank and the Golden West Cowboys rented a complex of three houses on South Thirteenth Street in Nashville, and we began our stay living close together.

The Opry had already been going for about twelve years when we arrived. According to George D. Hay, "the Solemn Old Judge," it began at eight o'clock, Saturday night, November 28, 1925, when he invited an old-time fiddler named Uncle Jimmie Thompson to do a program on WSM. The response was tremendous. WSM had just gone on the air the previous month, and Hay realized the wealth of folk music in the Tennessee hills and countryside. The show was originally called the "WSM Barn Dance," but about two years later Hay nicknamed it the Grand Ole Opry. His country music show followed an opera broadcast from New York, and when he opened the show one night he said, "Well folks, you've been up in the clouds with grand opera. Now get down to earth with us for a four-hour shindig of Grand Ole Opry." The Solemn Old Judge not only named the show that night but defined its down-to-earth music. He once called the Opry "as simple as sunshine," and he fought to keep it pure and simple. He even fought me when he thought I was polluting and diluting his brand of country music.

WSM was owned by the National Life and Accident Insurance Company, and its call letters were the company's slogan, "We Shield Millions." The Opry soon became a gold mine for the company because it was a door opener for their insurance salesmen who traveled all over the South. They'd knock on the door and say, "I'm from WSM's insurance company. We bring you the Grand Ole Opry every Saturday night. Did you catch Roy Acuff's show last week? That man knows how to sing and fiddle." Chances were very good that the family on the other side of the door heard the Opry every week and were fans of Uncle Dave Macon and Hank Williams and Minnie Pearl and all the others. Now here was a man on their front porch from the company that made it all possible. So, of course they were going to be polite and invite him in, and maybe even buy some insurance from him.

A lot of country people made the trip to Nashville in their rattletrap cars and trucks and heard the Opry live at the WSM studios, the Fatherland Tabernacle, the War Memorial Auditorium, and later at the Ryman Auditorium. When we arrived at the Opry, admission was still free. People would arrive early and eat the dinners they'd brought from home on the grounds. I remember vividly seeing hundreds of people lined up at the Fatherland Tabernacle before the doors were open, and then they'd be let in about six o'clock to the tabernacle, with its sawdust on the floor and homemade benches to sit on. One time Mr. Frank was looking out at the throng of people waiting for the free show to start, and he said to the Opry announcer, David Stone, "You're missing the boat. You should charge a small admission price, maybe a dime or a quarter." Mr. Stone said, "Why should we charge them? We're getting a lot of valuable advertising out of these free shows." Mr. Frank said, "When you give something away, people don't value it as much as they should; but if you charge even a small amount, they know it's something special." Most of the people who came to the Opry were too poor to pay much, but not long after we arrived, the Opry began to charge a small admission.

Another major asset in making Nashville Music City USA was the Ryman Auditorium, which was the home of the Opry from 1941 until Opryland opened in 1974. During those thirty-three years it was the "Mother Church" of country music. To many ordinary people it was a sacred place where they could hear people like themselves celebrate their lives of trials and tribulations and triumphs in music and comedy. In fact, the Ryman was originally built as a church, the Union Gospel Tabernacle.

The story is told that a riverboat captain named Tom Ryman docked his boat one evening in 1891 along the Cumberland River, which flows through Nashville. Captain Ryman had a reputation for being a heavy-drinking brawler, and that night he and some of his crew decided to have a little fun by breaking up a tent meeting where a popular evangelist, the Reverend Sam P. Jones, was preaching. Apparently, Brother Jones was waiting for him because as soon as he and his gang walked in, the preacher launched into his tear-jerking sermon on Mother. It must have been a rip-roaring success because on the spot the lost soul was saved. Not only was he converted from the paths of sin, he dedicated himself to doing the Lord's work and promised to build a great tabernacle for the Reverend Jones to use. He was true to his word, and the following year the tabernacle was opened. Church services were still being held there when I was on the Opry, but it had also doubled for a long time as a concert and lecture hall.

WSM started renting the tabernacle for the Friday and Saturday night Opry because they had outgrown the War Memorial Auditorium. There was also a lot of trouble with litter scattered around the building, which is close to the state Capitol. The Ryman was convenient, cheap, available, and could seat more than three thousand people. Another reason the Ryman was an ideal place for the Opry was its acoustics. I don't know the technical explanation for why the sound was so incredible, but I have my own theory. I believe the wood in that auditorium absorbed the sounds of the music, and it just stayed there. The walls and floor soaked up layer after layer of music and gave it a richness, a kind of patina, like a piece of furniture that improves with years of use and becomes an antique. It was like being inside an old violin, surrounded by good, seasoned wood. A big music hall like the new one at Opryland that is made of concrete won't resonate the sound like wood. The sound was so good at the Ryman that, even with all the scuffling and shifting in the audience, you felt like you were in church. It didn't matter where you sat, downstairs or in the balcony that covered about half of the lower auditorium. It didn't matter if the roof was leaking, which it did every time it rained. The sounds of music in the Ryman were always lively and rich.

Not even the backstage noise could destroy the sound. And talk about noise! It was like a free-for-all back there. In fact, a lot of the talking and tune-ups and rehearsing took place in full view of the audience. Sometimes the only way to tell who was performing was to see who was at the microphone at the center of the stage. It was like organized chaos, but somehow the audience heard just what they were supposed to.

There were almost no dressing room facilities, just one area for men and one for women. There were two washrooms to accommodate as many as two hundred performers in one night. During the summer the heat inside would get up close to 100 degrees. I'm sure young performers today wouldn't put up with such facilities, but it didn't bother us. I never heard any complaints. We were proud to be on the Opry and proud to be performing at the Ryman. Nothing else mattered. When I'd finish my part on the show, I'd pack up my instrument and go out in the alley and head toward my car. Then I'd turn around, look back at the Mother Church of country music and say, "Well Lord, I hope I did my best tonight." It was so appropriate that the Ryman was built as a church because Saturday night at the Opry was, for most of us on stage and in the audience, like being in church on Sunday.

There were no lounge facilities at the Ryman where we performers could get together and talk, so we'd agree to meet in the alley and go to a nearby bar or café to relax. One time I saw Loretta Lynn come over to the boy's side of the dressing area and holler out, "Roy, I want to see you." Roy Acuff said, "All right, Loretta, just give me a minute. I'll be out directly." She said, "No, I don't mean now. I mean after the show." Roy said, "Okay, where can we meet?" She laughed and said, "How about my office in the alley?"

After meeting in the alley, a lot of us would walk a few yards over to Tootsie's after she opened on Broadway about 1960. If the Ryman was our church, then Tootsie's Orchid Lounge was our shrine, complete with a priestess and holy pictures on the wall. The icons were photographs of Opry performers after they got famous. The last time I was down there it was still open, but it looked a little seedy. It went downhill after the Opry moved in 1974 and after Tootsie died in 1978. It was a regular tavern, but it had a small stage big enough for two or three people to play and sing. I never played there, but it was popular with people like Willie Nelson, Tom T. Hall, and Roger Miller when they were trying to break into the Opry. If they couldn't play the Opry, they could maybe play at Tootsie's. Even

stars who were down on their luck would play there for a few dollars; and if they were hungry, Tootsie would feed them and put it
on the tab until they could pay. They could even borrow some money
from her. She'd say, "Well, I reckon I can let you have forty dollars,
but you be sure to pay me when you get back from the tour." I never
got that desperate, but a lot of well-known Opry stars did.

In those days country musicians didn't have deep pockets to
tap between dates, and they had to depend upon the generosity of
others. I have often been tapped by desperate musicians. One time
when Billy "Crash" Craddock was just starting out in the business
and was working a date with us close to York, Pennsylvania, his bus
broke down. A mechanic looked it over and said he could fix it, but
he wouldn't take a check. Crash asked the man to drive him over to
the auditorium where we were playing, and he said, "Pee Wee, I
don't have enough cash to have my bus fixed, and the man won't
take a check." So after the show I paid him his fee and lent him a
few more dollars; then I took him over to pay the mechanic and get
his bus, and he was okay until the next crisis. Sometimes an Opry
performer would get stranded without any money and would have
to get a family member or friend to wire him some. Merchants, hotel managers, and other people you'd meet on the road didn't like
to take checks from country musicians. Sometimes the checks would
bounce.

I never had any serious money problems on the road. While
he was alive, Mr. Frank made all the arrangements for us. He rented
the show hall, hired the ticket sellers, and kept close tabs on sales
and expenses. We didn't always make our guarantee because of a
snowstorm or a windstorm, but we were never stranded for lack of
money. The Good Lord must have been looking out for me!

I think Tootsie was from around Nashville. Her husband was
a singer and performed over WLAC in Nashville and did shows at
high schools and festivals in that area. Tootsie looked like a typical
housewife, and she served as a substitute mother to many country
entertainers. She was always ready to listen to their troubles and let
them cry on her shoulder. She was a good manager and ran an or-
derly place. If two fellows had too much to drink and wanted to
fight, she'd send them out to the alley. She also served good food,
the best roast beef and barbecue sandwiches I ever ate. Tootsie was

just one of a number of women around Nashville who befriended
musicians who were down and out. Another was Mom Upchurch,
who ran a boardinghouse on Boscobel Street right near where I once
lived. A lot of her boarders were Opry people because she was within
walking distance of the old Fatherland Tabernacle. So many of the
boys lived from day to day and were lucky to get help from women
like these.

I arrived at the Opry with an organized western band. Most of
the Opry stars performed individually and were not part of a band
or group. If the singers needed a band to back them up, they used a
staff band with catchy, hick names like "the Possum Hunters," "the
Fruit Jar Drinkers," the "Mud Creek Ramblers," or "the Gully Jumpers."
The players were loosely organized, if they were organized at all.
In those early days there was more string music than vocals, with a
lot of old-time fiddling. Much of the instrumental music was for
square dancing, but there were never any square dancers on the stage—
that is, not until Mr. Frank decided to spruce up our act by having
the Kentucky National Champion Square Dancers to perform. The
Solemn Old Judge was shocked. All that dancing didn't set well with
him and the other straight-laced Opry managers, and they didn't
allow square dancing on stage again for a long time.

The Golden West Cowboys never fit in very well with the hillbilly
string bands that filled the Opry stage. We played a lot of western
swing music and used instruments like the accordion and drums and
horns and electric guitars. Some people say I "electrified" country
music. Back then, most people thought that to be a country musician you had to play a fiddle, a guitar, a banjo, or a mandolin. Gradually,
we helped to change ideas about what country and western music
should sound like. We certainly proved that country music doesn't
have to sound old-timey. It could be just as up-to-date as a new Ford
or Chevrolet. But it was not easy to get the Opry to modernize.
George D. Hay was very resistant to any kind of change. The first
time he heard me play my accordion, he said, "What is that thing
you're playing?" I said, "It's an accordion." He said, "That's not a
country instrument." I said, "Well, it's a western instrument, and
we play country and western music. If you see a Western movie with
music, you'll generally find not only a guitar but a fiddle, a harmonica, and an accordion." Of course, we soon helped to wipe out

the line between country and western music, just as we helped wipe out the distinction between country and pop.

Every time we'd introduce a new instrument on the Opry, the Solemn Old Judge would get upset. His glasses would come down on his nose. He would call me over, and I knew I was in for a lecture. That's what he did when we did a show with a drum the first time. He said, "Pee Wee, there's no room on the Opry for a drummer." I said, "But Judge, that's how rhythm got started." That's the way he reacted when we used a trumpet for the first time on the Opry. I was substituting for Roy Acuff on his show in April of 1945 when President Roosevelt died, and I had Buddy Harrell bring his trumpet from the bus and play "Taps" while I played "My Buddy" on the accordion. We had everybody in the audience in tears. Then Buddy went straight into "Bugle Call Rag," and Mr. Hay almost jumped off the stage. Afterwards the Judge said he wanted to talk to me about some things I still needed to learn about the Opry. I said, "I'm sorry, Judge, I don't have time right now. We are leaving immediately for a show in West Virginia. Anyway, you asked us to do our regular stage show, and that's what we did." The Judge said, "Pee Wee, I don't know where you get all your answers, but you sure got 'em." What I was trying to get across to Mr. Hay and the Opry generally was that music, like everything else, has to change with the times. Not to change is to die. I think the Judge, however, finally saw what I was trying to do. A few years later, after "Slow Poke" became a national hit and blurred even more the line between country and pop, he said to me, "Pee Wee, you've always been at least ten years ahead of your time." I said, "Thank you, Judge. You've seen the light at last."

When we were performing on WAVE and WHAS in Louisville and WNOX in Knoxville, we always got paid for our work. As members of the musicians union affiliated with the American Federation of Labor, we were supposed to be paid a minimum scale. But the Opry didn't pay its performers in those days and didn't make an exception for us. Our income had to come from personal appearances. Our "pay" was that we became known as Opry stars and could announce our show dates on the air.

It was a hustle to get in our personal appearances and get back to play our regular shows on the Saturday night Opry. Near the end of each week, we'd try to schedule shows near Nashville, and sometimes we'd even try to sandwich in shows while we were performing on the Opry. It was similar to what we called "bicycling," that is, booking two towns on one night and running from one place to the other, just as if you were racing on a bicycle. For example, we'd book a show in, say, Kosciusko, Mississippi, and another show in nearby Philadelphia. We'd do our first show in Kosciusko at six o'clock; and while they showed a Gene Autry Western, we'd run over and do our show in Philadelphia at eight o'clock; then we'd rush back and do a ten o'clock show at Kosciusko. Sometimes we'd even transport the featured movie from one theater to the other. That was three shows in two towns in one night. You have to be young and willing—and maybe a little hungry—to take that kind of wear and tear.

When we played towns close to Nashville, we could sometimes do the Saturday night Opry and two shows at, say, Franklin, which is about eighteen miles south of Nashville. We might do a matinee in Franklin at the movie theater, then go do our early spot on the Opry, then go back to Franklin and do another hour for them, return to the Opry for our second show there, and finally go back to Franklin and close the theater with a show from eleven o'clock to midnight. The first time we tried it, the manager said, "Mr. Frank, these boys can't make that schedule. They won't get back in time. There's no way they can do these shows and the Opry shows too." Mr. Frank said, "Don't tell me what my boys can do. They're going to do the Opry and your show. You can count on that." Sure enough, we were always at least five minutes ahead of time. Of course, if we'd got caught in a traffic jam or had a flat tire, we couldn't have made it.

One time the band was a little late, but it had nothing to do with bicycling. It happened because the boys played crime-stoppers. For several years our Opry spots were at nine and eleven, so we had about an hour to kill between shows. One night between performances several of the Golden West Cowboys went out to a target practice range to do a little rifle practice and were rushing back the Opry to do our second show. Just as they pulled up in front of the building, a thief was in the act of robbing a passerby. The would-be thief looked up, saw the boys dressed in their cowboy uniforms and carrying rifles and dropped his victim's wallet and fled. That incident made them a few minutes late, but somebody covered for them. Their picture was on the front page of the next morning's newspaper.

There were other times when we were late for road shows because of car trouble. One time when my twin sons Larry and Gene were three years old, they decided to help Daddy gas up his car—I had a big Cadillac limousine then—and the truck we carried the instruments in. The only problem was they were gassing us up with sand and gravel from the driveway. We were headed to Shreveport from Nashville to be on the "Louisiana Hayride," but both vehicles stopped dead on us a few miles out of town. We finally got them pushed to a filling station, and the mechanic took one look and said, "Fellows, you ain't gonna get to Shreveport on these vehicles tonight. But I tell you what I'll do. I'll loan you my truck and by the time you get back, I'll have everything ready. I got to take the gas tanks off before I can clean them out; then I have to let them dry before I can solder them back on, or we'll all go up in flames." We crowded into the truck cab and onto the truck bed and finally got to Shreveport. Our booking agent was waiting for us and said, "Pee Wee, I knew something was wrong because you're always on time." I said, "We were cutting the time close to begin with, and once we got started again I couldn't afford the time to stop and call you." It wouldn't have mattered much if we had been playing a local stage show, but you can't delay a live radio show. As luck would have it, Kitty Wells and Johnny and Jack were also on the "Hayride" that night, and they took our place, and we took their spot later on.

During the ten years we were regulars on the Opry, we played with wonderful people—Uncle Dave Macon, the Delmore Brothers, Roy Acuff, Minnie Pearl, Hank Williams, Patsy Cline, just to name a few—just about everybody in country music at that time. Of course, the ones who performed with my group, like Eddy Arnold and Minnie Pearl, have a special place in my memory. Two of my other favorites were Sarie and Sally, a comic sister act. Sarie was Edna Wilson from Chattanooga and Sally was Margaret Waters of Memphis. They were already on the Opry when we arrived. Mr. Frank said to me, "Pee Wee, we're newcomers down here, and we need to work with an established act first to give us legitimacy. Sarie

and Sally know the ropes, and we'll hook up with them for a while."
So they were the first act I worked with at the Opry. When they
weren't available, I'd try to get the Delmore Brothers, who were
big names in the late 1930s and had some hot records. Sarie and
Sally were older women with grown children, but they were real
troupers. They weren't afraid of driving roads covered with ice and
snow to make a date. One time Mr. Frank said, "I'm going to put
together a show featuring the Golden West Cowboys and Sarie and
Sally and book you in the Sudicum chain of theaters all over the
South." It turned out to be a very successful tour, but it left us all
exhausted because we did a lot of bicycling. We almost broke our
necks running from one show to another, especially when we were
playing the Opry on the same day.

It was hard to do road shows and the Opry too, but we all had
to do it. We had to be on the Opry for the prestige and the publicity, and the road shows gave us our income. We knew we had to be
on the Opry stage when we were scheduled. The only legitimate
excuses were death and extreme illness. Many a time we have driven
all night long to get back to Nashville for the Saturday Opry. A lot
of performers couldn't take the pressure and resigned from the Opry.
Soon after we arrived, the Delmore Brothers left to start their own
barn dance in Raleigh, North Carolina. It's still a grind today for
Opry stars, even though they get paid and have better Opry schedules. The management at the Opry is more flexible than it was in
my day. The Opry, like country music itself, keeps changing. The
music has broadened. The new young musicians are revolutioniz-
ing the whole business.

In 1974 the Opry got a new home out at the Opryland amusement park, and I was there to say farewell to the old Ryman Auditorium and the thousands of memories it had locked within its walls.
Opryland is a giant enterprise, an amusement park with dozens of
rides, a luxurious, four-star Opryland Hotel, craft shops, a petting
zoo, the Acuff Country Music Museum, and, of course, the Opry
auditorium, where the Grand Ole Opry is broadcast over WSM and
TNN, The Nashville Network. Every time I go to Opryland, I can't
believe what has happened to country music in my lifetime. The
new Opry house seats about 4,700, and it's always jam-packed to
the rafters during the Opry broadcasts. It has a red curtain that rises

and falls between acts. The seats are a lot more comfortable than the ones at the Ryman. The architect tried to make a continuity between the old and the new when he set into the stage some of the floorboards from the Ryman. The commercials are still read for Dollar General Store and Goody's Headache Powder, the way we used to advertise Royal Crown Cola and Prince Albert Smoking Tobacco on my Opry shows. The old stars and the new stars play together on the stage, so you'll hear Bill Monroe and Porter Wagoner and Little Jimmie Dickens along with Ricky Skaggs and Garth Brooks and Alan Jackson and Kathy Mattea and Marty Stuart and Tom T. Hall. But somehow as I sit on the front row for the annual Hall of Fame show, in the middle of all that luxury and glitter, I don't have the same feeling I had when we were playing back at the old creaky, uncomfortable Ryman. But now we can have a piece of the past along with the conveniences of the present. In June 1994 the Ryman reopened after a multi-million-dollar renovation. Now there is air-conditioning and even cushions on the seats, and you can tour the Ryman Museum and see special stage shows and broadcasts. Of course, we can never again hear within its walls the legendary sounds of Hank Williams and Patsy Cline and Roy Acuff and Ernest Tubb; but somehow I think their sounds are still there reverberating in the stillness.

Opryland and TNN are state-of-the-art for country music fans of a new generation. In the old days country music was a Saturday night thing for most people. Now you can have it any time you want. You can go to Opryland in the summer and hear afternoon concerts by Opry stars like Loretta Lynn and Jerry Clower. You can tune in TNN any time, day or night, and get country programs. The Opry is still on WSM radio on Friday, Saturday, and Sunday evenings. You won't find a lot of traditional Opry programming on TNN because Opryland wants people to come and see the shows in person. But you will see shows that appeal to people who like country music and culture. There are cooking shows, variety shows, talent scout shows for new performers, fishing and hunting shows, country dancing shows. I enjoy watching some of them. Ralph Emery does a good job with his interviews, but I've seen him so much now I can predict what he's going to say. Most of his guests are on the show to plug something—their show dates, a book, or a new album. I don't mind that. After all, that's about what we were doing in 1937.

I think TNN is having a very big—and mostly good—influence on country music. Shows like "You Can Be a Star" have opened doors for a lot of performers and given them a chance to be heard. There are thousands of people all over the country, from Smithville to Farmer City, who want to get on television, and some of them have talent. TNN provides a lot of opportunities for young and up-and-coming county musicians to perform. Dwight Yoakum got a hell of a break on TNN. Marty Brown from over near Owensboro, Kentucky, got national exposure on TNN, which he parlayed into a good-paying promotional job with Wal-Mart Stores. TNN has allowed all kinds of new talent and innovations, and that's good. I only hope that country music doesn't lose its soul with all these changes. Already a lot of the traditional sounds are gone. One of the few younger Opry performers still close to his country roots is Ricky Skaggs. His music blends the best of the old and the new. While I applaud TNN for the good work it is doing, I have to confess that my favorite country music show is *Austin City Limits* on PBS. That show has sparkle and excitement and the best country talent today.

Country music is a billion-dollar business now, and it's run like one. There's a lot of market research and not as much plain old experimentation and chance-taking as there used to be. The Opry, Opryland, TNN, and a new network called Country Music Television—and even the stars themselves—are now financial properties to be bought and sold by financiers like Edward L. Gaylord and his wife Thelma. The Gaylords owned a lot of newspapers and broadcasting stations, as well as the TV series, *Hee Haw*, and bought WSM and the Opry properties when it came up for sale. Gene Autry was interested in bidding, but he never had a chance against the Gaylords. At one time he was interested in building a country music center in Dallas, but I think he's dropped all such plans now. Texas would have been a good place for a country-western entertainment complex because it's filled with people who like cowboy music, cowboy looks, cowboy dress, cowboy atmosphere and style. But it'll be up to someone else to do that now. Gene's too old to take on such a major project.

I can't fault the Gaylords for their takeover of the Opry enterprises. They did a good job with *Hee Haw*, one of the best country variety shows we've ever had. Talented entertainers like Roy Clark, Buck Owens, Archie Campbell, Grandpa Jones, Junior Samples, and the preacher comedian Grady Nutt made it a tremendously popular series. But the Gaylords wanted a country music and culture empire, and they had $650 million to spend to buy it. Opportunity is the name of the game in business, even the business of country music.

Of course, it's hard for old-timers like me who want to stay active to find an audience nowadays. We're not invited to play state fairs or any of the big-paying concerts. One of the few places where we are welcomed is another country music empire, the one in Branson, Missouri. You can see younger stars like Reba McEntire and Ricky Skaggs there, but you can also see Mel Tillis, Tanya Tucker, Glen Campbell, Johnny Cash, and Willie Nelson. Some of the older stars have come to Branson to settle down. Johnny Cash built his own theater, he said, "Because I'm looking forward to sleeping in the same bed."

One of my oldest and best friends, Boxcar Willie, has one of the most popular music halls at Branson. I go back a long way with Willie. Before he got to be famous, he was a disk jockey at a radio station in Omaha. I was doing a show there one frigid winter and was supposed to be at his studio at five o'clock in the morning for an interview. At that hour a visitor had to punch a bell to be let in. Boxcar was in his enclosure and didn't see or hear me outside in the freezing cold ringing the bell. I kept punching and getting colder. Finally, as I was about to give up, he remembered I was coming and came to the door and let me in. "I thought you might not show up," he said, "and I just forgot. Most of the stars don't want to get up and come over here at this hour." Afterwards, he and I appeared on each other's shows many times. Many other stars have their own theaters at Branson, and there's also the Grand Palace, which seats more than four thousand people and attracts such new stars as Vince Gill, Emmylou Harris, and Patty Loveless.

The country music shows at Branson go back to the early 1960s, but it wasn't until Roy Clark opened his music hall there in the mid-1980s that it really took off and became a serious rival to Nashville as the country music capital. It's cut deeply into attendance at Opryland,

and it's already the center of country music in the Midwest. People are swarming there from all over the country.

Branson has become popular for a lot of reasons. First, as I've suggested, older fans can see and hear and meet a lot of us senior musicians there. It's not nearly as expensive as Opryland, where the hotel can cost you several hundred dollars for a weekend. It features a range of country sounds, from traditional to bluegrass to gospel. You can find fancy musical revues with a heavy patriotic flavor, pop music, and even a Japanese fiddler named Shoji Tabuchi, who has a very popular variety show. Middle-class people like it because it has clean family entertainment. Most of the places don't serve liquor. Most of all, the traditional country music stars and fans feel at home when they go there. I certainly do.

Of course, I felt very much at home when I lived in Nashville, despite the snooty attitudes of some of the natives. Attitudes in Louisville and Nashville toward country music back in the 1930s were very similar. A lot of people in both cities looked down their noses at what they called hillbilly music. Some Nashvillians didn't like the image that country music gave their city of being a hick town. Most of the rich people, the movers and the shakers, and the university crowd didn't pay us much attention. They didn't go to the Opry. They had their own little cliques and circles, their golf tournaments, symphony concerts, card games, and dances. People who lived in the fashionable sections of Nashville, like Belle Meade and the West End, had little to do with the early Opry stars. Sometimes we'd get the cold shoulder from people who thought we weren't worth fooling with. They seemed to be saying, "You're not in my class. You're not educated and cultured. Why should I spend my time with you?" It's true that most of the hillbilly performers were from farms and little country towns and didn't have a lot of education. Stars like Loretta Lynn, Patsy Cline, Hank Williams, and many others didn't even finish high school.

Of the early superstars, Minnie Pearl was a major exception. She went to finishing school and college and helped to bridge the gap between the Belle Meade set and the Opry performers. While she was appearing on the Opry, she was also hobnobbing with the upper crust. She moved in both circles without any trouble or strain. She was never embarrassed by her performances as an Opry star.

She was show business all the way, a real professional. She was like a ballplayer who puts on his uniform to play out on the field, then takes it off when the game is over. I don't think she set out to be a cultural bridge. It happened because Minnie was at home with upper classes and lower classes and all of us classes in between. She was so well educated and such a good and decent person she could appreciate all kinds of people and adapt to any situation.

Minnie was just getting established when I met her. She was trained in serious music and drama, and she wanted to be an actress. She was touring with a tent show when she discovered the character she developed into Minnie Pearl. Ophelia Colley, Minnie's real name, already knew who she was and didn't have to prove anything to anybody. She had so much self-confidence she could play a country woman, add touches like the tag hanging from her straw hat, and not feel self-conscious about it. As a professionally trained actress, she knew what would appeal to the audience. After all, that's what all entertainment is about—how to get people to like what you do and come out to hear you. Minnie Pearl was a God-sent opportunity for Ophelia Colley. How many actresses ever have the chance to create a living character known and loved by millions of people?

Another country star who made his way into the higher social circles of Nashville was Eddy Arnold. There were also people like Jimmie Davis, the country musician who was elected governor of Louisiana in 1944 and wrote "You Are My Sunshine." But for most of us, it was like living in those early days in two cities, the city of the Opry and the rest of Nashville. The attitude that country music was lowbrow spilled over to the fans. I've seen them go into record shops and buy a Frank Sinatra or a Jo Stafford record and sneak an Eddy Arnold or a Pee Wee King record in the pile. For a long time it wasn't fashionable to admit in public that you liked country music.

I don't think many of us Opry people ever worried about it. In fact, we didn't have a lot of time to think about it because we were usually on the road doing shows and didn't have much time to get involved in Nashville's social life, even if we'd wanted to. I know I never felt inadequate. I've met a lot of people at parties and fundraisers and social and fraternal organizations that are just as ignorant of show business and show business people as we are of them. We all specialize in something. My expertise is show business. If you ask me about other things, I'm limited in what I can say. But that's not been a real handicap. After they get to know me, people accept me for what I am. Everybody's limited in some way. Everybody's ignorant of some things. Character and personality make you what you are. You can have a long family pedigree, a pile of college degrees, and be a millionaire, and you can still be a rotten human being.

The country music people I've known who felt insecure and inadequate were that way for reasons other than their profession. I know Hank Williams felt very insecure, especially around Audrey. He was so much in love with her that he was always afraid she would leave him. It made him feel inadequate and gave him an inferiority complex. "If I'm so good," he seemed to say, "why can't I keep Audrey?" On the other hand, maybe it was this uncertainty, this living on the edge of their relationship all the time that made him such an original genius as a songwriter and performer. You can feel the insecurity and heartbreak and longing in songs like "Lovesick Blues" and "Your Cheatin' Heart." His hurts and fears came out in his songs. With his great talent, Hank is assured of a place with the immortals. He was not inferior to anyone. Even the big symphony orchestras play his songs now. A lot of us country entertainers of Hank's generation may have been lacking in some education and social graces and felt ill-at-ease in the mansions of Belle Meade, but we were the ones who put Nashville on the map.

My ten years on the Opry were good years. I developed musically, socially, and personally. I met a lot of good and talented people who became my friends for life. I helped to play a role in the reshaping of country and western music into a music that could appeal to a broader audience and become the music of America. I sometimes had to fight conservatives like George D. Hay, the Solemn Old Judge, who resisted a lot of the innovations I brought to the Opry. But let me credit him with something important. About our kind of music, he used to say, "Keep it close to the ground. Keep it simple enough for people to understand it." He was right. Adaptation and change are the laws of life, whether you're operating a hardware store or playing music. In the Germantown neighborhood of Louisville, the people don't care anything about bluegrass music, but if you play a polka or a waltz, they will sing and clap and dance. You have reached their level. An entertainer has to remember that he's there to please the audience and not himself. They bought the tickets. If you compose and play for yourself, you won't have a job long. The Solemn Old Judge, as narrow-minded as he was, was right about one thing. You've got to keep your music close to the people.

Mr. Hay was just one of the many people I met in Nashville and at the Opry that taught me a lot about country music. But after ten years, it was time to move on to other challenges. I had enjoyed living and working and even playing in Nashville. I had played on the National Life softball team and pitched it to a winning season in 1940. But it was time to move on—or back—to Louisville and the new challenge of television.

Before we go back up the road some two hundred miles north to Louisville, however, I want to tell you more about some of the friends I made in Nashville and other places during my career in country music. I also want to talk about other aspects of my career—radio, recordings, songwriting—that I had developed already before I returned to Louisville, where I have lived right up to now.

Country Friends

I'VE WORKED WITH DOZENS OF STARS, from Rudy Vallee to Judy Canova to Perry Como, but most of my friends have performed on the Opry, either as regulars or guests. I'll begin with one of the younger stars and one of the best, Randy Travis, whose wife, Olivia, discovered him when he worked in a nightclub she owned in North Carolina. She became his manager and brought him to Nashville because she said, "Whatever happens in country music happens in Nashville. That's where we've got to go." When they arrived, he supported himself while he was trying to break into the music business by frying catfish and washing dishes at the Nashville Palace Restaurant near the Opry. The restaurant has a popular floor show, so when he wasn't frying fish he was on the stage playing and singing. He was soon noticed by the right people and got invited to be on the Opry. I've never been on the same bill with Randy, but a few years ago I was playing up in Hamilton, Ontario, right after he had done a show, and he left me a note that said, "Dear Pee Wee, I plugged your shows. You can thank me when you get back to Nashville." So that's what I did, and I got to meet Olivia, who is still his biggest fan and supporter. Randy is just one of the many, many talented stars who are taking country music to larger and larger audiences.

I've liked all the people I've worked with in the business, and I've worked with most of them. I liked them all, but some of them were hard to work with. Take Lynn Anderson. Some years ago we were doing a show with her at the fairgrounds up in White Plains, New York. She had just done the *Lawrence Welk Show* and arrived late from the airport. She rushed up to me and said, "Here's my music." It was an arrangement of her new song for a twenty-piece orchestra. I said, "Lynn, we don't have a twenty-piece orchestra. Look out there and count them—two, four, six, maybe eight—that's what we've got." She said, "I plugged my new record on *Lawrence Welk*, and I announced I was going to be here tonight, so the crowds will be coming to see me and hear my new song." I said, "It's almost time for you to go on, and we don't have time to rehearse your new song. Give me a list of your old songs that the boys may know and the keys you sing in, and we'll practice some of those quickly. Then you'll just have time to dress and put on your makeup." She said sort of haughtily, "Well, thank you." But she knew that's all we could do. She went in and dressed, came out, and we all struggled through her part of the show. We never played her new song, and she didn't like it at all.

Most of the performers I've worked with have been just as cooperative and considerate as possible. Jan Howard, for one, was a lady of class and quality. One time we were serving as her backup band, and she came backstage and said, "How many boys in the band can read music?" I said, "They all can. Just give us your chord charts." So she brought them out, the boys put them on their stands, and I introduced her: "Now folks, from the Grand Ole Opry, here is Jan Howard, one of the finest singers you'll hear anywhere. We know she's going to please you. How about a good hand for the young lady?" Jan came out and did a beautiful job with the ballads she had made into hits, with my band backing her up without a hitch. Everything went smooth as silk, and the audience loved her. After the show, she came over and said, "Pee Wee, your boys played the heck out of my music. If I'd known they were that good, I would have used them on my recording sessions." You see, these situations were similar. The difference was in the two performers.

I've had a few problems with stars on the road, even the ones I like. Donna Fargo, for instance, is a sweet girl; but one time she threw a monkey wrench into a show we were doing in Green Bay, Wisconsin, and caused us to lose money. Actually, it was her husband who was responsible for the trouble. That was when "The Happiest Girl in the USA" was a national hit, and she was to be the featured star on our show. We had booked her for a late December show;

then her wacky husband said, "No, we can't come up there for one date. I won't bring her up unless you can get her two days." I said, "Well, I'm sorry. We can't use her for two days. I'll just have to get somebody else." We already had Kitty Wells scheduled, and I managed to get Bill Anderson, who was pretty well-known up there. They were both popular performers, but it was a hard sell without a top recording star like Donna Fargo and a current big hit. We were desperate to sell tickets. We were playing the Packer Auditorium, which seats around seven thousand, and we could only sell 1,700 tickets. For a month we had advertised Donna Fargo as the headliner, and when she canceled, the people stayed away in droves. We're still polite and speak to each other, but I never tried to work with her again. Her husband was responsible, but I think she could have overruled him. I don't carry grudges long, and I don't know anybody I wouldn't speak to, including him.

I've always tried to help other entertainers when they were down on their luck and needed a break. I learned from Mr. Frank that, regardless of how big a star you become, there are times when you need a favor. One time when we were doing a Canadian tour he brought in a Monogram cowboy star named Eddie Dean. He was a singing cowboy from Texas and made such movies as *Stars Over Texas* and *Song of Old Wyoming*. In the 1940s he had been one of the top cowboy stars, but when he was with us he was down on his luck. He was a spellbinding entertainer, one of the few I know who could go on stage by himself and hold an audience for an hour and more, with them begging for him to stay. But when he worked with us, he was just another talented entertainer without a job.

Some entertainers simply get too big for their britches. Sometimes they get bitter because of a bad review. Some of them are mad because they aren't as far up the ladder of success as they'd like to be. I've known performers who get so cocky they come to a show unprepared. One time we were doing a show with a singer who was going to lip-sync her records, and she didn't even have a record player to use. So we wound up having to back her up, and we hadn't rehearsed with her. She did a miserable job just trying to stay up with the band. Today, of course, tapes are used and performers don't have to use record players or backup bands.

A real pro and one who won't sing with a tape is Wayne Newton. He insists always on having a live band. When I watch Wayne work, I can understand why he was the leading entertainer in Las Vegas for seven years in a row. And to think he started out as a hillbilly steel guitar player, fiddle player, and singer with his brother! My band and I worked with the Newton brothers one time in a hillbilly park in Newark, Ohio, and another time in West Virginia, just when they were starting out. I could tell even then that those two boys had the talent and drive and discipline to be a great success. Soon after that, the boys split up, and Jackie Gleason discovered Wayne as a solo act. His brother tried to start a western-style nightclub near Muscle Shoals in Alabama, but it didn't last long. Wayne helped him a number of times and bailed him out of several financial messes, but he finally gave up on him.

Wayne is a one-of-a-kind guy. He sees you once and never forgets you. One time when Colonel Tom Parker was my manager, he booked us at the Golden Nugget in Las Vegas, and Wayne was playing the Fremont Hotel across the street. We had Monday night off, so I went over to hear Wayne. During his break I went backstage and said, "I'm Pee Wee King." He said, "Pee Wee, don't pull that stuff on me. I know it's been a long time since we played together, but I know who you are. I'm so glad you stopped by." Since then, we've seen each other many times on the road and in Las Vegas.

Wayne is such a good entertainer I could see him perform every night. He uses his band for music and for comedy. When he was performing in Owensboro, Kentucky, one time, he had a drummer from the boondocks of West Virginia, where Wayne is from. After one of the numbers the drummer said, "Hey, Mr. Boss Man." Wayne said, "Who? What's my name?" The drummer said, "Wayne." Newton, in a fake stutter, said, "Why-why-why-why-why don't you call-call-call-call me Wayne?" And the drummer said, " 'Cause you're my boss man, that's why. You're the boss, and I got a problem and I need help. The saxophone player plays and gets a hand. The lady sings and gets a hand. I want to play my drum and get a hand." Wayne said, "You've been playing your drums all during the show." He said, "Yes, but I want to play my drum all by myself and get a hand." Wayne said, "Why?" He said, "Because I got a date here in Owensboro waiting backstage for me, and I want to show off." Wayne said, "Oh, all right, go ahead and play your number." So the drummer played his solo with cymbals and a lot of showmanship and pizzazz. When he finished, the audience applauded madly, and Wayne said, "Now, are you satisfied?" The drummer said, "Yeah, but I don't think it did me any good with my date. He's already gone." That tore the house down, and everybody laughed. They knew it was an act and kind of silly, but it was still effective. Wayne always knows how to size up an audience, pull them in, and draw them close to him.

What can I say about Marty Robbins? He was one of the greats, right up there next to Eddy Arnold and Roy Acuff. He was a gentleman who knew how to make love to his audiences, and they loved him right back. He established a bond with them immediately, and by the end of the show they were eating out of his hand. He was often the last performer on the Opry, and the audience would beg him to do one more song. He would continue for another hour, then go out to the autographing bar and sign programs and pictures and pose for photographs until everybody was satisfied.

Another of the superstar legends of country music is Patsy Cline, and her reputation seems to grow every year since her tragic death in March of 1963 in the crash of a private plane. The only time I ever worked with her was the year before she died, at the fairgrounds in Stilton, Wisconsin. She was at the height of her popularity at that time with hits like "Walkin' After Midnight," "I Fall to Pieces," and "Crazy." She was the first female country singer to perform in the Hollywood Bowl and at Carnegie Hall. I think she was the best country singer of her time, certainly the biggest female star. She flew into Madison, and we sent a car over to pick her up. She was cordial and polite to me, but she spent most of her time in her dressing room, and I didn't see much of her. When she finished her show, she flew right back to Nashville. She'd had a rough life, and you can see it reflected in the way she interpreted her songs. She may have been a little rough and racy in private, but when she sang her heartbreaking songs in public, her voice was like silk. She sang from her heart and made every song her own. She recorded one of our songs, "You Belong to Me," so I asked Owen Bradley, who was production manager for the movie about Patsy, why he didn't use the song in the movie. He said, "I think the song is too pop to represent Patsy's style." I said, "Well, when she recorded it, she didn't think so."

I like Patsy's work very much. Like all great artists, she had a unique talent. But we never got to know each other as well as Dolly Parton and I did. I got to know Dolly very well when she and Porter Wagoner were still doing their syndicated television show. Finally, she broke with him to try it on her own. It was a bad time for both of them. At the time he lost Dolly he was also having a lot of trouble with his band. I think Dolly did what was right and picked a good time to strike out by herself. It was Porter's show she was leaving. She was the featured singer, but he was the star. She knew that she could never become a superstar by playing second fiddle to Porter or anyone else. The way her career took off proved that she was right. It wasn't ill will that split them up, and she and Porter are still friends and make occasional joint appearances on television.

Soon after Dolly and Porter broke up, she and I were booked by Hap Peebles, a great promoter, and we spent several days working together. It was at the Threshers Association at Fairfield, Iowa, where more than forty thousand people came into that little town for the fair. It poured down rain from the time we got there to the time we left. The fairgrounds were flooded, so we did our show at a schoolhouse. They fed us at the school cafeteria, and Dolly and I sat together. She said, "Pee Wee, what's wrong? You never stop to talk to me." I said, "Hell, Dolly. I can't ever catch up with you. You move too fast." She said, "I know. I'm going through a lot of bad things now that I have to straighten out. In ten years I expect to have everything I want. I don't want people to say when I'm old and forgotten, 'Remember Dolly Parton? She used to be on Porter Wagoner's show. Well, there she is walking over there by herself. That pitiful old woman.'" I said, "Dolly, I don't think you'll ever have to worry about that." Sure enough, she had it made in a lot less than ten years. Now when she sees me, she says, "Pee Wee, I'm not quite ready to rest. I have to hang on for five more years."

Dolly knew she wanted stardom when she left Porter, and she knew that in order to get it she had to create her own particular image. That's important to all performers, but it's crucial for someone like Dolly, whose appearance is a major asset to begin with. Early pictures of Dolly show her to be a lot less endowed than she is now. Everyone thinks Dolly has had some work done on her breasts, but she swears she hasn't. That's her business. It's her body, what-

ever she wants to do with it. I do know that the hair she wears is
not her hair. She wears wigs in public all the time and changes them
sometimes three or four times a day. She is very strict about main-
taining her image. I've never seen her without a wig or makeup,
and neither have the boys in the band. She's always extremely professional. When she left Porter, she knew she was going somewhere,
and she was willing to do what it took to get there. She's succeeded
beyond belief. She's a superstar now with top recordings, a movie
actress with several hits, a top draw at live shows, a major attraction
on television, and she's the force behind Dollywood, the amusement
park near her home at Pigeon Forge, Tennessee. She's certainly no
longer Porter Wagoner's tagalong. She's made it, but she's still the
same friendly, down-home girl I knew before she became a superstar.

I know a lot of people who had the talent and the drive but
bad timing. Jan Howard left Bill Anderson at a bad time and tried
to make it on her own, but she never made the big time. Connie
Smith was also discovered by Bill Anderson, and chose a bad time
to leave him. When he found her, she was on a barn dance at Wheeling,
West Virginia. He groomed her and gave her television exposure;
then after she got her record contract, she said to Bill, "It's time for
me to go." For a while she was popular around Nashville, but she
never became a superstar. Some people make it and some people
don't. It's not always timing or talent either. It's management and
marketing and a whole lot of other factors.

Loretta Lynn is another one of my favorites. She works too
hard, and she's fragile, not tough like Patsy Cline or Kitty Wells.
Back in the 1970s I did a sellout show with Loretta at the Indianapolis Music Hall. I've always enjoyed working with her because
she's so sincere and genuine. Whatever she does it's with total commitment—even her marriage. She's been married to Mooney almost
all her life, and she couldn't leave him now even if she wanted to.

I've met a lot of entertainers while I was on tour. When the
Golden West Cowboys and I were playing Riverside Rancho in
Hollywood, I met Merle Haggard who was working for Buck Owens
at a tavern in Bakersfield. Merle knew my business partner, Charlie
Adams, and said to him, "Why don't you bring Pee Wee out to the
club when he's not busy?" So we drove out to Bakersfield, and I saw

a great show. We stayed overnight, and the next day we played golf and enjoyed the spectacular scenery, especially the big mountains in the distance from the golf course. Most of the stars like Merle Haggard that I met on tour I later played with on the Opry.

Bill Haley and I were friends a long time. Our paths crossed many times when he was playing the bars up and down the Jersey shore. He had a western band that played music much like my own. When I told him how much I liked his music, he said, "You should. I stole a lot of it from your band." One time Jolly Joyce, who was Bill's booking agent, asked me about booking the Golden West Cowboys overseas as a rock 'n' roll act. The only hitch was that we had to change our name. I said, "Nothing doing! I've worked hard to make our name mean something, and I'm not about to change it. Anyway, why should I want to become a rock 'n' roll band? I can play rock 'n' roll any time I want to and still call our band the Golden West Cowboys."

Before he went into the army, I worked a concert date with Eddie Fisher at the Hollywood Palladium. We had a wild crowd. Eddie introduced us, and we played "Sentimental Journey" to start off, but I could tell it was too slow for the crowd. Then we played "Slow Poke" and the people came alive. Eddie said, "That's it, Pee Wee. You're hitting it on the nail now. That's what the people came for." We began to play several two-step numbers because most of the people wanted to dance. At that time Eddie was working for a gold record with "Anytime," and we were working on a million seller with "Slow Poke." In those days I knew all the artists at the top of the best-selling charts—Eddie, Perry Como, Eddy Arnold, to name a few—because I wanted to find out what their secrets were. I suppose they were also watching me to find out what my hard-earned secrets were—just as Bill Haley admitted to me. A few months after I did the show with Eddie, he was drafted. He was a nice-looking fellow back then, but he certainly hasn't aged well. I know I won't win any beauty contests either.

Another guy I liked very much and worked with a number of times was George Gobel. He taught me something important about show business. One time I was on the bill with him at Cincinnati River Downs, along with a group called Borah Minivich and His Harmonica Rascals. The Rascals had a midget harmonica player who

would run up to the leader and pull his pants down to get his attention so he could play. The little fellow did this several times, and
each time the leader would say, "Go back to your place at the end
of the line and stay there." Finally, he let the midget play a solo,
and he stole the show. George was the featured act, so he made sure
the Harmonica Rascals followed him. He said, "Pee Wee, don't ever
follow or try to compete with a midget or an animal. They will always take the spotlight away from you. Perry Como discovered that
a stage drunk will also steal the spotlight, as he found out when he
took Foster Brooks with him to Las Vegas.

Bob Wills and I were good friends, though we played similar
music and were in friendly competition with each other. He had a
lot of influence on the development of country music. He had a
western swing band that he called the Light Crust Doughboys and
later the Texas Playboys. They brought together the folk sounds of
the fiddle with the sounds of the Big Bands and Dixieland jazz. Like
me, Bob added a dancing beat to country songs. He included "Slow
Poke" on one of his LP recordings called "Bob Wills Plays the Greatest
String Band Hits," and at the end he says, "This is a tribute to you,
Pee Wee. I hope you like it." I always liked Bob's music. We saw
eye-to-eye and heard ear-to-ear on a lot of what country music needed
to make it more popular.

It goes without saying that Hank Williams is one of the immortals of American music—not just country music. During my Opry
years we got to be good friends. Between shows he and I would
often go to a nearby bar and have a couple of beers and talk. He
was person-smart, but he didn't give a damn about business. And
he didn't give a damn about his own health. He knew he had a bad
hip and a bad back, yet he kept pushing himself and abusing his
body with alcohol and drugs. He was unstable and unhappy most of
his life, certainly during the part of his career that I knew. We were
friends, but he was basically a loner and didn't buddy-buddy with
anybody. He and Audrey had a strife-filled relationship, from the
time they met while he was appearing in a medicine show in Banks,
Alabama, until his death. She helped him book dates and sell tickets, and I know she inspired him—often in a negative way—to write
some of his best songs. At the time of his death at twenty-nine they
were divorced and he had married Johnny Horton's widow. But I

know he loved Audrey until the very end. He couldn't get along with her, and he couldn't live without her. Hank told me he drank because of his problems with her, and she said his drinking caused their problems. Who knows which came first? Maybe there are some people who are born to be unhappy.

One time Hank came to Louisville's old Parkway Field Ball Park as part of a road show sponsored by a patent medicine named Hadacol. Bob Hope was paid by the Hadacol people to be the star, but everyone came out to hear Hank, who was supposed to be the warm-up act for Bob. Hank sang his songs and started to go, but the audience wouldn't let him leave the stage. Finally, Bob came out in his big cowboy hat and started his routine anyway. It was a tense moment, but he managed to get control and do his act. I'll bet he never followed Hank Williams again.

Hank was scheduled to appear with Lefty Frizzell and me in a New Year's Eve show in Baltimore exactly a year before he died. He'd just had a serious back operation, and his doctor wouldn't let him travel. But he sent his band and got Jimmie Davis to stand in for him. He also recorded an apology, which Audrey brought to the show and played to the audience. Hank had been practicing horseback riding at a stable in Nashville and hurt his back. His publisher, Fred Rose, tried to protect him from riding accidents, but he was not able to protect him from himself.

One year later on the way to a New Year's show in Canton, Ohio, Hank died in the back seat of his Cadillac convertible. He had abused himself to death. He died with one great unfulfilled ambition, which was to make a movie—and not just any kind of movie, but a Western. That was why he had been practicing his horseback riding skills. He had signed a contract, and the movie was in the embryonic stage when he died. It was to be produced by MGM because he was their big recording star and they wanted to keep him. I think Hank wanted to do a movie because to him, as a little country boy growing up in Alabama, a movie star was the most glamorous thing he could imagine. And, after all, Johnny Mack Brown, who was from his section of Alabama, had made Westerns, so why couldn't he? Elvis came along a generation later, and he wanted to make movies too. The difference was that he had a manager named Colonel Tom

Parker, and he lived long enough to make them. I think Hank had as much acting talent as Elvis and could have made good movies.

I have a photograph taken on the stage at the Opry in 1951, with me, Audrey, Hank, and others, including Governor Gordon Browning of Tennessee, George Morgan, Fred Rose, and Tex Williams. It's a picture I treasure. Hank was a simple country boy who had the genius to write and sing everybody's songs. But he didn't know how to handle love and fame.

There are so many friends that have left me with such fond memories. Kitty Wells has been called the Queen of Country Music, and that's what she was. People loved to listen to her sad, sincere voice in such smash hits as "It Wasn't God Who Made Honky Tonk Angels." She was the third woman inducted into the Country Music Hall of Fame, after Patsy Cline and Minnie Pearl. It was a richly deserved honor.

Another very good friend I've known most of my career is Whitey Ford, who called himself the Duke of Paducah. He was a part of Gene Autry's band as a comedy act, but he decided not to go with Gene to California in 1934. He was born in Desoto, Missouri, and was given his stage name by a radio salesman in St. Louis. He never even lived in Paducah, Kentucky, but after he became famous, the mayor made him an honorary citizen. He got started back in the early 1920s in Hot Springs, Arkansas, when he called himself Benny Ford and His Arkansas Travelers Radio Train. Back around 1930 he was a member of Otto Gray and His Oklahoma Cowboys, which is said to be the first hillhilly cowboy band on radio. He was a very versatile performer and could play the harmonica, the banjo, and the mandolin; but everyone remembers him best as a comedian with the tag line, "I'm goin' back to the wagon, boys; these shoes are killin' me." When I first knew him he had a huge collection of jokes and joke books and got most of his corny stories from them. He used to get big laughs with lines like this: "Maybe I don't look like no matinee idol, but I'm really a lady's man. Even if she ain't no lady—I'm still her man."

Many country stars I've just known professionally, but others, like Roy Acuff, Eddy Arnold, and Minnie Pearl, have become my intimate friends; and we've visited often in each other's homes. I think the first time I was entertained in a star's home was in 1938 when the Golden West Cowboys and I were out in Hollywood making *Gold Mine in the Sky* with Gene Autry and Smiley Burnette. Smiley invited the whole band to his house and had a big cookout. His specialty was Caesar's salad, and he made it a full-scale, four-star production, selecting and cutting up all the ingredients in a big wooden bowl, pouring over the dressings, and then stirring and serving them with huge wooden spoons.

My relationships with Roy, Eddy, and Minnie lasted a lot longer. I knew Roy when we were living in Knoxville and he had a late afternoon show on WROL. We met when we were both working a dance at Riddle Springs Golf Course. They wanted a hillbilly jamboree and hired both our bands. Roy had started out with Doctor Hauer's Medicine Show, selling bottles of patent medicine that could cure anything from constipation to a pain in the side. It had a large alcohol content and made people feel good at least for a while, so Roy said. Roy's radio show was sponsored by a big department store owned by a man named Caswell Walker, who did his own radio commercials. Everybody knew Cass, as he liked to be called, and he once got elected mayor of Knoxville. He could have run for governor and probably won, but he said he didn't need the job.

Roy's band was first called the Tennessee Crackerjacks, which he renamed the Crazy Tennesseans because they did a lot of novelty songs. Roy's unique country voice got them a contract with Columbia Records while they were still in Knoxville. His yo-yo tricks were popular with audiences even then, but it was his sad country songs that won him a big following. I liked Roy very much, but I never could appreciate his mournful music. It just wasn't my kind. I couldn't have continued to play and sing all those sad songs over and over. They depressed me just listening to them. To sing his kind of songs, I'd have had to learn to cry on stage. Like Hank Williams, Roy had a cry in his voice. Overall, his sound was very different from mine. Where I used an accordion, he used a steel guitar, and he sang in a country twang, which I suppose he got naturally growing up in the Smoky Mountains. He used to actually cry while he was singing, especially if it was a sentimental religious song like "The Great Speckled Bird." But Roy was no fool. Like Gene Autry, he was a shrewd businessman and owned radio stations, road shows, an interest in Acuff-

Rose Publishing Company, a lake, and a hotel resort. We lost a giant of country music when he passed away.

Mr. Frank was the man who gave Roy his first big boost. After we moved to Nashville in 1937, Mr. Frank contacted Roy and said, "Man, you're missing the big boat. You don't have to be stuck in a little town like Knoxville. Come on down to Nashville. With your recording contract, you can go national." Roy was skittish about leaving Knoxville, especially since he'd already been turned down by the Opry once. Finally, he came over to be my guest on the Royal Crown Cola Opry show at nine o'clock one Saturday night. He was on three times. The first time he sang two songs and got a healthy round of applause. The next Saturday he sang two more songs and got more applause. The third time he got a standing ovation. That was enough to convince the Solemn Old Judge, and Roy was invited to join the Opry family soon after that. Then Mr. Frank said, "Roy, there's no reason for you to commute between Knoxville and Nashville. Move to Nashville, and it'll be easier for me to book you from here." That's what Roy did. He was on his way to becoming a country music legend.

The last time I saw Roy was in April 1992, just a few months before he died. He was very feeble and had glaucoma. Someone had to lead him around, but he was determined to perform. He knew the Opry stage by heart. He was led to the microphone, and he took over from there. Yes sir, Old Roy did all right for a man who thought his life was over when he suffered a bad case of sunstroke as a boy and couldn't play professional baseball. Like me, Roy was hell-bent for music. If anybody had offered him a regular job, he wouldn't have taken it. He never regretted having to give up baseball for music.

Ernest Tubb was like a lot of us pioneers of country music. He didn't have a lot of formal education and training. He was educated in the school of hard knocks. As a boy in Crisp, Texas, his idol was Jimmie Rodgers, and Ernest learned much of his own style from listening to his records. Many years later Jimmie Rodgers's widow gave Ernest her husband's guitar as a sign of her approval of the way he had followed in Rodgers's footsteps.

I met Ernest when we were playing a date in San Antonio in 1945, and I developed a hell of a toothache. Somebody sent Mr. Frank and me over to a dentist whose office was in the same building that housed the studios of radio station KONO. We took an elevator up to the dentist's office, had my bad tooth packed, then got back on the elevator to go down. That's when we met Ernest. He had just finished his radio show for a local beer company and was still wearing his stage costume with "Ernest Tubb, the Texas Troubador" embroidered on the back of his shirt and printed on his guitar case. We recognized his name because he'd already recorded "I'm Walking the Floor Over You," and it was a big hit. But he had never been to Nashville. We all talked a few minutes on the elevator and then went our separate ways. A few hours later, Mr. Frank said, "I just hired Ernest Tubb." I said, "Really?" About a week later Ernest was on his way to Nashville when his rickety old Chevy broke down in Brownsville, about 150 miles west of Nashville. He called Mr. Frank and said, "My car's broke, and I'm stuck without much money in this little town. Can you send somebody here to pick me up?" So Mr. Frank left immediately for Brownsville and had a wrecker tow his car to Nashville. That wasn't a very promising entrance into the city where he would live most of his life and become one of the superstars of country music.

Ernest knew he was taking a big chance when he quit his job at the radio station in San Antonio and gave up the good-paying gigs he played in the honky-tonks around there. But he hedged a bit. He left his wife and children behind and told them that he would try out Nashville first to see if he liked the new city and the new job before he moved them. At that time we were doing a lot of tent shows, and Mr. Frank needed good acts for them as well as the Opry and our other radio shows. With Ernest Tubb and Roy Acuff, we had two big talents to show off. Or as Mr. Frank put it, "Now I got two more acts to pay for and worry about."

Roy had already built up a big following from the Opry, and it didn't take Ernest long to become popular. Within a few weeks he was getting bushels of mail from Opry listeners, and he went on to become a tremendous hit on the Opry with his western honky-tonk sound. It was the kind of white blues music that people could dance to in the dance halls where he played. It was a forerunner of the kind of music that Hank Williams was soon to make even more popular. All I know is that Ernest had a certain spark that set the Opry on fire every time he played. Soon he put out a songbook and was swamped with orders. Mr. Frank knew right away that Ernest had star appeal and formed a band for him. He brought in the Short brothers, Jimmy and Leon, from Texas and took several fellows who had played with my band—Ray "Kemo" Head, Toby Reese, Chester Studdard, Johnny Sapp—and they formed the Texas Troubadors. All of this happened very fast—before the end of 1945. I used to kid Ernest, "You've got a fellow in your band named Leon, so why don't you ever say, 'Take it away, Leon'?" Ernest said, "For the good reason that it's not my line. It belongs to Bob Wills. He started that with Leon McAuliffe, his steel guitar player. If I used that line, he'd accuse me of grand larceny."

For a period Mr. Frank had a star-studded cast of performers—Eddy Arnold, Roy Acuff, Grandpa Jones, Minnie Pearl, Ernest Tubb, the Golden West Cowboys, and Cowboy Copas. When he hired Cowboy Copas, he said to me, "Copas is coming to work with you." I said, "Can we afford him? What are we going to pay him?" He said, "Promise him a hundred dollars a week and pay him fifty." So that's what we did. Before long, the boys started breaking off and forming their own groups or drifting over to other bands. That's the way it was—a lot of shifting around from one band to another, from one town to another, from one radio station to another, from one show to another, from one manager and booking agent to another. Contracts were not common in those days, so everything was loose and flexible. A man like Ernest Tubb was bound to succeed in whatever he did—as a band leader, recording artist, Opry star. In 1946 he opened his record shop on Broadway across the street from where Tootsie's is now, and it's still going. He said he wanted to see his name in lights on something, so he started the music store. Despite a few misunderstandings over the years, I felt I lost a close friend when he died from emphysema in 1984 at the age of seventy.

In 1938 I met one of my best and oldest friends in the business when we were playing the Kiel Auditorium in St. Louis. Skeets Yaney, the most popular disk jockey in town, came backstage during our matinee show and said to Mr. Frank, "There's a young boy in town that you ought to take on and manage and get on the Grand Ole Opry. He's the hottest country singer around here. But he'll never amount to much if he stays here. He needs to go to Nashville. You won't be sorry. He's a clean kid." Mr. Frank said, "When can I meet this fellow? Is he going to be at our show tonight?" Yaney said, "He's out in the audience now. I'll go get him."

Yaney went out and in a couple of minutes he came back and introduced us to a very young Eddy Arnold. "Eddy," he said, "this is Mr. J.L. Frank, the best promoter in country music. I want you two to talk. Eddy, tell Mr. Frank how much you want to go to the Opry." Eddy said, "Yes sir, Mr. Frank. I really do want to go to the Opry. I feel it's time to leave here and try someplace else." Mr. Frank said, "Have you got your guitar with you?" Eddy said, "Yes sir, it's outside in my old Plymouth." He came back in a couple of minutes, did a quick audition backstage, and Mr. Frank said, "How would you like to do our show tonight?" Eddy said, "Yes sir, I'd like to do two Gene Autry songs, 'Gold Mine in the Sky' and 'Silver-Haired Daddy of Mine,' and I can do them in the same keys Mr. Autry uses." That night I introduced him: "Ladies and gentlemen, here is a young local singer who is said to have enough talent to get him on the Grand Ole Opry. Let's see if he does. Here he is—Eddy Arnold." Eddy came out, sang his two songs, and got a huge ovation. Mr. Frank came up to him and said, "That's good enough for me. I think you'd do good on the Opry. Can you be in Nashville on Saturday night?" Eddy said, "Yes sir, I'll be there."

Before we left St. Louis, I told Eddy to try to get to Nashville by Friday so he could rehearse with the Golden West Cowboys for the Saturday Opry. I also told him, "We can't guarantee you anything, but the going pay is three dollars a day and five dollars on weekends. And for that money you may sometimes have to do five shows a day, at ten in the morning and at one, four, seven, and nine. Then we may have to drive five or six hundred miles to our next day's work." He said he was eager to take a chance. In fact, he was so eager he didn't wait until Friday to start. On Tuesday afternoon I heard a knock on my door in Nashville. I opened it and there was Eddy with his little Plymouth parked out front. He said, "Well, here I am. I wanted to make sure I got here on time." I sent him to Mom Upchurch's boardinghouse nearby and told him to come back the next day for an early rehearsal. After a few days he was a regular with the Golden West Cowboys.

A couple of years later, he moved his mother from their small Chester County, Tennessee, farm into Nashville, and they lived in a small house on Dickerson Road. Two of my boys lived about half a block from Eddy's house, and they would pick him up every morning and take him to WSM for our daily show. One day Mrs. Arnold said, "Edward, these fellows can have biscuits and coffee with us every morning, can't they? Then you all can leave for your radio program." He said, "Yes Mama, they can. I didn't think of that." So every morning they all ate breakfast with Mrs. Arnold, and she charged them fifteen cents a piece. They loved her as much as Eddy did. She used to kid them, and they kidded her back. At their first breakfast she said, "You fellows do eat white gravy, don't you?" And they said, "Yes ma'am, is there any other kind?" Eddy came from a very modest background and has always been kind and helpful to family members. He had a half-brother who was a barber in St. Louis; and every time we played in that area, Eddy paid him a visit.

Eddy only went to school for about nine years. He started singing and playing on a borrowed guitar when he was ten. He would work in the fields all day and play his music at night. He told me that when he went with his mom and dad to Jackson to shop, it was his job to carry the kerosene can and get it filled up. They didn't have electricity and used kerosene lamps to light the house. When he was eighteen, he left home to find something better. His first job as a musician was on WTJS, a small radio station in Jackson. He was the rube comedian with a rag on his toe and blacked-out teeth with a band called the Arizona Cowgirls. That job didn't pay enough to live on, so he got a job at a local funeral home, where he began to prepare to be an undertaker, driving the hearse, helping dress the dead, and serving as a general handyman. More and more he began to see himself as a musician, not a mortician, and started calling himself the Tennessee Plowboy because that's what he was. He went to Memphis to work at WMPS but was fired after two weeks. From there he went to St. Louis, where we found him.

After Redd Stewart left for the service in World War II, Eddy became the star soloist for the Golden West Cowboys. He toured with us as part of the Camel Caravan during the war, and he was with us when we worked a political campaign in Florida. Although he was the featured singer of the Cowboys, he used to say he spent as much time selling songbooks and sweeping out the auditoriums as he did playing and singing. Throughout his time with me, he remained the courteous, cooperative young man who was so eager to go with us to Nashville. One time we were playing the jukebox operators show in Chicago and were staying in the ritzy Palmer House Hotel. Eddy came up to me in the lobby one day and said, "Pee Wee, come over here and see these shoes." We walked over, and he showed me a pair of Florsheims. He said, "Aren't they pretty?" I said, "Yes, they are. Buy them if you want to. You can afford them now." He said, "Pee Wee, I think I will. I just wanted you to tell me it was okay."

Eddy met his wife Sally Gayhart when she worked behind the soda fountain at Woolworth's in downtown Louisville. She became a good friend of my own wife Lydia, and we had them over a number of times to our house when they were courting. They hit it off right away and were married on November 28, 1941, at a time when, as Eddy tells it, she was making more money then he was. One day he came to me and asked for a ten-dollar raise. I said, "Eddy, I just can't afford it. No way. I might be able to go five dollars, but there's no way under heaven I can afford ten dollars a week more." He was making five dollars a day for every day he worked. In fact, I'm sure that's what led him to leave the Golden West Cowboys. He had his mother and his wife to support and needed more money. I also think that after he married he wasn't so eager to be on the road so much.

Eddy came to me one day in 1943 and said, "Pee Wee, I'm giving you six months' notice. I want to go out on my own." I thought he was kidding, but six months later he came back and said, "Well, this is the last time I go out with you." I said, "Are you serious? I thought you were kidding." He said, "I've been to see Harry Stone at the Opry, and I told him I was thinking of leaving the Golden West Cowboys, but I told him I'd sure like to stay with the Opry. He told me that I would still have a place and that I should form my own little group. I told him I already had one." When Eddy left with my good wishes, he also left with two of my players, my steel guitarist Roy Wiggins and fiddler Speedy McNatt. He knew it was a big risk to go out on his own. He didn't know whether he could succeed on his own, but I knew he had the makings of success. He had top-drawer talent, a lot of experience, and a steel determination. He was already making records that were showing up on the popularity charts. When I met him in St. Louis he was a professional, but his career really took off during the time he was with me.

Leaving me was a smart professional move for Eddy. Sometimes a person has to grit his teeth, close his eyes, and plunge in. Unless he does, he'll never know whether he will sink or swim. It was soon obvious that Eddy was going to swim. He got a daily show on Mutual radio for Purina. He made a generous deal with the Opry. And soon his recordings went to the top of the *Billboard* charts. From the beginning, he was able to get his records on jukeboxes when they weren't featuring many country songs.

Eddy was also lucky to have Colonel Tom Parker as his manager after he left Mr. Frank. Parker was good for Eddy, but Eddy was moving up the ladder and soon got a New York agent named R.J. Purcell, who handled a lot of the top stars. Purcell taught Eddy how to make more money with better contracts and how to invest the money he made. He's made good money in shrewd business deals ranging from a car dealership to an ice cream stand. He's done a lot better with his investments than I have! Eddy and Sally live on a beautiful farm south of Nashville now near Brentwood. They have two children, Dickie and Jo Ann. He's come a long way from the poor farm boy he was in Chester County. I'm glad I was able to give him a boost early in his career.

What can I now say about one of the joys of my professional life, Minnie Pearl? She has always been a thorough professional through thick and thin. She was a willing worker who never complained about the often primitive, embarrassing conditions we had to work under. If we were playing a mining camp, she would have to change her clothes in a coal bin with almost no privacy, but she never complained. It was the price she gladly paid to do what she loved best— that is, make people feel good with her innocent, homespun brand of humor. Minnie loved show business and she loved people. She used to say, "Lord knows, we're not in this business, Pee Wee, for the money. I just want to make people laugh and feel better." And the people loved her back. They would write to her about their problems, and she would answer with words of cheer. I've seen her sit in the back of our touring car and write dozens of one-cent postcards to her fans as we drove the hundreds of miles between shows.

Under her real name of Sarah Ophelia Colley, she studied dramatics in college and wanted to go on the legitimate stage, but she didn't have any kind of success until she developed her country character. Even as Minnie she wasn't an immediate hit. When she arrived in Nashville with her dad, mom, and sister and auditioned for the Solemn Old Judge, boy! was he surprised! He thought she played the guitar and sang and wasn't prepared for her wild makeup and tacky clothes and hat with the price tag hanging down. He said, "Miss Colley, I don't believe it will work. I don't think audiences will like it. They'll think you're making fun of them." She said, "Mr. Hay, I tried a comic act on the road with a chautauqua tent show, but nobody liked what I was doing. Nobody liked my comedy until I started playing Minnie Pearl. Now they love it. I believe the people who listen to the Opry will love her too." And, of course, they did.

Early in her Opry career, Minnie worked with Roy Acuff for about a week. She was still perfecting her now famous introduction that ran like this: "Howdeeeeeee. I'm just so proud to be here. I'm so proud I could come." Roy, who was the son of a Baptist preacher, said, "Minnie, you'll just have to leave off that last part. It's too suggestive." Roy didn't much like her act anyway. He also thought it might be a little risque to have a single woman traveling with his band. He said, "I've never had a girl on my show, and the boys' wives might not like having one going around with their husbands." Mr. Frank, who was booking Minnie at that time, said, "That's all right, Roy. I can put Minnie with Pee Wee. It won't bother him." At that time, around 1940, we were playing a string of about nineteen theaters of the Schine and Kemp circuits up and down the East Coast from Virginia to Massachusetts. We were also working for the Sudicum chain of theaters in Tennessee, Alabama, Georgia, and Kentucky. Our contract meant that we had to work all the theaters several times a year. It was backbreaking work. We did our live shows as half of a double feature with a movie, usually a Western. It was a grinding routine, but we were all young and happy to be working. All this time Minnie was refining her characters and trying out different routines. She was a tough, hard-working professional. As she reminded me often, Ophelia Colley was not Minnie Pearl. Although she never looked down on anyone, Ophelia was educated, cultured, and grammatical—just the opposite of Minnie. "Remember, Pee Wee," Minnie said, "it's Minnie Pearl who gets into trouble all the time and talks about it in bad English. Ophelia would never dream of doing or saying those things."

When Minnie first started traveling with us, she was not married. Then she began getting her own engagements and decided she wanted to rent a plane because she was tired of so many hours in a cramped car. The pilot she hired was the president of Capitol Airlines named Henry Cannon. He was from a well-off family and a bachelor. The first thing we knew they were dating and soon began talking marriage, even though by then she was around forty. She had a big church wedding and a reception in her apartment across from Vanderbilt University. A lot of her country music friends were there mingling in comfortably with her upper-crust friends. She was from a prosperous family in Centerville, Tennessee, and had graduated from Ward-Belmont College in Nashville. She never needed to support herself, either before or after she married, but she loved her career so much she had no intention of quitting until she had to.

It was a fabulous career. Sarah Ophelia Colley was able to do what few actors can. She created a legendary character and put her in a town named Grinder's Switch and filled it with fascinating, colorful people. By the way, there is a real town named Grinder's Switch about three miles from Centerville, but her stage town existed only in her imagination. Millions of fans got to know Minnie Pearl and her fellow citizens, like her brother, called Brother, her Uncle Nabob, Aunt Ambrosy, Coz Elmer, Lizzie Tinkum, and her special "feller," Hezzie. This was the way she would report the news to her Opry listeners: "People say, 'How did Brother get all them red spots on his face?' and I'd say, 'Well, we been teaching him how to eat with a fork.'" It wasn't intended to be sophisticated humor, but people liked its backwoods plainness and its gossipy kind of comedy. She'd say, "Well, in Grinder's Switch you don't read the paper to find out who was doing what. You already know that. You read the paper to find out if they got caught." In the mid-1940s Minnie put out a little comic paper called *Minnie Pearl's Grinder's Switch Gazette*, which sold for twenty-five cents, and in it she told you who got caught.

Even after Minnie was married, she continued to work with me and the band. But she loved to have Henry fly her to the shows. When we met the Collins Sisters at a fair in Ohio, she insisted that we ask them to join our group. She liked their singing and dancing, and she also wanted them to fly with her. "We've got plenty of room— just Sam and me. Henry's too busy flying the plane to talk to me, and that leaves me only Sam to talk to." Sam was her poodle. We agreed we'd talk with the sisters' parents about them joining the show and flying with Minnie. The parents said, "Yes, it sounds like a good job for them. But is Henry a licensed pilot?" I said, "Sure he is. He's the best. He's only had one crash landing—in Knoxville— but nobody got hurt, much." That was the beginning of a happy two-year relationship with the Collins Sisters.

My relationship with Minnie lasted until her stroke in 1991 in Joliet, Illinois, where we were doing a package show of Opry stars. She was rushed to a Nashville hospital, then later allowed to go home, where she has to have twenty-four-hour a day nursing care. For a while, it looked like she might recover enough to return to work, but I talked with Henry a while ago, and he said her right side is still paralyzed and she's unable to speak. She's so sick she can't have visitors. I know now she'll never return to the stage.

A couple of years after her stroke, a tribute called "Hats Off to Minnie" was produced by a guy from Chicago, and I went down to Nashville to be a part of it. It was a sad and joyous occasion for a lot of us old-timers, with stars like Jimmy Dean, Roy Clark, Pat Boone, Jim Nabors, Grandpa Jones, Roy Acuff, Jimmy Dickens, Bill Monroe, and some younger stars mixed in to improve the ratings. Even the governor of Tennessee was there. It was a sad reunion because we were celebrating a woman we all loved and probably would never see again. I was lucky to know Sarah Ophelia Colley and Minnie Pearl. They both enriched my life.

Finally, I want to say something about the African-American friends I have made through country music. I know that sounds almost like a contradiction because country music has never been very popular with black people. We never had more than a few blacks in our audiences, and I think they came mostly out of curiosity. I did have a fairly large black audience for my television shows in Louisville. I frequently had black entertainers like Mahalia Jackson and the Ink Spots on my television shows in Cleveland and Cincinnati. One time the NCO Club manager at Ft. Campbell, Kentucky, called to book us for a show, thinking I was B.B. King. I said, "No, I'm not B.B. King, but I believe we can entertain you." He said, "Okay, come on anyway." During most of my career, however, our music didn't seem to be their kind of music. Whenever blacks came to one of our shows and bought a ticket, we never turned them away. Of course, in the South and a few other places the usher would take them to back seats or to a special section or to the balcony; but that was the law.

Sometimes we had blacks working with our road crews. I've also worked with a few black performers in country music. Some orchestras had black performers, but they were usually buck-and-wing dancers or tap dancers. I remember a buck-and-wing dancer with Francis Craig's orchestra who was called Little Pee Wee, but I never knew his real name. O.B. McClinton, a blues singer, did some country shows and appeared with me at the Kentucky State Fair one year and was on the Opry several times. He was from Mississippi and sang the old black blues the way they used to be sung. He made several good records but died young of cancer.

The first black performer that I know of who appeared on the Opry was DeFord Bailey, who played the harmonica. Audiences always wanted to hear his two signature songs, "Hot Water Blues" and "Cold Water Blues." DeFord toured with both Roy Acuff's band and mine. He was a good-natured fellow, and we liked to play jokes on him. One time we were touring down in Florida and were about to cross a long toll bridge where the charge was ten cents a person. We were driving my long stretch limousine then and had a trailer hitched behind it. Before we got to the bridge, DeFord said, "Mr. King, I know how I can save myself ten cents. You lock me up in that trailer and let me out after we get across." So we put him in the trailer, drove up to the toll booth, paid for the rest of us, then crossed the bridge and kept on driving way beyond where we should have stopped to let DeFord out. After a few miles we could hear him pounding on the sides of that trailer and hollering, "Let me out. Let me out." Finally, we stopped, opened the trailer, and DeFord jumped out and said, "Golly me, I never knew a bridge that was that long." We had a good laugh at his expense. But he did save ten cents.

Roy told me that one time DeFord was with his band on their way to do a show in Chattanooga, and they noticed that every chance he got he would sprawl out and go to sleep in his seat. So the boys found a bucket and slipped it over his head while he was asleep. When they hit a bump in the road and he woke up, he said, "Lordy me, it's done got dark. Have I done missed my supper?" So they pulled the bucket up, and the handle hit him in the jaw. Roy said, "DeFord, we shouldn't have done that to you. We could have knocked out some of your teeth and then you wouldn't be able to play the harmonica." We all enjoyed being with DeFord and he liked us, but in those days, especially in the South, he couldn't room with us on the road. When we'd get to a town where we were playing, we'd start looking for a boardinghouse or a private home that took in blacks.

The most famous African-American in the history of country music is my friend, Mississippi-born Charley Pride, who broke the racial barrier in country music in the 1960s. He was the first black entertainer to perform in country music on equal terms with whites. When I met him in the 1960s, he said, "Mr. King, I know you're not going to believe this, but it's the gospel truth. I have always loved the Golden West Cowboys, and I can name every one of them and their instruments right now." And he did. Then he said, "Do you believe I grew up on your music?" I said, "Yes sir, I believe you did." We've been friends on the stage and golf course many times since then.

Charley has made it big in county music because he's got charm and style and he plays genuine country music, but almost all his fans are white. Not many blacks come to his shows or buy his records. I don't think you'll find many blacks in the audiences at his Charley Pride Theater in Branson, Missouri, where his matinee and evening shows are sellouts. When you think about it, it is remarkable that Charley has such a large following among people that are considered to be the most racist in the country. I've never witnessed any racial incidents when I was with Charley socially or professionally, and he's never told me of any problems he's had. I think that, by and large, his fans love him for his great musical talent and don't pay any attention to his color. He simply performs the kind of music country music fans like, and most of them happen to be white. And he just happens to be black.

There simply is not a big audience for what most blacks consider a white man's music. To most blacks country music is closely tied to the rural white culture of the South. Country music came mainly out of the hills and mountains where mostly white people live. Western music is also mostly about a white culture and the plains, the sky, the stars, horses, and ranches. For many blacks their own forms of popular music, like blues, jazz, and gospel—and now rap—are rich enough to satisfy them. Why should they buy Patty Loveless when they can have Aretha Franklin? On the other hand, blacks have made it big in mainstream pop music, which is not so closely tied to a culture or region. Nat "King" Cole, Johnny Mathis, The Ink Spots, and Sammy Davis, Jr., are just a few of the many blacks who have become pop superstars.

Because blacks and whites have lived so close together, particularly in the South, there is, naturally, some crossover of influences. Hank Williams owed a big debt to the music of the blacks he grew up with, especially blues and gospel, and some of his songs, like "Lovesick Blues," come close to the kinds of music that attract black audiences. Black blues singers and fiddlers also influenced such pioneers of country music as Bill Monroe and Bob Wills. On the other side, we know that many black bluesmen in the 1920s and 1930s played songs by Jimmie Rodgers, and we know that Ray Charles has said that when he was a boy in Georgia he used to listen to the Opry on the radio.

In 1980 Charley Pride recorded his tribute to Hank Williams, "A Little Bit of Hank in Me." It is a beautiful, sensitive interpretation of some of Hank's great songs by one of our best country singers, black or white. Country music is a democratic music. It is the music of ordinary people, and performers are judged by their talent—not by their education, their pedigrees, or their skin color. At least, that's the way it's been with me and my friends.

Country Roads

IN MY DAY—and it's not much different today—if you wanted to make a living as a musician, you had to take your show to where the people were—across town or on the road. You couldn't make it on records alone. In fact, your records wouldn't sell unless you did live shows. You couldn't support yourself on radio work because most radio stations paid very little, or nothing. Furthermore, people liked to see their favorite country stars in person, and they would gladly pay twenty-five or fifty cents for the privilege. Since most of the fans couldn't go to the Opry or to other radio stations to see us live in the studio, we had to go to them. We made most of our income from ticket sales and from sales of souvenir programs and songbooks. Even in this day of country videos, The Nashville Network, and hundreds of daily radio and television programs, fans still want to see their country stars at state fairs, concerts, college homecomings, and trade shows.

Public appearances have always been a vital part of sales promotion. Gene Autry knew how important it was for him to do tours when he started making movies. He said, "We make our movies out in California, but they are shown in theaters all over the country. We have to go where the audiences are. Every time we do a live show in Wheeling, West Virginia, we take in a little money, but more important is that we also build an audience for our movies. The people who see us in person become our fans and buy our records and see our movies." Whenever he made a new movie, therefore, Gene went on tour in his van with "Gene Autry and Champion" written in large letters all over it. He would do shows all the way from Hollywood to Madison Square Garden. Gene knew how to increase his income through promotion. Country stars still do it the old-fashioned way he used and perfected.

That's one of the important lessons I learned from Gene, and I've performed literally from the Atlantic to the Pacific and from Canada to the Caribbean, from Constitution Hall in Washington to the inmates of the Jefferson County Jail in Kentucky. I think I've played in every state except Alaska and Hawaii, and I was invited to go to Alaska but fortunately said no. One time a disk jockey up there turned promoter, and he persuaded Cowboy Copas and Ferlin Husky to go up for some hotshot Alaskan tour. It was a disaster. When they got there, they didn't find diddly-squat—no people, no money, nothing. There weren't many people up there to start with, and the few they found just weren't interested in country music. The disk jockey was a good kid, but he misread his audience potential. When Copas and Husky got back, they said, "Pee Wee, don't go to Alaska. It's not worth it." I said, "Don't worry. There's enough to keep me busy in the lower forty-eight."

Of all the places I've played, my home territory in Wisconsin holds special memories. They all knew me and turned out in droves when I came. The Midwest generally has been good to me, and Iowa was a special place. In the 1960s I gave my band a vacation and for a couple of months I worked Iowa with Andy Doll and His Orchestra, which sounded a lot like Lawrence Welk. In fact, we opened each show with Welk's theme song. It was a small group, but the six men played seventeen instruments. It was like a vacation for me because I didn't have to worry about anything. Andy made all the arrangements, and he had all the headaches. Not me.

Usually the touring headaches were mine, especially after Mr. Frank's death. At our peak—say in 1954—we were playing almost thirty separate locations a year, all the way from Billings, Montana, to Montgomery, Alabama. We played little towns, like Shepherdsville, Kentucky, and big cities, like Indianapolis and Philadelphia. Imagine all the details involved in arranging for that many shows in so many different places! My Louisville office did the paperwork, but I was responsible for the overall success of each show, artistic and financial. By the late 1940s we were traveling by car, by van, by bus, by train, and by plane—whichever was most practical. It was a fast-paced life, with a different town every night—you know: "If it's Friday, this must be Sheboygan." For example, on October 30, 1954, we played Tulsa, then Oklahoma City on the 31st, Enid on November 1, and Norman on the 2nd. After that, we had to fly home to Louisville to do our television show in Cincinnati the next day. The next night we played a date in Lexington before we went back the next day to Cincinnati. It was exhausting! We didn't have much time to rehearse on the road, and we learned to try out new numbers and arrangements in our hotel rooms. Most of our appearances were one-night stands—which I always preferred to being tied down for a three- or four-week job—so we at least could do pretty much the same show each time.

In addition to my office, we had managers and booking agents to help with the arrangements. Mr. Frank was, of course, the best of the lot; but there were many others who made touring a lot easier for us performers. In the early 1960s we used a booking agent in Nashville named Lucky Moeller, who put together a package show with Minnie Pearl, the Collins Sisters, and Pee Wee King and the Golden West Cowboys, and arranged a cross-country tour of fairs, auditoriums, parks, and festivals. It went off without a hitch. I also had occasional contracts with other booking agents, like the super-efficient Don Romeo Agency in Omaha. When I was playing a date near Omaha, I would call Don to see if he could get us a fireman's picnic or a church carnival to play while we were close by. It made our trips more productive and brought us additional income. Those guys kept us from having too many dead spots in our schedule, and they were well worth their 15 percent of our take.

Because of all this touring, our wives were road widows for much of the year. Fortunately, we were able to do a lot of shows close to home, whether we were living in Nashville or Louisville. We had a lot of competition from other country stars in the Nashville area, but since we moved back to Louisville in 1947, we've booked dozens and dozens of shows nearby. I've played state fairs all over the country, but most often at the Kentucky State Fair in Louisville, where I've done shows with Tom T. Hall, Crystal Gayle, and many other top talents. My favorite big local show was the Philip Morris Derby Festival Music Show at the state fairgrounds around the first of May each year. I worked with the Philip Morris promoters for a number of years in attracting top country stars and providing musical support for singers with the Golden West Cowboys—stars like Anne Murray, Ray Stevens, Mickey Gilley, Patsy Cline, Jimmy Dean, Glen Campbell, Tammy Wynette, and Carl Smith. One year I put together a band of about eighteen players; and we paid tribute to the music of Duke Ellington, Cab Calloway, Fats Domino, and Louisville native Lionel Hampton. Other local shows that I worked with include the William H. King Sport, Boat and Vacation Show, where I enjoyed working with people like football great Paul Hornung.

I can't overemphasize the importance of promotion in any entertainer's success. You can have the greatest musical talent God ever gave anyone, but if people don't know about it, they're not going to come hear you and buy your records. Like my mentor, Gene Autry, I've always tried to take advantage of every opportunity I had to promote my own shows and those of other country performers. Back in the 1950s, when I had a monthly column in *Country Song Roundup* called "Pee Wee King's Korn Fab," I tried to plug as many shows as I had room for. I also found it very useful to get to know disk jockeys in towns all over the country, and I made myself available to them for interviews. Promotion. Promotion. Promotion. In the music business, you can't have too much!

Even with a lot of local support from fans who came to our shows, I couldn't make a living in my own backyard. That meant that most of my income had to be earned on the road. When I was with the Opry, tent shows were popular, and I did a lot of them. They were traveling shows we performed under a large tent, which our crew would put up and take down at each show location. We had to have a special truck just to carry the tent and folding chairs and other equipment. It was hard and time-consuming work. They began to fade out in the North in the early 1950s but continued fairly strong in the South for another ten or so years.

This was the procedure we followed. We'd send an advance man into a town, say, Calhoun, Georgia, and he would say to the mayor or school official or local promoter, "I'm So-and-So, and I represent the Grand Ole Opry from Nashville, and we've got a show made up of Pee Wee King and Minnie Pearl and Eddy Arnold and the Golden West Cowboys. We'd like to rent a lot near the outskirts of town and set up our tent, put in seats, and sell tickets for our family show. We can give you a percentage of the show receipts, or we can pay you rent for the location." The local official would say, "Yeah, we like the Grand Ole Opry around here. Your show sounds like a good idea. We'll take it for 25 percent of your gross." Then we would move in according to the schedule, put up our tent, do our show, and move on to the next stop. We had a regular crew that raised the tent and put out the chairs, usually in the morning of the day we performed. Then the performers would arrive in the afternoon, set up their instruments, and tune them up. We had to be very careful. As we tuned them, the sun bearing down on the tent heated the instruments, and the cool air in the evening put them out of tune again. We were constantly adjusting to the changes in temperature.

Sometimes we'd make good money, and sometimes we wouldn't make expenses. One time Mr. Frank rented a tent from two blackface comedians and tried a circuit in Georgia, Alabama, and Arkansas, but that circuit had been played to death, and it was a disaster. Next, we got permission from the Opry officials to try a circuit in New England with our package show, but it was even worse. Up there we died the death of a rag doll! The best areas for our tent shows were usually in the Deep South, where the Grand Ole Opry was a magic name and where our six- to ten-day tours were almost always successful.

People in the little southern towns welcomed us with open arms. They were glad to see in person stars they'd heard on the Opry the week before. Our audiences were responsive and courteous. Occasionally, Mr. Frank might catch a couple of boys trying to sneak in under the tent. He would step up behind them, grab them by the collar, pull them back out and say, "Hey, what are you boys trying to do? Get in without a ticket? Go buy one." If they said, as they usually did, "We can't 'cause we ain't got no money," he'd say, "Well, here's some." They'd take it, buy their tickets, and go inside with sheepish grins on their faces.

On the road we'd sometimes have a singer or player want to join our show, and we took a few on for a while. We never had many second-rate entertainers approach us because they knew we were top of the line and our standards were high. One time when we were playing Glasgow, Kentucky, a country clown who called himself Uncle Bozo wanted to join our troupe. After he worked a show free, we could see that he had good potential and took him with us. He stayed for a few weeks and did good work, but he soon drifted back to Glasgow, and we never heard from him again. He was like a lot of people who think show business is all glamour, money, and fame, but when they get a taste of how hard they have to work just to keep a job, they decide there are easier ways to make a living. I tell young people to go into show business if they have to. Otherwise, get a regular job.

Everyone worked very hard on our road trips, and each one of us had his own job to do. As long as each person did his job, every show went off as planned. One time I overheard a conversation between Mr. Frank and an engineer from WSM who was in charge of the sound system for the Camel Caravan. The engineer was in a tangle of tripods and speakers and wires he was connecting. Mr. Frank said, "Why do we have so much trouble at each stop getting the electrical equipment ready? Why do you have to splice down the voltage from 220 to 110 every time we set up? Can't you get a ready-made plug and use it every time?" The engineer said, "Mr. Frank, I want this job. I don't want to go back to Nashville until this tour is over. By me splicing these wires every time, I've got a job that nobody else can do. I don't tell you how to manage the show, and I'll thank you not to tell me how to manage the sound system. Just let me know if it doesn't work right. Anyway, I'm under contract to Camel Cigarettes, and it doesn't cost you one red cent."

That's a good lesson, especially when you're dealing with professionals and a tight schedule. You do your job and don't bother someone else who's doing his job. If he's an expert, he doesn't need your help. If he's not doing a good job, he won't be with the show long anyway. One time two of my band members were arguing with each other about how to do a certain song. I said to one of them, "Don't you tell him how to play his guitar," and I said to the other one, "Don't you tell him how to sing. I'm the boss and I'll decide if either of you is not doing his job right."

On the road not only was the work hard and the schedule grueling, but often our accommodations were deplorable. We'd usually stay in boardinghouses or in tourist cabins like those tepee cottages at Horse Cave, Kentucky—just anywhere we could get rooms that were not expensive. Some of the boardinghouses catered to traveling entertainers and salesmen, but most of them served a general clientele, and we tried to fit in like everybody else. They were like the bed and breakfast arrangements that are so popular now. Of course, after motels became popular, our accommodations improved and were more comfortable and convenient. It was easier to make telephone calls home to our wives and families too. When we lived near Nashville at Goodlettsville, we always had problems when we tried to call home. The telephone operator would ask, "Now, how do you spell Goodlettsville?" One time, I said to Mr. Frank, "I think we're just going to have to move to a town with a simpler name." He said, "No, I think it'll be easier if the operators learn to spell Goodlettsville."

I'm a registered Republican now, but I've never been much of a political animal. In fact, I've campaigned on both sides of the street, Democratic and Republican. There are good candidates in both parties. I went on tour to help the Republican nominee for governor of Kentucky, Louie Nunn, and at our shows I would introduce him as the next governor of the state. I don't know whether I helped him, but I do know he was elected. Roy Acuff even came up from Nashville to work in the campaign. It was a kind of dress rehearsal for his own campaign several years later—one that he lost.

I did my best for Roy. He called me before he announced his candidacy, and said, "Pee Wee, you're a Republican, and I want you to come down here and help me. I'll throw in fifty thousand dollars of my own money, and we'll draw crowds like you've never seen. We'll play all the little foothill towns and country towns and courthouse squares all over Tennessee, and I'm confident we'll win." Well, he was right about drawing the big crowds. Everybody came out to hear Ol' Roy sing—whole families in a bunch—but they didn't vote for him. He got whipped by the Democrats two to one. I flew down in my airplane and joined his campaign at Winchester. Roy got up and made a beautiful speech about what he'd do as governor, and the people listened to our music. But they just wouldn't vote for him. A hillbilly musician as governor of Tennessee? Apparently, not even the hillbillies voted for him!

I don't think Roy's loss sent much of a message to other country music stars who wanted to run for governor of Tennessee as a

Republican. At least, Tex Ritter didn't seem to hear it. Around 1982 I went down to Nashville and rode the bus with Tex for two days when he was running for governor. Tex slept in the back of the bus. When we stopped he'd come out looking horrible, but what people said about him was even worse. One fellow said to me, "Where does this guy get off? Why does a Texan want to come over here and be governor of Tennessee? We ought to run him back to Texas." I said, "Do you know Tex?" He said, "No, and I don't want to either." Well, we who knew him loved and respected him. He had moved to Nashville from Hollywood and had lived in Tennessee about ten years before he ran for governor. He was sincere and unselfish about wanting to serve his adopted state. His son John, who is now a big television star, grew up in Nashville. Those two failed campaigns proved to me that Tennesseeans like to keep their music and politics separate.

I had better luck working with two Democrats back in Kentucky. I supported both Wendell Ford and Martha Layne Collins for governor. I even played at Governor Collins's inauguration in Frankfort. I campaigned for Governor Ford from a flatbed truck all over the state. At one stop he forgot how high the truck bed was from the ground. He walked up the steps to the truck bed, where we had the microphone, and I introduced him, as usual, as "the next governor of Kentucky, the Honorable Wendell Ford." He came to the podium and spoke about his plans for Kentucky, then said, "Now Pee Wee, will you play 'My Old Kentucky Home?'" I struck up the band as he left. I expected him to take the steps down as he did when he came up, but instead he jumped straight from the truck bed to the ground. When he hit, his knees buckled and he fell flat to the ground. I jumped off and picked him up to check his injuries. He said, "I don't think I have any broken bones, but I feel like my ankles are embedded in my loafers." He was lucky not to get hurt and lucky that there was no photographer close by to take his picture on the ground. He could have been carried off on a stretcher. I could imagine the photograph in all the papers next day and the headline: "Gubernatorial Candidate Wendell Ford Takes a Great Fall." I was still afraid that voters would think he was too clumsy to be governor, but they elected him anyway.

The longest political campaigning I ever did lasted several weeks in 1939 in Florida. We had been performing at the Flags, a big convention center complex in St. Augustine, where they had all kinds of business and professional meetings and conventions and political rallies. It was near the Fountain of Youth and across the street from the snake and alligator farm, where they'd milk the snakes for the tourists. We'd play the Opry on Saturday nights and drive down to St. Augustine in time for a Sunday matinee. The owner of the Flags was a good friend of Mayor Walter B. Fraser, who had heard us perform and said, "Boys, I like the way you look and sound. I'm running for the Democratic nomination for governor of Florida, and I'd like to hire you to play for my campaign. We'll pay you a good salary and get you all the sound equipment and transportation you need." We liked the offer. It gave us steady work and it relieved us from having to play a different little shotgun theater or schoolhouse every night, and then hurrying back to Nashville to do the Opry on Saturday.

At that time there were five of us with the Golden West Cowboys, plus Texas Daisy and including Eddy Arnold. We started in early 1939 and worked until just before the Democratic primary in early May. Mayor Fraser called himself the businessman's candidate for governor, and his motto was "Vote for a Business Man with a Business Plan." If elected, he promised to reduce car tags to three dollars each.

We campaigned all over the state—in rented halls, on courthouse steps, public squares, and at business places. The guy who drove our main truck had worked in political campaigns before, and he knew the best fruit and orange docks to play. Mr. Frank made up the schedule and all the arrangements. He'd check with the front office to make sure we didn't interfere with work times. At lunch periods we'd have large crowds who'd eat and listen to us play. We'd set up our sound system and instruments on a loading dock where they shipped out oranges and other citrus fruits. We'd play for about half an hour, then I'd introduce the candidate: "Ladies and gentlemen, I have the privilege of introducing the mayor of St. Augustine and the next governor of Florida. He's going to reduce your car taxes and everything else. He's your man. Vote for Mayor Fraser." We even wrote a jingle for the campaign. I don't remember how it went, but I bet Eddy Arnold can still sing it.

We were based in St. Augustine, where we stayed at a downtown hotel. We tried to get back to our rooms every night because the hotel kitchen always prepared us such good seafood dinners when we'd get in late from a show. Lydia, our daughter, Marietta, and I stayed in one room, and Mr. and Mrs. Frank had the room next to us. Texas Daisy had her own room, and the fellows were all single and roomed together—Speedy McNatt, Joe Zinkens, and Eddy Arnold. Actually, Joe was married, but his wife refused to leave home and stayed with her mother in a little town in Indiana. I was the emcee of the shows until the salt air irritated my throat and I lost my voice. I was emceeing five or six shows a day and singing with the trio, and I just ran out of voice. Eddy took over for me as emcee.

When we were too far from St. Augustine to return for the night, we stayed in a hotel or tourist cottage near where we were performing, whether it was Sarasota or Miami or Gainesville or Tampa. We performed anywhere we thought we could get a crowd. One of our best places was in front of a courthouse. We'd set up our instruments on the top level and the audience would sit on the steps below or stand on the ground. One of our biggest crowds was at a big sponge business near Naples. One day we were campaigning in downtown Hollywood in front of a big bank building, and the temperature hit 112 degrees. We were wearing satin shirts, cowboy pants and boots, and cowboy hats. Man, were we suffering! Mr. Fraser could see that we were about to pass out from the heat, and he came over and whispered, "Pee Wee, have the boys take off their hats." So I turned to the audience and said, "I've just been told by the next governor of Florida that it's too hot to wear our cowboy hats today. So boys, take 'em off." The audience cheered. In those days, men wore hats like they wore their shirts. You hardly ever saw a man outdoors without a hat on, regardless of how hot it was.

Another incident on that campaign trail also involved a hat. Our daughter, Marietta—we called her Tootie—was just old enough to be toddling around, and we used her in our act. Mr. Fraser, whose trademark was a Panama suit and hat, would get Tootie to hold his hat while he made his speech. But at this particular stop, his hat was soaking wet, and Tootie laid in on the sound system while he was talking. When he finished, she picked up his hat and took it to him, and he tried to put it on. He was a big man with a big head, and his hat had shrunk to about half its regular size. He looked at the hat, put it back on his head and said, "Tootie, are you sure this is my hat? It looks like Pee Wee's hat." The audience went wild. Mr. Fraser had a good sense of humor and never failed to compliment us for our work. We worked our buns off for him.

As we got closer to May the heat began to be a bigger problem. It really got to us as we raced from one stop to another. We began to have trouble with our instruments, especially at night. The dew would rise as the temperatures cooled; and all that salt water and air would clog the instruments, particularly my accordion and the bass fiddle and guitar strings. My accordion was damaged so much by the weather that when we left Florida, I had to send it to Milwaukee to have it reconditioned.

We had a number of other interesting experiences during the campaign. When we were in Miami, we had one night off, and we all went to see Mickey Rooney in a stage show at a big amphitheater. After the show the boys and I went backstage to meet him. He didn't know who I was, and Eddy Arnold didn't have a big name then either. I told him we were on leave from the Grand Ole Opry and working a political campaign. He said, "Oh yeah, I know about the Grand Ole Opry, but I don't go in for that hillbilly stuff." A few years later when I went out to California to make a movie, I got off the plane at Los Angeles airport and who should be in the waiting room but Mickey Rooney. I said, "Hey, Mickey!" He looked at me and said, "Do I know you?" I said, "I'm Pee Wee King. We met in Florida." He said, "Oh yeah, I remember you. We're the same size." Actually, he's a little shorter than I am; but he's a better actor.

In those days if a candidate won the Democratic primary in Florida, he was considered elected. There were so few Republicans they didn't even have a primary. So if anybody really wanted to be governor, he ran in the Democratic primary; and it was usually overrun with candidates. Most of them were not taken seriously, and not many of them had enough money to do much campaigning. My candidate, Mr. Fraser, and another one, Spessard Holland, had a lot of money backing them and didn't ask for contributions during their rallies. But I remember a preacher candidate who did. He'd say: "I don't have no country music bands to play for me. I don't have nobody to make speeches for me. I don't have no money to advertise in the newspapers and on the radio. I don't even have the money to pay my expenses. What I do have is a big barrel right here where you can drop your donations in as you leave. Now don't be timid. I'll welcome anything you can give. If your love gift jingles when it hits the bottom, that will suit me fine. It's just as good as that folding money the big shots give. I'm grateful for anything."

Spessard Holland and Mr. Fraser were friends and business partners, and before the primary election they agreed to stop running against each other. Mr. Fraser pulled out of the race and threw his support to Mr. Holland, who won the Democratic nomination and, of course, the election. Although our candidate didn't become governor, we felt that we had won anyway because it was a change of pace for us. We also had time to be tourists and enjoy the Florida sights. It was one of the most pleasant jobs we ever had.

While we were campaigning in Florida, the Prince Albert tobacco company was putting together an Opry show to be broadcast coast to coast. After they auditioned a lot of people, they chose Roy Acuff. Roy asked me and the Golden West Cowboys to be the first guests on his new show. Afterwards, the show's producers asked Mr. Frank, "Why didn't these guys audition? They're a sharp outfit and play the kind of music we want." Mr. Frank said, "They've been working in Florida and were not available for an audition. Anyway, they're about to go to Hollywood to do a movie."

We didn't have many special assignments like political campaigns or movies. Most of the time we were on the road, doing our shows all over the country—NCO clubs in air force bases in Oklahoma or Texas or Kansas, the Ohio Sweet Corn Festival, a police ball in Peru, Indiana, a concert at the Corn Palace in Mitchell, South Dakota, truckers' shows, bowling alleys, Masonic theaters, a hillbilly jamboree in Boston, a mountain festival in Hiawassee, Georgia, a concert at Myrtle Beach, South Carolina, a series at Riverside Rancho in Los Angeles, state fairs from Maine to Minnesota, and rodeos galore. For several years I performed at the Jimmie Rodgers Memorial Festival in Meridian, Mississippi, and served as chairman of the celebration honoring this grandfather of country music. I enjoyed doing rodeos, but they were hard on my voice. My lungs would get clogged up with all the dust flying about, and I'd lose my voice. When I think back now, I am amazed that we played so many places for so long and had so few problems.

One of the most unusual engagements we ever had was in the Texas State Prison in Huntsville in October of 1946. For the entire month the Golden West Cowboys and San Antonio Rose and I put on a Sunday afternoon show as part of the Texas Prison Rodeo. The prisoners did contests in calf roping, saddle bronco riding, bareback bronco riding, bull riding, wild mare riding, and other kinds of animal tricks.

Another of our unusual assignments was in 1965, when we played at the Wild Pony Roundup on Chincoteague Island on the Eastern Shore of Virginia. We were doing a show for ABC television in Cleveland, and the network called and said, "Pee Wee, can you and the boys do some shows for us on Chincoteague Island? We have a kind of freakish show to do in connection with the wild pony roundup and auction." Well, I'd never heard of Chincoteague Island or the ponies that run wild there and have to be thinned each year with a roundup and auction, but it sounded like fun, and we did it. We taped for television three shows a day, a half hour each time, with the two-hour horse auctions in between the shows. The annual event attracted more than thirty thousand people every year. The wild horses were paraded in front of the platform, and people would walk around, look at the ponies, and buy one for their kids. I almost bought one, but they weren't fully broken, and I knew I couldn't take home a wild pony.

In January of 1961 we played an engagement I never want to repeat. Our booking agent, Colonel Tom Parker, had heard that a casino in Las Vegas needed a western band, and he said, "Pee Wee King has one of the best." So he made the arrangements and we went out and played the Golden Nugget for two weeks. Boy, was I glad when it was over and we could head home. It was like working in a salt mine. We did the night shift from eight until two the next morning. When we finished a set, we climbed up the stairs to our dressing room to wait for the next set. Those hours got longer and longer. One time the manager said, "You fellows don't seem to be enjoying yourself." I said, "Well, not much. We're not used to a schedule like this." He said, "Well, you're committed for two weeks, so you'd better learn to like it." I said, "Oh, don't worry. We'll get used to it. We'll give you your money's worth."

We were well paid. Homer and Jethro played there just before us, and Homer said, "Pee Wee, let me give you a little advice. Ask the management for advance money every night, and then pretend to go down to the gambling tables and slot machines and spend it. They'll think they're getting it all back, and it'll make them feel good. They'll think they're getting free entertainment, and they may even give you a bonus." So that's what we did. But instead of gambling it away, we sent it home, the way Homer did.

It was good money but hard-earned. When you play a dance, you've got motion on your side. When you play a theater, you've got a responsive audience who've come to hear you. But when you work a gambling joint, you've got gamblers who don't give a damn who's up there trying to entertain them. Some of the casinos had big concert rooms, but at the Golden Nugget we were mixed in with the gamblers in the same room. Our stage was at one end of the gambling area, and we tried to put on a good show of songs and instrumental music. There were maybe fifty chairs near the stage area where people could sit and listen, but most of the people went right on gambling and talking while we played. We had very few people who sat and listened to us for more than a few minutes at a time. Even when they sat down to listen, they would soon drift away to the gambling tables to play the roulette wheels or slot machines. We were like background music that nobody listened to. The Golden Nugget now has a concert hall without the gambling, and people can come to hear the music. Entertainers don't have to compete with the noises of gambling.

After we finished our two-week run, the manager gave us our final pay. We sat down and he bought me a drink and said, "I'll say one thing, Pee Wee. You're a hard-working band, and everybody liked your shows. But you weren't as bubbly as I expected." I said, "Well sir, I'm sorry, but it's hard to be bubbly at one o'clock in the morning." He said, "Would you rather do one-nighters?" I said, "Yes, I do. We like playing to a different audience at a different place every night. It's always fresh." Then he said, "Well, I doubt if you'll ever want to play back here again, but let us know if you do." I never called him back. The Golden Nugget was not our kind of audience.

Being a bandleader on the road is a big responsibility. I felt responsible for what happened to my band members and tried to help them in emergencies. When we were in California one time,

Gene Stewart became seriously ill. We thought he had a stomach ulcer, but the doctor said, "This boy doesn't have an ulcer. He's dying of malnutrition. You need to get him home to his family." It seemed that Gene's problem was that he was grieving inside and not eating properly. We had been away from home for long periods doing movies and working at the Riverside Rancho, and the long absences were beginning to take a toll. At that time we had four days left on our contract with the Riverside Rancho. But we sent him home, where he rested and recuperated for a couple of months. We continued to cover his salary just like he was working. We also paid his brother Al, who sang and played the violin, bass fiddle, and guitar and covered for him while he was absent. Show business is very stressful on families. I was lucky that Lydia was used to the pressures of the business when I married her, though after our second child was born she started staying home to raise our family. During periods when we had local radio and television contracts, we could stay at home more. We weren't always saying good-bye to our wives and children and talking to them so much by long distance.

It wasn't always the loneliness of separation that made touring so difficult. We had accidents and boredom and other problems to contend with. The times we toured by bus were a nightmare. The boys played cards and shot dice and wouldn't sleep, and by the time we got to our destination, they were dead tired. Sometimes our problems were matters of misjudgment when a driver would go to the wrong place. Once we were touring by car and playing a fair in Martinsville, Illinois, but when we got there, one of our cars was missing with half the musicians and instruments. The second car had gone to Martinsville, Indiana, and I had to quickly fill out the band with pickup musicians.

Accidents could be dangerous in two ways. First, we could get injured in the accident itself, and then we could get hurt while trying to repair the damage done to the car. Mr. Frank warned me against trying to do any roadside repairs. "Let me tell you something, kid," he said. "You make your living with your hands playing the accordion. If you injure them, you can't work. If you have a flat, don't fix it yourself." During the war we were always having flats because the tires were made of synthetic rubber that wasn't very durable. We'd take the tire off, hitch a ride to a filling station, get the tire repaired, and bring it back. We spent a lot of time waiting by the road getting tires fixed.

One time when Minnie was traveling with us and we were headed back to Nashville, we had a flat on a bridge near Henderson. We'd already had twelve flats on that trip, and we were hot and tired and frustrated and late; and there we sat on that bridge with a flat tire. I was mad as hell. There was nothing we could do until somebody stopped to give us a lift. Suddenly, I said, "All right, everybody get out. I'm going to throw this tire tool through the windshield, and I don't want anybody in the car when I do it!" Minnie said, "Gus, I do believe Pee Wee is upset." Gus was my brother-in-law and road manager. He said, "Minnie, I've never seen Pee Wee mad at anything before, but I think you're right. He's cussing in Polish." Minnie said, "Well, I thought he was either using cuss words I've never heard before or jabbering in some foreign language." Somebody stopped and rescued us before I broke out the windshield, but I was mad enough to do it. Traveling by bus or car during those war years was slow and dangerous. It's a lot safer and more comfortable now, with $250,000 Silver Eagle buses that have every convenience and luxury you can imagine.

We didn't know whether we'd make it for our next show on time during the war years. One time Eddy Arnold was with me when we were on our way to do a live radio show at WSM in Nashville. I was driving my rickety old car, and just as I got to the top of a hill and stopped for a red light, the transmission fell out. Eddy looked like he would have a fit. But I got out, looked the situation over, and said, "I got an idea. Get out and let's push." So we started the car downhill, jumped in, and rolled to a stop in front of a car dealer. In a few seconds a salesman came up, and I began to put my plan in operation. "Just looking," I said. "I don't have enough money for a down payment on another car." The salesman looked out at my car at the curb and said, "Your old car will do for a down payment. Just let me test drive it first." I said, "No, I never let anybody drive my car." Well, he bought my story hook, line, and sinker. Eddy and I drove off in a new car and got to the station just in town for the show. When the salesman called me next day to cuss me out, what could I say? I said, "Well, you see what happens when I let some-body else drive my car."

In times of gas rationing and scarcity, we had trouble getting enough gas to get us to our dates out of town. Ernest Tubb hit on a good idea during the war. He wouldn't play a date unless the pro-moter filled his gas tank for the trip home. I had luck with a varia-tion of that deal. I'd stop at some remote gas station out in the country and say, "How would you folks like to have passes to the Grand Ole Opry?" They'd say, "Yes, we would. What do we have to do?" I'd say, "Just fill up my car with gas and don't ask for coupons." We had other problems from time to time, including theft. In 1979 some thieves broke into our van at the Holiday Inn in Reading, Pennsyl-vania, and stole all our instruments. We had to borrow substitutes from people around town and buy replacements when we got home.

When we were so busy in the early 1950s with road shows, television and radio shows in several cities, and numerous record-ing dates, I decided we needed an airplane to make our jumps. So I went into partnership with a pilot, Art Greenamyer of Kentuckiana Aircraft, and we bought a twin-motored, ten-passenger Lockheed Lodestar, and on its sides we painted "Pee Wee King and His Boys." It was a real lifesaver, except for once when it almost cost us our lives. It was on December 11, 1951, and we had just finished doing some network shows and an engagement at the Riverside Rancho in Hollywood. We were flying from Burbank to Chicago, but we had agreed to stop by Salt Lake City as a favor to Bob York, who was RCA records distributor for the territory west of the Missis-sippi River. He was celebrating the opening of a new RCA distri-bution warehouse and asked us to stop by for a couple of hours. Art, who was our pilot on the trip, said, "Sure, that's no problem. We've got plenty of time." So we took off from Burbank and flew over toward Las Vegas, with the boys hollering, "Hey, let's go down and play a little dice and some blackjack and 21." I said, "I'll 21 all you guys. We don't have time. We've got to get on up to Salt Lake City, do our job there, and get to Chicago." We had to be in Chi-cago by the next afternoon to tape a television show called *The Old American Barn Dance*, where we were to be special guests.

We passed over Las Vegas and headed for Salt Lake City, but we never got there. We heard on the radio that there were heavy snow showers between Salt Lake City and Provo, and we knew that the further south we stayed the better off we were. The mountains around Provo are all thirteen to fifteen thousand feet high, and a small private plane with no oxygen just can't go up much above twelve thousand feet, or your eyes will bug out like a pinball machine. Suddenly Art said, "Pee Wee, we've got to go down. It'll be a forced landing and dangerous, but I've got to have the wings de-iced. So all you guys hold tight and hope and pray that everything goes all right." So down we went, all of us holding on for dear life, and touched down about fifty yards short of the runway, landing on a frozen lake. We hit the ice, skidded, and rolled onto the runway, where several dozen pheasants were flying around scared to death. I don't know what they were doing there—probably looking for food—but we were lucky they didn't get sucked into our motor, and they were lucky too.

We spent about two hours at the little Provo airport, with Art and Mr. Frank and two of the boys trying to figure out how to de-ice our wings and get us up again. The rest of us were inside the hangar and could hear the emergency calls coming in. The airport guys were saying, "Sorry, we can't be bothered right now because Pee Wee King's plane has been forced down here, and we're trying to get him going again." Finally, I asked one of the men, "What's going on?" He said, "Oh, haven't you heard the news? Fred Waring is in trouble. He's got two buses covered in an avalanche outside of town. He was on his way to Salt Lake City too. But he's already taken care of. The highway department has sent a road crew out there with snow shovels to dig them out." So there we were, two entertainment troupes trapped by snow in the mountains around Provo, Utah. Finally, one of the airport radiomen got through to Salt Lake City and said, "Pee Wee King and his plane force-landed here at Provo and are having their wings de-iced so they can take off again." The fellow on the other end said, "Well, it's too late now. AP and UPI have sent out news flashes all across the nation that Pee Wee King's plane is lost and presumed down in the mountains of Utah."

Art and Mr. Frank and I got together to make a game plan. The snow was still coming down, and the ice was still forming on the plane. Finally, Art said, "Well, we know it's clear in Vegas, so we'll just have to go back there." We took off, and Art managed somehow to dodge between those mountains and pilot his way safely through that sleet and snow and finally we arrived in Las Vegas. Art got emergency clearance from the runway and we landed. The first person to greet us was a fellow from the FCC, who demanded, "Who owns this plane?" Art said, "It's ours. I'm the pilot." The guy from the FCC said, "You're the man I want to talk to. You violated all the rules taking off from Provo and coming back down here." Art said, "I thought the man at Provo notified the FCC that we were coming here." We soon got our problems patched up with the FCC and tried to do some damage control in other places.

The first person I called was Lydia in Louisville. She said, "Oh Pee Wee, I'm so relieved. Where on earth are you?" I told her we were in Vegas getting ready to go on to Chicago. She said she would call the other band members' families immediately. The wives had been calling her after they heard on the radio that our plane was missing. Lydia had said, "Don't worry. I know they're safe and sound somewhere or I would have heard. At a time like this, no news is good news." Her hopeful words had not cheered anybody, including herself.

Bob York in Salt Lake City was also worried that we hadn't shown up and hadn't contacted him. I called him and told him we'd had to change our plans. He then called Charlie Adams, my partner back in Burbank. Charlie had said, "Oh yeah, I've heard about Pee Wee. My little friend is gone. He crashed in the mountains near Provo." Bob said, "Good news, Charlie. Pee Wee's all right. They found him and his band in Provo and he's now in Las Vegas. He plans to bypass Salt Lake City and fly directly to Chicago." We filed a new flight plan and took off for Kansas City, and then up to Chicago. As soon as we arrived, all the boys called their families to say they were safe and ready to do the television show the next day. After the show, we flew home to Louisville exhausted and happy and ready to relax until the next road trip—which we hoped would not be so stressful.

We were still traveling a lot by car and bus, but when we had to make big jumps around the country, the plane was the only way to go. We knew the risks of air travel, but it was necessary. We were appearing on national television shows like *The Perry Como Show* all over the country. We had just completed our thirteen-week run as summer replacement for Sid Caesar and Imogene Coca. One time we played the Orpheum Theater in Wichita, then had to go directly to New York to be on *The Kate Smith Show*. We had to use a plane to meet schedules like that. Air travel was a luxury we all enjoyed. Road trips by car can get awfully long and boring when you're on the go all the time. Whenever you're under stress, as we usually were, any kind of travel is dangerous. Risks of all kinds are part and parcel of show business.

One of the most exciting and rewarding tours I ever did was for Uncle Sam during World War II. I didn't know what role I could play, but I knew I wanted to support the war effort in some way. At first, I thought I would be doing my share as a soldier. In 1940 and 1941, when we were getting closer and closer to war, all my friends were getting drafted, and I assumed I would be too. I decided I would try to get into the navy and went for a physical examination. Soon after the physical I was playing a St. Patrick's Day dance at a post near Nashville, and I ran into a doctor I knew who was stationed there. He said, "Well, how did you make out with your service exam?" I said, "I don't know yet, but I asked for the navy so I could maybe be stationed on the Great Lakes and be close to my parents." He said, "You did what? You get in the navy and they'll send you out to the middle of the ocean somewhere, and your mother and dad won't know whether you're dead or alive." I said, "Well, what should I do?" He said, "Tomorrow morning you come back here and I'll put you through the army exam again, and I'll recommend that you organize a band and do USO shows." So four of us musicians went back the next day and took the physical. The three other guys were drafted quickly and spent the duration of the war in the Army. Before I could be drafted, Congress passed a law that excused married men over thirty with young children. But I did get to serve my country in a small way. I spent a lot of time on military bases entertaining the troops.

Country music has long been a favorite with soldiers, and stars like Roy Acuff, Ernest Tubb, and the Duke of Paducah toured posts and camps at home and overseas during and after the war. Finally, I got to do my part when I got involved in one of the biggest entertainment ventures of the war. In October of 1941 the Opry organized a troupe of about two dozen entertainers called the Camel Caravan to tour installations in this country and in Central America. We had held auditions on a flatbed truck in Shelby Park in Nashville and put the show together in late summer of 1941. Then we brought it up to Ft. Knox to try it out to see how it would go over with the servicemen and with the Camel Cigarette people. It was a complete dress rehearsal, with sound, lights, and all the acts we intended to use. We made a few adjustments and did a second tryout at Ft. Campbell. Both shows passed review with flying colors. We then felt we were ready to take our show on the road anywhere, and for nineteen months we played for military audiences in this country and even went down to Panama, Guatemala, Nicaragua, and Tobago Island. We had our own sound system and lighting equipment and a special crew to work them. We traveled in four new automobiles and a house trailer, which we used as a dressing room.

What a sight we were on the highways and streets—the four bright red automobiles, the house trailer, and the stage truck! On the side of each vehicle were the words, "Camel Caravan," with pictures of Camel cigarettes and Prince Albert smoking tobacco, whose slogan was "The National Joy Smoke." As we passed, people would wave and blow their horns at us. People came up to thank us in hotels and restaurants. We tried to do two complete shows a day, a matinee in a sports field outdoors, and an evening performance in a base theater or auditorium. We'd also split the cast into small groups and tour the base hospital wards. I think we did good work for the Opry, for military morale, and for our tobacco sponsors.

Our cast of twenty-one entertainers featured Minnie Pearl, Eddy Arnold, Grandpa Jones, Cowboy Copas, Redd Stewart—until he got drafted, as well as Pee Wee King and the rest of the Golden West Cowboys. Redd only got to tour with us for a few weeks before he was drafted. We had Kay Carlisle, a singer from Nashville who later became a big name, and a girls trio who sang like the Andrews Sisters—"Don't Sit Under the Apple Tree" and songs like that. We also had a specialty dancer named Dolly Dearman, a singer named Eva Nichols, whose stage name was San Antonio Rose, and four girls known as the Camelettes, who were dressed in skimpy costumes and did an opening number and later in the show passed out cigarettes and matches to the audience.

Our managers were Mr. Frank and Ford Rush from the Opry, who made all the arrangements. Mr. Rush opened the show, and I took over as emcee. Minnie was our cast director and girls' chaperon. She was the soldiers' favorite. After the band had played several numbers, she'd jump out and give her signature greeting, "Howdeeeeeeeeee," and the fellows would answer back, "Howdeeeeeeeeeeeeee." Then she'd say, "Gentlemen, I'm just so proud to be here. I didn't know I had so many 'fellers' here until I looked around and saw so many of you wearing my initials, M.P." Minnie was our head comedian, but sometimes the boys in the band would do comic routines—like the bass fiddler who'd hold onto my accordion while I played "Hold That Tiger." Minnie had been trained in dance and voice as well as dramatics and sometimes she'd do a novelty song like "How to Catch a Feller." When Minnie came to our band, Eddy said, "She's not a singer, is she? I hope she's not going to sing, is she?" Minnie overhead him and said, "Yeah, I sing too. What do you do?" That became a standing joke between them. Minnie would sometimes do a buck-and-wing dance, which is sort of like a square dance with clogs.

We toured the South first, then went up North. One of the biggest crowds I've ever seen in my life was at our show at Ft. Benning, Georgia. Another memorable stop was in San Antonio, where we were scheduled to do shows at Kelly and Randolph fields and Ft. Sam Houston. It was December 7, 1941. We were on stage doing our show when the announcer interrupted with the shocking news that Pearl Harbor had been attacked by the Japanese and that President Roosevelt had asked Congress for a declaration of war.

But the most impressive performance of my life was at the stadium on Lake Erie in Cleveland the following year. The stadium seated seventy-two thousand people and was jam-packed with service men and women and Camel employees and civilians from that area. At the end of our show, the announcer said that all the lights in the stadium would be turned out, then at his signal the person at the left end of each row would strike a match, followed by each person to his right in turn. In a matter of a couple of minutes, while Kay Carlisle sang "When the Lights Come on Again All Over the World" with our band, that stadium went from pitch dark to daylight bright with the light from those thousands of tiny matches. It was like seventy-two thousand little fires lighting up the darkness. When Kay finished her song and the lights came back on, I'll bet there wasn't a dry eye in the whole stadium. It was the highlight of the entire tour.

There was another Camel Caravan group that played pop music, but we soon discovered that our music, which included some pop songs, was liked by all the soldiers. In the training camps there were boys from all over the United States—Yankees from New England, Jewish boys from New York, Georgia corncrackers, Tennessee hillbillies, Louisiana Cajuns, Midwestern farm boys—all mixed in together, and on Saturday nights they would hear the Grand Ole Opry on the radio. Country songs like "You Are My Sunshine" and "I'm Walking the Floor Over You" were national hits. So when we would arrive at a camp, all the boys were eager to hear us. We could tell that country and western music was already developing a national audience. When San Antonio Rose sang "I'm walking the floor over you, / The reason is needless to say," the boys went wild. She was a nice girl from St. Joseph, Missouri, but had a tragic life after she left the Camel tour. She divorced her first husband and married again, but was killed when her second husband ran their car into a concrete mixer in St. Joseph.

Every week the Opry Camel Caravan got more popular. In March of 1942 we received orders from our New York booking agency that we were going to the Panama Canal Zone and Central America, where there were many American military and civilian personnel. Because it was wartime, travel anywhere outside the country was dangerous, but we were eager to do our part. We got all our immunization shots and left for New Orleans, where we stayed at the Roosevelt Hotel until we shipped out for Panama. On board the *Veragua* of the Great White Fleet, we were under curfew every night, which meant we could have no lights. We tried to do some rehearsing, and I remember thinking one time how appropriate that Kay was singing in the pitch dark "Blues in the Night." The captain told us to keep our life jackets handy in case of an enemy attack. Our bass player, Joe Zinkan, wore his all day and slept with it on at night. Nighttime was something else! Imagine being out on the sea on a ship about a block long with no lights except for an occasional flashlight.

It was chilly in New Orleans when we left, but when we arrived in Cristobal, Panama, on March 9, it was downright hot. We were a sight disembarking with our topcoats and winter clothes. We stayed in the Washington Hotel and were taken to our concert locations by jeep and small school buses. From Panama we were taken to Guatemala and stayed at the Grand Hotel. It was Easter Holy Week, and from our rooms we could see the daily parades and religious processions with huge statues of saints carried through the streets on the men's shoulders.

One of our most unusual experiences occurred after we navigated through mine-infested waters to an American outpost on Taboga Island. Most of the soldiers hadn't seen an American woman for over a year, and they went crazy when our girls got off the boat. The commandant said, "We want you to put on a good show for the fellows, then we'll go eat. I know you're hungry. We've got a tasty dinner prepared, a good dessert, and a little gin or whiskey to take with you." He was right. We did our show and got thunderous applause throughout. Finally, after the encores we were exhausted and as hungry as wolves and hurried over to the mess hall to the feast that had been promised. We all sat down. The food was brought to us, and man! it looked good. The meat was white and looked like boned pork chops. We dug in and ate, stopping only to comment on how good it was. We ate the meat and all the trimmings and everybody was full and happy. Then someone said, "What *was* that delicious meat we just ate?" Our host said, "Is everybody finished? Let's wait until we're all finished. Then we'll have dessert, and I'll give you the menu." Suddenly, before we'd finished our ice cream, the news went around like wildfire—"Iguana!" Holy cow, we had been eating iguana! Just like the lizards that had crawled in through our windows and that we had been chasing out of our rooms! I looked around me to see how the others were taking it, to see if anybody was getting sick. But we all managed to hold it down. In fact, once we got used to the idea, we admitted that iguana steak wasn't such a bad meal. We knew also that the boys stationed there would never go hungry even if the Germans blew up all the supply ships from the States. There were iguanas aplenty to last the duration of the war. We had seen them crawling everywhere. As we left to return home, we thanked our hosts for our unexpected treat. But

I've never had an iguana meal since—and I've never really wanted one!

When we got back to Nashville, we made a few personnel and schedule changes. But we maintained a good troupe until our contract ended during the Christmas season of 1942. During our last months, we traveled mostly by bus, with a stage truck following with our equipment. After our nineteen-month caravan was over, we finished with a giant public square dance in Nashville. We had traveled more than fifty thousand miles, covered more than nineteen states, and had done 175 shows in 68 camps, hospitals, air fields, and naval and marine bases. Someone said to me that we did for the stateside soldiers what Bob Hope and the USO did for them overseas. In addition to aiding the war effort, I think we did a lot to spread the good word about country music. We took Opry music to people who had never heard of the Opry before they were in the service and who thought that all country music was of the barefoot hillbilly variety. We showed them how good country music could be. We were becoming a bridge between country and popular music at a time when they were still distinct and separate. It was just one result of the gypsy lives we had to live. We took our kind of music to the people wherever they lived, in war and peace.

"The Tennessee Waltz" and Other Country Sounds

ALONG ABOUT 1950 HANK WILLIAMS and I were talking backstage at a show in Montgomery, Alabama, and he said, "Pee Wee, I believe one of us is gonna have a pop record before long." He was right. Soon Tony Bennett had made "Cold, Cold Heart" into a pop hit, and Patti Page had taken "The Tennessee Waltz" to the top of the pop charts. Then other pop singers—Kay Starr, Margaret Whiting, and others—were taking country songs to huge audiences. Of course, there had been some crossing over from one music field to another for a long time. One of the first country music stars was Vernon Dalhart, who had been trained as an opera singer. But before the 1950s there wasn't much crossover from one kind of music to another. You either liked pop music or country music or blues or jazz or something else. You were either a pop musician or a country musician or something else. The performers and their audiences tended to stay with their own music. But I've never paid any attention to dividing lines. I've always felt comfortable crossing from one side to another, as the occasion required.

Beginning in the 1950s many singers and songs and bands crossed over easily. Marty Robbins was popular with pop audiences as well as country music fans. He had a smooth, easy, gentle voice that everyone liked whether he was singing a high school prom song or a western ballad about the dust and sun. Johnny Cash, Glen Campbell, Tennessee Ernie Ford, and Roger Miller are just four more country singers who played both sides of the street. With singers like them, country composers no longer had to depend on pop singers to make their songs big hits. On the other hand, there is Ray Charles, who at thirty-one surprised a lot of his fans when he did an album of country music called "Modern Sounds in Country and Western Music," with songs like "Bye, Bye, Love," "Hey, Good Lookin'," and "Careless Love," an old folk song that he wrote his own lyrics for. Bing Crosby recorded country and western songs for years. He's like other talented performers: he could do different kinds of music in his own unique style, from rhythm and blues and jazz to pop and country. The time was, therefore, right when I started writing successful songs that could appeal to both country and pop audiences.

Like most musicians, I wanted to be a composer. I wanted to write my own songs. I knew that it was important to write my own songs, then publish them as sheet music, play them on the radio, get them recorded, and bring out a songbook to sell to fans. It was a good way to get recognition and to make money. There's hardly any country musician you can name who hasn't written—or tried to write—songs. Here in my basement study, I have dozens of pieces of sheet music and songbooks written by my friends in country music—Mel Tillis, Merle Travis, Jimmy Wakely, Marty Robbins, Gene Autry, Bill Monroe, Dolly Parton, Loretta Lynn, Tammy Wynette, Willie Nelson, Bob Wills, even Eddy Arnold. The list goes on and on. For years I had tried to write successful songs, but it wasn't until I moved back to Louisville from Knoxville in early 1937 that it all started coming together. For the next twenty years I was to have a part in the composition of some of the most popular songs in American music.

It started partly because of a natural disaster, the Ohio River flood of January and February 1937. The newly formed Golden West Cowboys had planned a big debut early that year after we returned from a year in Knoxville, but the flood kept us from doing anything but sitting in our rooms and apartments in downtown Louisville and watching the water rise higher and higher. With all that time on our hands, some of us boys would get together and go through country and western songbooks to see if we couldn't figure out what made songs popular. After all that unscientific research, I am convinced that every country and western songwriter has composed at least one song about his mother—or someone's mother—usually about a no-good son who runs off from home, gets into trouble, and longs to see his saintly mother before she dies—or before he dies, usually by hanging.

Most of my early songs were very forgettable. My first modest success was called "Darling, How Can You Forget So Soon?" which was recorded by Gene Autry. Another of my early songs that Gene recorded was "The End of My Roundup Days." Mr. Joe Frank and I wrote some fairly good ones, especially religious songs like "Singing as I Go," "Lilies of the Field," and "Temple on the Hill," which Eddy Arnold recorded. The war inspired a lot of our songs, including "My Cowboys Are Riding Now for Uncle Sam," a song that Mr. Frank began with the title; then the two of us wrote the words and music. It became a common routine with us. We'd be driving down the highway, and he'd think up a title, write it down, and hand it to me, and say, "Now you think up some words and a tune for that song." One day he handed me the title, "Darling, How Can You Forget So Soon?" which we later wrote into a song that was recorded by—in addition to Gene Autry—Grandpa Jones and Eddy Arnold. Bill Monroe recorded one of our songs, "Dog House Blues." We also wrote a lot of western songs, including "Covered Wagon Lullaby" and "Last Go 'Round," a song about how bad company will take you to an early grave. Our other coauthored songs include "I'll Forgive You But I Can't Forget," which Roy Acuff recorded; "Don't Forget"; "Don't Blame It All on Me"; and "You'll See the Day," which became the theme song for Johnny Mack Brown's movie, *Flame of the West*. A lot of our songs had titles like "I Just Don't Care Anymore" and "The Heart That Is Breaking for You," songs about separation and broken relationships—experiences that I didn't really know much about firsthand.

Of the more than four hundred songs that I've written or coauthored, the most successful ones were written with Redd Stewart and Chilton Price. Redd and I wrote "The Tennessee Tango" and Mr. Frank and I wrote "My Heart's Below the Mason-Dixon Line" and "My Roamin' Days Are Over, Little Girl," both recorded by

Cowboy Copas. We wrote many others as well, but the big one, the really Big One that Redd and I wrote was "The Tennessee Waltz." It's now the official state song of Tennessee and has been recorded more than five hundred times, including the version that went to the top of the charts, the one made by Patti Page in 1951. Governor Browning of Tennessee did a recording of the song with our band backing him. "I'll sing it and take it to the legislature and try to get them to approve it as our state song," he said. But nothing happened until several years later, in 1965, when Governor Frank Clements got it adopted. Redd and I were playing a date in Columbia, South Carolina, when we got a call from Wesley Rose, our publisher. He said, "You fellows better hurry on home." I said, "Oh my God, what's happened now?" He said, "Nothing bad, but something good is about to happen to you and Redd. Just be here in Nashville tomorrow morning. The governor has proposed 'The Tennessee Waltz' as the state song, and the legislature will vote on it. Everyone is sure it will pass."

Redd and I rushed out to the Columbia airport the next morning, and I asked a fellow if there was any way we could get a plane out of Columbia that morning for Nashville. He said, "There's a guy here who's servicing a private plane right now, and he's headed that way." So we hitched a ride and arrived at Nashville, where a taxi from the Acuff-Rose Publishing Company was waiting to take us to the Capitol. It was February 17, 1965, and we were there when the Tennessee legislature made our song the official song of the state. It was a beautiful moment for Redd and me. It was especially meaningful to Redd since he's a Tennessee native. We never dreamed what we were doing when we were writing the song that night in 1946 in the truck coming back to Nashville from Texarkana, Texas. Even now I can hardly believe that we wrote such a song. When I hear Patti Page's recording or the song played by a hundred-piece band, I get goose pimples all over. It was a great thrill when Governor Clements got to do the keynote speech at the Democratic National Convention in 1956, and the band played "The Tennessee Waltz" as he walked to the podium. Another thrill is to hear the big marching band of the University of Tennessee play "The Tennessee Waltz March" at football halftime on network television. One time Redd and I were in Boston in a big office building waiting for an elevator. When the door opened, the Muzak sound system began playing "The Tennessee Waltz." Redd turned to me and said, "Pee Wee, now this is really going too far."

I'll try to recall as accurately as I can how "The Tennessee Waltz" came to be created. It was close to Christmas in 1946, and the Golden West Cowboys had just played a date in a large high school in Texarkana, Texas, just across the Arkansas border. We were driving a stretch airline limousine that could carry nine passengers and a panel truck for the luggage. Redd and Chuck Wiggins were in the truck, and I was in the limo with the rest of the boys. Redd smoked big old black Cuban cigars that smelled up the car. He knew if he rode in the limo there would be a mass revolt, so he rode in the truck with Chuck. They were good friends, and Chuck was studying Masonry. Redd, who was already a high degree Mason, was giving him a lecture. But I knew that not even Chuck could put up with Redd's heavy cigar smoke very long, so I flashed my limo lights a couple of times and we pulled off at the next service station. I offered to trade places with Chuck, and he gladly accepted. I got in the truck and we took off, with Redd driving.

I turned on the dome light and started working out our itinerary—where we would be playing, where we would stay, what songs we'd use, the costumes we'd wear, where we'd eat—all the details connected with the shows for our next road trip. Since it was a Friday evening, we were headed back to Nashville to be on the Opry the next night, as usual. We were getting close to Memphis and had the radio playing and tuned to WSM's 50,000 watts, when we heard the disk jockey say, "I want you folks to hear Bill Monroe's new song dedicated to his home state of Kentucky. It's called 'The Kentucky Waltz.'" While the record was playing, Redd said, "Pee Wee, I've got an idea for a song. Trade places with me and drive, and I'll get that kitchen matchbox that I light my cigars from out of the glove compartment, and we'll write a song about Tennessee. After all, I was born in Ashland City, Tennessee, and we both live here now. We can write a Tennessee waltz." So we stopped and swapped places. I had used up all the blank paper I had for our itinerary, so Redd got the matchbox, turned the top over, borrowed my pen, and started writing.

He said, "I've got an idea. Let's use our theme song you wrote,

'No Name Waltz,' and I'll hum it as I put down lyrics that will match the melody. I think it'll work out that way." "No Name Waltz" was a signature tune that Opry listeners could identify us with, but it didn't have any words. So we began to think up words for the melody, and Redd began to write: "I was waltzing with my darling to the Tennessee Waltz." Then he paused and wrote, "When an old friend I happened to see." Redd kept on: "O, the Tennessee Waltz; O, the Tennessee Waltz." He continued to write until the song was finished. Then he stopped and said, "I think that's it. That's the way it should go."

Redd sat there writing the words on the matchbox as we both hummed the melody we knew so well. We'd hum along, and Redd would write a word down. Every once in a while he'd say, "How does this sound?" and he'd sing the words to the melody. Finally, we had the words pretty much the way everybody knows them today. There wasn't much changing left to do, with either the words or the melody, just a little fine-tuning here and there. We finished it up that night in the truck. It was a song with simple words, with a simple sentiment, set to a simple melody. Little did we know that we were making music history out there in the cold dark somewhere between Memphis and Nashville.

We drove on a few miles after we finished with the song, and the more we thought abut it, the more excited we became. The other boys were ahead of us now, and we tried to flash our lights to get them to stop, but they kept on going. None of them saw us, or if they did, they didn't pay us any attention and went on. I said, "To hell with them. Let's stop and get some coffee and donuts; then we'll go on home." When we got home, late as it was, Redd got out his guitar and began putting down the words and the notes so we could show our new song to Fred Rose, our publisher, the next day. When we took it over to his office, he liked it immediately but suggested a major change. He changed the bridge from "O, the Tennessee Waltz; O, the Tennessee Waltz" to "I remember the night and the Tennessee Waltz." Then it was ready to be accepted or rejected by the public.

We were about ready to do a recording session with RCA Victor and wanted to use our new song on one of the records, but Steve Sholes, our A & R man, didn't like it. He said, "Do Bill Monroe's

'Kentucky Waltz.' It's going to be a big hit and you can jump right on the bandwagon because you're already known for your waltzes." I said, "Steve, I don't want to be known as 'the Waltz King.' We've already got Wayne King. We've written our own waltz, and we want to do it." He said, "No, we can't do your song at this session." I said, "All right. But just wait a while. You'll be sorry." Now, here was the main guy who helps all the artists decide what to record, from Perry Como to Pee Wee King, and he wouldn't let us record "The Tennessee Waltz" because we already had four songs chosen for the session. I don't even remember now what those four songs were.

We were always having arguments about songs he'd picked up in New York and promised publishers he'd get me to record. We'd run over the songs and sometimes make demos until we were sick of them. Demos were demonstrations or trial records that we made to test to see if they would be good for commercial release. Sometimes during a recording session we would go through eight or nine tunes to see if there was anything that would suit us. If we found something we liked and made a demo, we had to wait maybe fifteen weeks before we could decide whether to record it for the market.

The Golden West Cowboys finally recorded "The Tennessee Waltz" with the vocal by Redd Stewart at a 1948 Victor session in Chicago on the same record with a novelty song called "Helegged Hilegged." Our record sold over half a million copies right off the bat and was number six in the folk category on the charts. It was also a hit for Cowboy Copas, who was still with the Golden West Cowboys. He liked the song so much he went to his recording company, King Records in Cincinnati, and got permission from Syd Nathan, the owner, to record it. Nathan decided to get the jump on our recordings and released his first, even though it violated our verbal agreement. Back then, a lot of agreements were based on a handshake, so we didn't have any legal documents to back us up.

We also had some trouble over the song with my good friend Ernest Tubb. He recorded "The Tennessee Waltz" with the Short Brothers and released it. He also had his publishing company issue a pirated sheet music version. Ernest didn't get our permission to do any of that, either to record it or publish it. He just took the song as his own. We were flabbergasted! Not only had he not gotten our permission, he had not even given us credit. Hill and Range in New York published it with the Short Brothers name on it as composers. Finally, as a last resort, we had to bring suit to protect our property. Fortunately, Acuff-Rose had already published and copyrighted the song in our names, and we knew their lawyers would fight to protect our rights. A lawsuit was filed in Nashville and also one in New York because Mercury Records, which had issued Patti Page's recording, decided to hold all royalties until it was decided legally who the rightful owners were, whether it was Redd and me or Ernest Tubb and the Short Brothers. It was all a big stink, and I didn't like it at all. But it had to be done. It was the lawyers and the publishers fighting it out, and we remained friends with Ernest throughout the lawsuit. I never did find out all the details, but the lawyers cleaned it up in six or seven months. What it amounted to was a stalemate. The lawyers on both sides suggested we all pull back, and we agreed. The case could have dragged on for years, and only the lawyers would have won. We didn't get any damages, but we put an end to their pirated record and sheet music. Most important, we didn't make enemies out of our friends. I didn't hold a grudge against Ernest, even though his company recorded and published the song illegally. Ernest and the Short Brothers made a mistake, but I don't think it was an honest one. I believe they knew that they were doing something morally wrong and illegal. They were putting us to the test to see if they could get away with it. I've never heard the Short Brothers recording. I don't know how it sounded, and I don't want to know.

Copas's recording and our recording of "The Tennessee Waltz" were good sellers, but then its popularity died down. It wasn't until about Christmas of 1951, when Patti Page recorded it as a pop song, that it became a smash hit. Country songs were just beginning to cross over into the pop field. Tony Bennett helped to pave the way for crossovers when he made pop versions of Hank Williams's songs a little earlier. Eddy Arnold's songs were also being bought by pop fans.

Patti's recording was by accident, but it was a lucky accident for me. Jack Rael, who was her manager, selected "The Tennessee Waltz" for her to record with a song that Mercury thought would be the Christmas hit of the year, something called "Boogie Woogie

Santa Claus." One day Rael bumped into Jerry Wexler, a record reviewer for *Billboard*, on a New York street. Wexler said, "Jack, I want you to hear a new song I have here. It's called 'The Tennessee Waltz' and it's been recorded by Erskine Hawkins." Erskine was a black bandleader who had recently played a month's engagement at the Coney Island Ballroom in Cincinnati, where he had heard Cowboy Copas's recording of the song. He liked it and decided to do his own version. That's the recording that Wexler played for Rael at his office at *Billboard*. Rael said, "I like it. Don't let anybody else hear it. I've got an idea." Rael was not only Patti's manager but also a musician, and he thought he smelled a winner. He immediately called Patti to New York, and they began working on an arrangement. When they were ready, he recorded her with his own orchestra in three voices, then in two, and finally in one. Patti listened to all three versions and said, "I like the two voices. Let's go with it." So that's the version that ended up on the B side of Patti Page's new recording for Christmas 1951. Patti later replaced her loud and lively "Boogie Woogie Santa Claus" with a peppy rendition of "Long Long Ago" on the A side. I wonder what ever happened to "Boogie Woogie Santa Claus."

I heard Patti's recording before it was released, and I flipped. I instantly knew it was going to be big. I liked everything about it, especially the way her molasses alto voices blended. Sure enough, the recording came out like a shell out of a shotgun. Talk about sales! As soon as the record went on the market, it was a hit; and the first three million went like hotcakes before the Christmas season was over. It sold all through the following year and by late 1952 *Billboard* listed "The Tennessee Waltz" as the nation's number one hit. The same issue shows it to be the most popular record played by disk jockeys, with Patti's recording at the top. In eighth place and twenty-third place were recordings of our song by Jo Stafford and by the Fontaine Sisters. It was also the best-selling sheet music and the most popular song played on jukeboxes.

I had not met Patti before she recorded the song. About three months after its release, I was in Chicago at the Mercury Records office and Jack Rael said, "Pee Wee, you wanna meet Patti? Come on." I said, "You know I do." She is a sweet, pretty lady with a warm, outgoing personality. She was at the office to discuss the promotional campaign for the record, the television and radio shows, and interviews she would do. Later, she and Redd and I sang the song at a stage show in Austin, Texas, and on a special show at the Opry. Man was it fun! Redd and I still thank the Lord for the day that Patti Page got together with our song.

"The Tennessee Waltz" was my first real invasion of the pop field, especially after it was recorded not only by Patti Page but by dozens of others, including Guy Lombardo, Sammy Kaye, Les Paul and Mary Ford, Jo Stafford, Anita O'Day—even Spike Jones, who gives it his usual souped-up treatment with bells, shots, and whistles, but this time in a Yiddish-flavored parody. It even became a big hit in Japan in a Japanese-language version.

What I do know is that our song is now a part of American music history, and its influence has been widespread. At the beginning, "The Tennessee Waltz" was labeled a hillbilly song, but after Patti Page recorded it and it went to the top of the pop chart, it helped open the door for the general acceptance of country music. At the Country Music Hall of Fame in Nashville, visitors can quiz themselves on the history of country music. One of the questions is, "What is the most popular country music song of all time?" The answer, in case you haven't guessed, is "The Tennessee Waltz." And it keeps on selling. There is even a ride at Opryland called the Tennessee Waltz. It is a revolving swinging ride, with forty-eight swings suspended in a carousel made in Austria. Some friends told me that Baryshnikov closed a ballet performance in Las Vegas a few weeks ago by dancing to "The Tennessee Waltz." I ask you: how much higher on the hog can you get?

Last week, I went down to the Jefferson County clerk's office to get a new sticker for my license plate renewal. The clerk recognized me and started singing, "I was waltzing with my darling to 'The Tennessee Waltz.'" I smiled, got my renewal sticker, then took one of the forms called "Comments on Customer Service," and wrote: "I suggest that everybody come to the county clerk's office just to hear Terry Shaw sing 'The Tennessee Waltz.' She's almost as good as Patti Page." I handed the form to her. She read it and broke into laughter. And to think that all this came from a few minutes Redd and I spent together on the way home to Nashville from Texarkana and the few words he wrote down on a nickel matchbox. Our song is now a part of American culture.

"Bonaparte's Retreat" was another song Redd and I put together that became a national hit, but not quite as popular as "The Tennessee Waltz." We were rehearsing some square dance numbers with a boy from Texas, and he showed us a recording of a Texas square dance tune called "Bonaparte's Retreat," which had a sort of Cajun beat. It was a folk tune in the public domain, so Redd and I took part of the melody, put a bridge or middle to it, wrote some words, and reshaped the whole song, building on its folk base. Our recording with the Golden West Cowboys had good sales, but it didn't become a smash until Kay Starr did her recording. She heard the song by accident as she and her husband were driving across country and stopped at a restaurant and heard our version on the jukebox. She asked the restaurant owner to sell the record to her, but he refused until she told him who she was. Then he gave it to her when she promised to send him an autographed copy of her version. She had already made up her mind to record it.

It was also in the early 1950s, about 1951, that Redd and I teamed up with Chilton Price, who was a songwriting librarian at WAVE radio, where we were working. One day she came by the studio and handed me a brown envelope containing about half a dozen of her songs. She said, "I wish you'd take these with you and see what you think of them." I said I'd be glad to and put the envelope in my accordion case and took them home. They stayed there for a couple of weeks because I was using another accordion and didn't open up the case with her songs. When I finally opened it, I saw the songs and took them over to the piano, and started picking out some of the melodies. Lydia, who was looking over my shoulder, said, "Here Pee Wee, try this one called 'Slow Poke.' I think it might be a good one for the band. As I punched out the tune, Lydia sang the song. We knew instantly that it could be a winner, so Redd and I took what Chilton had written, did some reshaping of the words and the melody, and it finally became a national hit and sold more than two million records. It was our first and only gold recording.

In 1952 we collaborated with Chilton on "You Belong to Me," which was recorded by a number of top singers, including Joni James, Jo Stafford, and Patti Page. It was used as the background theme in the 1954 Tony Curtis-Joanne Dru film, *Forbidden*. Chilton wrote complete songs, and they were beautiful, but since she doesn't sing, she didn't know how they would sound. She called "You Belong to Me" by another name, "Hurry Home to Me," and it was about soldiers and pilots in the war. Redd and I took her songs and played them, singing and humming, changing words and notes here and there until we'd get a version easier to sing. At the time it was hard to get war songs recorded, so we gave "Hurry Home to Me" a new name and changed it into a kind of universal song about separated lovers. We took the best of her songs and made records and published them. She also sent songs to publishers and promoters in New York, and some of them were recorded by Perry Como and Bing Crosby, but I don't think she has gotten any big hits out of those songs.

Chilton is still writing good songs. I was recently over to her house here in Louisville and over a cup of coffee she showed me a little tune she called "Holly the Jolly Hippopotamus." It's a cute song, and I hope I can get someone to record and promote it for her. Who knows? It could become another surprise hit like Gene Autry's "Frosty the Snowman."

I can never predict which songs will be hits and which will be misses. A popular singer doesn't guarantee a hit, but it helps. I suppose it's a combination of things—the song, the singer, the arrangement, the timing; but even with all that going for it, a song can still fall flat. You simply have to write the best song you can and dress it up with a good arrangement, a good band, a good singer, and then run it up the flagpole and see if anybody salutes. It's a wonderful experience when it happens.

A good song is composed of the right words and the right music. But if you forced me to tell you which I think is more important, I'd say, without hesitation, that it's the music, the melody, the tune. It's the nonverbal part, the part that crosses national and language boundaries and retains its essence. It's the part you can hum and whistle. The words can change, but the tune is the song. That master songwriter and singer Leadbelly used to say, "You gotta get the tune first, then the words; then I play the song on my guitar." Now, you know you have to listen to a man who wrote "Goodnight

Irene," which we recorded, by the way, and "Rock Island Line" and "Kisses Sweeter Than Wine."

Words are important to my songs—of course, they are—but they are always secondary. A song is written with a melody and words. It is performed. Then the words die out, but the melody lingers on. You can write new words, new stanzas. You can rewrite the words to update them or to make the song into a satire or a parody. You can change the words to make them more politically correct. Look at how we've changed the words to "My Old Kentucky Home." We used to sing Stephen Foster's song the way he wrote it:

> *The sun shines bright on my old Kentucky home.*
> *'Tis summer; the darkies are gay.*

But now we sing:

> *The sun shines bright on my old Kentucky home.*
> *'Tis summer, the young folks are gay.*

Yet every year when the band plays Kentucky's state song at the Derby and the people sing the new words, everyone recognizes the same old song because no one has changed the melody. Indeed, you cannot change the melody because that's the vital part. That's the part that makes the song. Try saying the words to any song. Even if they're good as poetry, you don't have a song until the melody is added. You may forget the words to a song, but you can remember the melody. You can listen to the instrumental version of a song and dance to it. You can't dance to the words alone.

I'll leave it to the critics and music historians to analyze my music and decide whatever innovations and contributions I've made to American music. I do, however, have some personal observations about the kind of music I've tried to make. I'll share those with you. Remember that I never called myself, strictly speaking, a country musician. After I met Joe Frank and Gene Autry and began to develop an interest in folk and western music, people began putting me with country performers. Now that I'm in the Country Music Hall of Fame, for better or worse, I'm a "country" musician. I gladly accept the label because to me it now means that I'm an "American" musician.

I certainly came to country music not very well equipped to fit in with the likes of Eddy Arnold or Roy Acuff or Hank Williams. Our backgrounds were so radically different, and what's more, I didn't even play a "country" instrument. I started out with the violin—not "fiddle"—which I dropped for the accordion, which I felt I was more versatile for my purposes. When I took my accordion to the Opry, most of the string bands didn't understand what I was doing there with my squeeze box.

I'm not sure that anyone now can draw a line between country and western. I'm sure I can't. You could say that Gene Autry was western because that's the way he dressed and because he sang songs about the sky and the land and the animals and lonesome cowboys. You could say that Jimmie Rodgers was country because he dressed in a straw hat and jeans, and he sang about the everyday lives of poor farmers and ordinary working people. Western songs were also smoother and softer, I think, than the twangy sounds of the hillbillies. Over the years, however, there's been a lot of crossover between the two kinds of music.

Coming from the polka and waltz land of Wisconsin, I started out with a blended music; and it became a habit with me to mix in other sounds as I heard them—big band, western, swing, country, pop, blues, jazz, rock 'n' roll—whatever I liked and felt comfortable with. I found it necessary to change not only with the times but with the territory, as I moved around the country. I did polka music when I was in the Midwest and Cajun music when I was in Louisiana. Out in California, I did western swing. I tried to play music the people wanted and could dance to. In other words, I've learned from all kinds of music, but I never tried to copy any of them. If you want a band that sounds exactly like Kay Kyser, you get Kay Kyser. I tried to develop my own sound, a kind of smooth western swing, spiced with a lot of other sounds mixed in—like a Kentucky hash called burgoo.

The many experiments I tried with my band I believe helped open up country music, though it shocked traditionalists like the Solemn Old Judge at the Opry. I think drums and horns and electric guitars and accordions all added to the richness of the country music we have today, as did the sounds of boogie-woogie and rock 'n' roll. When I came south I didn't know much about country music and its traditions, and that's probably why I didn't hesitate to use new instruments and sounds. You could say that I just didn't know any better.

Some people have given me credit for influencing Elvis Presley and Bill Haley. Maybe. That's not for me to say. I do know that Elvis built upon the work of western swing bands that had elements of country, jazz, blues, and pop music in their style and used amplified instruments as we did. One mixture would become country boogie, which Elvis worked up into rockabilly. Elvis took the sounds of bands like mine and brought them together with his own style of singing and performing. The fact that he was a singer made a big difference. My music was mostly band with vocals. It was not focused on the singer. I was always a promoter of change, but in the mid-1940s I became a bit alarmed that rock 'n' roll could damage or destroy country and western music. I didn't want to throw the baby out with the bath water. Fortunately, country music survived rock 'n' roll and a lot of other influences that seemed for a time about to engulf it.

I've never been concerned about what labels people have given the music I have written and played, just so long as they liked it. When Louis Armstrong was playing a concert in Louisville in 1960, someone asked him if he called his music Dixieland. Louis said, "We just play good music. Call it whatever you want." I feel the same way.

The Country
of the Air

YOUNG ENTERTAINERS TODAY have some advantages we old-timers didn't have. They have television. But we did have radio. And we had 50,000-watt stations scattered all over the country. That's what Mr. Frank was always looking for—a centrally located 50,000-watt-clear-channel radio station—because he knew that was the best way to make his entertainers into stars. A well-located station could reach a potential audience of millions, especially at night. WLW in Cincinnati, KDKA in Pittsburgh, KMOX in St. Louis, WJR in Detroit, WGY in Schenectady, KMBC in Kansas City, KRLD in Dallas, WMC in Memphis, KFWB in Hollywood, XERF in Del Rio, Texas, WLS in Chicago, WSM in Nashville, and WHAS in Louisville—that's an impressive lineup of some of the powerful stations that featured country music shows when I was a young man just starting out in the business. WHAS was the reason Mr. Frank settled in Louisville and the reason I came here from Wisconsin.

Radio stations didn't pay very much, but they were nonetheless our lifeline because they made us known to a huge audience that would pay to see us in person. We took our radio shows seriously because that's where we made our image and our reputation. Take any country music star who started out in the 1920s through the 1940s, and you can follow his career from station to station. Hank Williams is a good example. He started out in 1942 on WSFA in Montgomery, Alabama, then in 1948 moved to KWKH in Shreveport,

Louisiana, to join the new "Louisiana Hayride," and finally he made it to WSM and the Grand Ole Opry in Nashville. It was a steady progression. Without radio exposure a country musician couldn't get anywhere at all. Little Jimmie Dickens got his big break on WKNX in Saginaw, Michigan. Roy Acuff got started on WROL in Knox-ville. And on and on.

I was in radio almost all of my career, from my King's Jesters days in Milwaukee until the mid-1950s when I had the "Pee Wee King Show" on the NBC Radio Network from seven to eight on Saturday nights. Radio taught us our skills as professional musicians and showmen. First, it taught me how to put together a coherent show following a logical pattern. Here is a typical show of the 1930s or 1940s: We opened with a fast fiddle tune, a square dance num-ber like "Old Joe Clark" or "Fire on the Mountain" or a shout song, which is one that all musicians sing together in gang style, like "Wait for the wagon; wait for the wagon; and we'll all go home." That would be followed immediately by a ballad by our principal male singer, usually Redd Stewart, which was followed by a yodeled song by someone like Texas Daisy, which was followed by a comedy song by three fellows in our band that we called the Bardstown Bucklebusters. Then I'd do a solo on my accordion. Finally, we'd end with an in-spirational song, such as "Beyond the Sunset" or one we called "Singin' as I Go." We'd mix in some jokes and comic sketches to break up the music. Of course, we'd have an announcer who would intro-duce us and read the commercials for a flour company, a feed com-pany, a soft drink company, a patent medicine, or a local furniture or used car dealer. It was a pattern that we changed very little after we went to television.

Many of the lessons I got from radio I learned from Mr. Frank, who taught me all the fundamentals. First, he said, you have to cre-ate an image in the listener's mind for everyone on the show. He'd say, "Pee Wee, you're the emcee, so this is the way you introduce a band member: 'Here's that cute little cowgirl Texas Daisy, who has her hair all done up in beautiful brown curls, and is wearing her sparkling white cowgirl outfit and boots today. She sings and yo-dels and does a little dance all at the same time.'" When Mr. Frank decided to nickname me Pee Wee, he'd say, "Here's little Pee Wee King. He's so short we have to get a Coca-Cola crate for him to stand on to reach the microphone. He's so little he has a hard time holding up his big, heavy accordion." People would then imagine what I looked like, even though it wasn't completely accurate. People always sympathize with the little guy. Of course, we'd designate someone to be the big guy, and Mr. Frank would say, "Coming up to the microphone now is Cowboy Jack, a tall, lanky fellow who looks like he just got out of the saddle. He's going to sing one of the songs he used to sing to his cows out on the lonely prairie." The imagination is powerful, and people could sit by their radios and picture vividly the performers as they heard us play and sing.

Another lesson I learned very soon from Mr. Frank is that you can have only one principal or headliner or star at the time, and he's the fellow or gal at the microphone. As long as he or she is there, you must not detract from him in any way. Whether you're on radio or on stage with a live audience, you don't cut up, crack jokes, make comments, ask questions, or do anything to attract attention away from the person at center stage. While he's at the microphone, he's the leader and it's his show. You may be bored silly, but you must appear to be listening and enjoying what he's doing. When you're on stage, you spend a lot of your time listening to others perform. That gets tiresome, but it would never, ever do to let it show. The performer is trying to make a good impression on his audience, and you must help, because your time is coming. You certainly don't want anyone yawning or fooling around when you're in the spotlight. When I first went on the Grand Ole Opry in 1937, Uncle Dave Macon was the star, and I knew never to try to upstage him or divert attention from him.

I don't have any recordings of our early radio shows from the 1930s. The only recordings we ever made were acetate discs that we might send to New York for an A & R man to listen to. Later, we made large sixteen-inch discs that could be broadcast at a later time. Some of the ones we made at WAVE radio in Louisville are still floating around. They had our usual mix of country, cowboy, and gospel songs, cornfield humor, and sometimes a slight story line.

I've done live broadcasts not only from radio studios but from any place we could set up our remote equipment. I've broadcast shows from Fontaine Ferry, a Louisville amusement park, and I've played gigs at Gypsy Village and the Madrid Ballroom. I once tried to do a series from the dogtrack across the river in Jeffersonville. We called it Greyhound Rancho after the ones out West where Spade Cooley and Tex Williams played. Bob Kay was our announcer: "From the beautiful banks of the Ohio, we bring you Pee Wee King and the Golden West Cowboys from the spectacular Greyhound Rancho." It was a good setup. Sometimes we had very good audiences, but we were always at the mercy of the weather. It lasted one year. On Derby Eve it poured three inches of rain on the track, and we sold thirty-five tickets. I turned around to the band and said, "Boys, we've had it. This is our last show from the spectacular Greyhound Rancho." To the owner I said, "I think we made a mistake." He said, "When you came to me with the idea, I didn't think it would work. But I'll say one thing: You've got guts."

A remote series I did from a Louisville used car lot was more successful. It was around 1957, when I was reshaping my band be-tween television series, and my good friend Bob Ryan of Bob Ryan Auto Sales said to me, "Pee Wee, why don't you get together three or four of your boys and let's do a Saturday morning show over WKLO from my lot." I said, "Okay. It's worth a try." We decided to do the show from his lot in good weather. In bad weather we'd do it from the radio studios. The show became very popular, and a lot of people came to the used car lot to hear us, and some of them even wound up buying a car. I sometimes think, however, that I have a bad habit of not leaving well enough alone. One day I said, "Bob, why don't we have a talent search, and whoever wins it gets a recording con-tract. We'll run it for a month or so and then pick a winner." He agreed, so we announced the contest and invited performers to come do their numbers in person or send in a demonstration record or tape. Man, were we flooded! I never knew there were so many would-be country music stars.

Every Saturday afternoon Bob and I would listen to the talent that came in that week. Most of it was just bad enough to be bad, but some of it was so bad it was funny. One woman sent in a tape that sounded something like this: "Mr. King, I don't sing too good, but I sure would like to have a record contract." We could hear a dog barking in the background and her saying, "Shut up, Spot." Then she said, "Mr. King, that was our dog Spot barking. I play the gui-tar a little, but the chords don't come too easy for me." Suddenly, we heard another noise on the tape and she said, "Oh, that's my baby Melvin crying." Well, it went on like that for several minutes. Then after a few false starts, she did her number, playing and singing it mostly off-key. By then, Bob and I were in hysterics. I said, "Bob, this is what I call dedication to show business. Here we are two grown men, reasonably intelligent, spending whole afternoons listening to these awful tapes. We don't *have* to do this, do we?" He said, "No we don't, Pee Wee. But it's giving me the most laughs I've had in a long time."

We finally chose a boy from somewhere around Mt. Washington, Kentucky. After we signed him to a contract, we found out that he was actually a semiprofessional and had done a recording for some outlaw label in Nashville. We were planning, in fact, to take him to Nashville to do his recording, but he said, "I can't go down there. I'm already signed up with a company in Nashville." We wound up publishing several of his songs, and they sold pretty well. But I think he and his talent faded, and I never heard from him again. Maybe he got a good, steady job at the Ford plant.

When we moved back to Louisville in 1947 from Nashville to try out that newfangled contraption called television, Mr. C.A. Craig, who was general manager of the Opry, said, "Well, kid, you go on up to Louisville and try that television, but I believe it's a passing fancy. It's a gadget that will never last." Then he added something that surprised and pleased me: "Son," he said, "if you don't make it, you just come on back to the Opry. We all love you, and we'll have a place for you." Believe me, that sounded good because normally if a performer left the Opry, he was never invited back as a regular. Mr. Craig and the other Opry officials had said they'd never allow the Opry to be televised. Nashville itself was slow in hooking into the new television medium, so there was no station where I could have done a show. I knew that the new medium was an experiment for us, and we might fall flat on our faces—the way a lot of silent movie stars did when they tried to make talkies. At the same time, I knew we had a lot of things going for us. We were entertaining. We were visual. We were danceable. We were good songwriters. A few of us had good business sense—well, Mr. Frank did. And we were willing to take a chance. We were young enough to risk failure on television. But it meant that we had to get out of Nashville.

The actual decision to return to Louisville was made because of an accident. Mr. and Mrs. Frank were driving through Shelbyville, which is about thirty miles east of Louisville, when they had a car wreck and both were hospitalized in Louisville. While Mr. Frank was recovering, Jimmy Cox, the sales manager for WAVE radio, came to see him and asked if I might be interested in returning to Louisville to work. Mr. Frank said, "Yes, I think he might be. He's getting restless in Nashville and could be available, especially if he can try out some television." Mr. Cox said, "We can offer him a radio and television package. We'll start out with the radio shows immediately and begin planning for television." That sounded just right for us, and on October 1, 1947, I quit the Opry and returned to Louisville with a one-year contract. I stayed for twenty-two years.

My radio shows were sponsored by Bensinger's Furniture Store, and we broadcast from their front show windows. The following year, in November of 1948, I was on the first TV broadcast in Kentucky. The cameras came on and I said, "You are watching WAVE-TV, Channel 3, the first television station in the state of Kentucky, and this is our first program. Take it away, boys." On an early show I had Eddy Arnold as a special guest and soon had Minnie Pearl and other friends from the Opry. Before long, I was also doing television shows in Cincinnati, Cleveland, and Chicago.

The first sponsor for my Louisville TV show was a furniture and appliance distributor named Peaslee-Gaulbert. The next one was Taylor's Drugstores, when they had only eleven stores. Now they must have way over a hundred. Later our show was sponsored by Oertel's Beer. At the beginning, the few people who had television watched us on eight- or ten-inch black-and-white sets. It was a marvel to see! We didn't have continuous broadcasting all day long. My very first show was on from 6:15 to 6:45 in the evening on Thanksgiving Day; then they took the cameras out to broadcast the St. Xavier-Trinity football game.

Our set was an imaginary Pee Wee King Ranch. We had a very thin story line about chasing desperadoes or being chased by them or being nearly hoodwinked by city slickers. The story was for laughs, but the main program was music. We mixed western with pop music to increase our audience appeal. Before long, WHAS-TV was on the air, and I had competition from Randy Atcher and his Hayloft Hoedown, with Cactus Tom Brooks, Tiny Thomale, Shorty Chesser, and others—a very talented group of country musicians, just as we were.

In 1952 we started our TV show for Oertel's Brewing Company, which was the biggest of a number of breweries that used to be based in Louisville. They sold more beer than all the others combined. Oertel's was the beer of choice in Louisville. We started out using a ranch set. We all dressed in cowboy suits, even our announcer Bob Kay. The show was on every Thursday night, with a studio audience of about fifty people. Featured players in my band were Redd and Gene Stewart and Neal Burris. I hired Neal because he could shuffle and sing and yodel. He and my brother Gene were good friends because neither one was married then. Neal cut several good records but soon left us and played with several other bands around town. Finally, he got a job working in a men's clothing store.

One of the most unusual guests I ever had on my Oertel's show was Elvis Presley's grandfather, who lived in Louisville. I had met Elvis when he came here in 1956 to do a show at the old armory. Colonel Parker, his manager, was an old friend of mine, and I went backstage to see him and met Elvis, who was staying at his grandfather's house. His grandfather worked at a factory where they made Coca-Cola crates, and he played the fiddle as a hobby. One day, out of a clear blue sky, Mr. Presley called me. "Pee Wee," he said, "by God, I'd like to be on that show of yours on WAVE. I can play the fiddle for you." I said, "Sure, Mr. Presley, I'd be glad to have you, but let me check with the station first." WAVE said it was no problem with them, so I set it up with Mr. Presley, then called my sponsor, Mr. Johnny Oertel, and said, "I'm fixing to do something way out in left field. I've booked Elvis Presley's grandfather to come on the show and play a tune for us on his fiddle." Mr. Oertel said, "That sounds fine to me, but is he any good?" I said, "That's a good question. I've never heard him play. But we'll all soon find out how good he is."

We made all the arrangements and set the date for Mr. Presley's appearance on our show. We put a rocker on the set to make him comfortable. I was about ready to introduce him when I heard a loud commotion outside the studio. It seems the rumor had gotten around that Elvis was going to be on the show with his grandfather.

We got the noise quieted, down and then I said to our live television audience, "Well folks, we couldn't get Elvis for the show today, but we got his grandfather to take his place. Of course, Mr. Presley is no competition for Elvis because he can't sing. But, come to think of it, Elvis can't play the fiddle." Mr. Presley did a fine job for us, playing a couple of square dance fiddle tunes.

I saw Elvis many times in Nashville. When he was just starting out around 1955, I got a wire from Bob Neal, his booking agent in Memphis, that he would give me Elvis for my Chicago television show for expenses only. Unfortunately, I had already booked a guest for the only Saturday Elvis was free.

Television shows are constantly undergoing changes in talent and format. Some turn out to be good and some don't. About 1970 Oertel's got a new advertising agency out of St. Louis, and those fellows had some cockeyed ideas about changing our show. The first thing they wanted to do was revamp the show and change the western format to a showboat revue called "Pee Wee King's Bandstand," featuring pop music with a rock 'n' roll beat. They also wanted to upgrade the commercials. The morning after the first new show I called Mr. Oertel and said, "I want to come and talk with you." He said, "I know what you have to say. I saw the show last night, and I don't think the boys are very comfortable in their new costumes. Come on over and we'll talk." In his office I said, "I just don't think people will like us doing a showboat series, with us dressing up like showboat people and wearing sailor caps. They are used to seeing us in cowboy suits for a country and western show. A one-time showboat special would be all right, but I don't think a series will work. But you're paying for it, so it's up to you. We'll do the thirteen-week series if you say so." Mr. Oertel asked me to talk with the agency man and give the series a chance. So we stayed with the showboat format for the entire series, but I never felt comfortable with it, even though most of our audience stayed with us.

I had a big run-in with the St. Louis agency over the commercials. I could tell from the start that I wasn't going to like the agency man who came over to supervise the show. After the first show, he said, "Mr. King, I know you guys have been writing commercial jingles for your show, but I don't want you to do it any more. Every week I'll bring the commercials and promotions we want used." The

A 1948 songsheet cover for "Tennessee Waltz," composed by Redd Stewart and Pee Wee King.

Above, Pee Wee King and his Golden West Cowboys were voted the number 2 western band in 1948. *Left*, Pee Wee King and Redd Stewart.

Above, Patti Page recorded Redd Stewart and Pee Wee King's "Tennessee Waltz" on Mercury Records. *Below left*, Pee Wee King with the "Singing Rage," Patti Page. *Below right*, Redd Stewart and Pee Wee King leave on his plane for a personal appearance.

Pee Wee King and Fred Rose along with Governor Browning, Bob Austin, and Lonie Bush, at the Grand Ole Opry in 1951 proclaiming the "Tennessee Waltz" the state song.

Pee Wee King with his daughter, Marietta Jo, and sons Frankie Pee Wee Jr. and twins Gene and Larry.

Above, a scene from
*The Pee Wee King Television
Show* in May, 1949.
Left, The Golden West
Cowboys appearing on
*The Pee Wee King Television
Show* in 1947.

Lydia and Pee Wee King
on horseback on their ranch
near Goodlettsville, Tenn.

A poster for Pee Wee King's *Country Western Hoedown*, released in 1967.

Pee Wee King as a Board of Directors' Member of the Country Music Association in Nashville, Tenn., in 1960.

Members of the Country Music Hall of Fame appearing at the Grand Ole Opry's "Reminiscing" in September 1981 (left to right): Grandpa Jones, Chet Atkins, Roy Acuff, Minnie Pearl, Eddy Arnold, Merle Travis, Pee Wee King, and Kitty Wells.

Minnie Pearl, Grandpa Jones, Roy Acuff, and Pee Wee King.

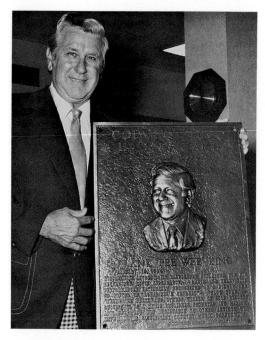

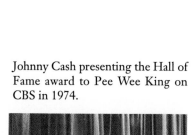

Johnny Cash presenting the Hall of Fame award to Pee Wee King on CBS in 1974.

Pee Wee King was elected to the Country Music Hall of Fame in October 1974.

Pee Wee King in 1992

first commercial he brought showed a guy dragging a six-pack of Oertel's '92 beer behind his boat. The voice-over said, "Keep your Oertel's '92 nice and cool. You don't have to measure. The pleasure's always there." After the show I said, "I hate to tell you, but that commercial won't reach our customers. The people who drink Oertel's '92 in Louisville work at Standard Manufacturing making toilets and sinks, or they work at Ford making cars. They don't have the time or money to go out on a lake and drag a six-pack behind their motorboat. They come home hot and tired and take off their dirty shirt and sit down in their sweaty undershirt and holler out, 'Hey Ma, bring me a Oertel's out of the icebox.'" He said, "You may be right, but I am the advertising expert." I said, "I know what you are, but I also know our customers a damn sight better than you do, and that commercial is not going to get to them! It's not the image we have built up for Oertel's as the working man's beer. I know the people who buy our beer, and they are not boat club people! The rich people out at the Louisville Boat Club on River Road are not drinking Oertel's '92." I was relieved when the thirteen-week contract with that agency was up. I felt we were betraying the audience we had already built up for our country and western music.

While we were doing the showboat revue, we were also playing concerts and dances as the Golden West Cowboys and dressing western for them. We had a topflight band that could play any kind of music, from pop to rock 'n' roll to country ballads. Our group had good chemistry. We had musicians who could lay down one instrument and pick up another and play it without missing a beat. They were all versatile as singers, comedians, and instrumentalists. We tried to have a special guest each week, sometimes a well-known performer and sometimes a good local talent like Cindy Hayes, the secretary of the local musicians union. She sang like Peggy Lee, like a bird.

I tried to give up-and-coming artists a helping hand by having them on my shows. When we were playing a date in Birmingham, a local singer named Sammy Salvo came backstage and introduced himself and said, "How about me coming up to Louisville and doing your show? I won't charge anything." I gave him a quick audition and said, "Sure, come on up, but we'll at least pay your expenses." We had him for a show and even took him with us for a show in Chicago. He was trying to promote a song he had recorded for Victor called "Julie Doesn't Love Me Anymore" and was doing very well for a while. He had a good voice and personality, but he never made it as a big star.

The 1950s were the high decade of my career. I was doing everything, everywhere. I was on television almost every day, with shows in Louisville, Cincinnati, Cleveland, and Chicago. On the first broadcast of *Flying W Ranch* over WLW in Cincinnati in 1953, my guest was Patti Page, and later guests included Julius La Rosa, Hank Snow, Minnie Pearl, and Jim Reeves. The "W" in the show name came from our sponsor, the Wiedemann Beer Company across the river in Newport, Kentucky. We had a similar show in Cleveland, which was promoted: "Channel 5, every Wednesday night, a full hour of music and fun featuring Pee Wee King and his RCA Victor recording band, brought to you by Erin Brew, Formula 1002. WEWS. Channel 5, Cleveland." In addition to my regular band, I had Neal Burris and six-foot-four "Little" Eller, who did comedy routines, singing, and dancing.

My WBBM show in Chicago on Saturday nights lasted from 1952 to 1957. In this business, like everything else, it's important who you know. When Gene Autry was doing his *Melody Ranch* shows on WBBM, the CBS station in Chicago, he became a good friend of the owner, Mr. Les Atlas, and introduced me to him one time. Sometime later, when I was doing a show in Birmingham, I saw Mr. Atlas again, and he said, "When you're in Chicago come by my office in the Wrigley Building and talk with me." A few months later Jack Soebel, our booking agent in New York, said he wanted me to go to Chicago and have dinner with Mr. Atlas to talk about doing a show there. "He already knows and likes you," Jack said. "And, man, that's a feather in your cap." So I went to Chicago and had lunch with Mr. Atlas at Henrici's, which was right close to the Garrick Theater. Mr. Atlas said, "Pee Wee, you and your band must be doing something right because your records are hotter than a pistol. I've got an idea. I'd like to rent the Garrick Theater on Saturday nights and put on your show from there. We'll bring in cameras and do a live broadcast. Jack will get the sponsors. I believe we can make a go of it."

To announce our show, WBBM made a big sign with our picture on it and stood it outside the theater. It said, "WBBM proudly presents Pee Wee King and the Golden West Cowboys every Saturday night." That's a spot of State Street where thousands and thousands of people pass every day. It's close to the Sherman Hotel, Henrici's Restaurant, and the Greyhound Bus Station. It's right in the heart of the city. On opening night we had a full house. But what made that first show a great success was a fire that burned down a little grill called Ham'n'Egger next to the bus station. Any fire in the loop area of downtown is a nine-alarm affair. We had finished our show, had stopped at Henrici's for dinner, and were leaving the restaurant when we heard the sirens and saw all the fire trucks and hoses all around us. All the Chicago newspapers were there snapping pictures, and there I was in the middle of things in front of the Ham'n'Egger, and there plastered up and down the street were posters advertising our show. The next morning I was on the front page of the Sunday papers along with my TV show posters. It was the best advertising we could have, and it didn't cost us a dime. Mr. Atlas said, "Kid, I thought Gene Autry had the best damn luck in the world, but I believe you got him beat." From that day on, I could ask Mr. Atlas for anything I wanted. Jack Soebel said, "Pee Wee, you sure made a hit with Mr. Atlas. I think you're on WBBM for as long as you want to be."

I've had pretty good luck all my life, but I wasn't lucky all the time. Before things began to go smoothly in Chicago, we had to learn some things about how the unions worked there. When we arrived for our first rehearsal at the Garrick Theater, the stagehands wouldn't let us unload our instruments. They said that was their work, and they got paid for it. It was new to me that other people had to unload your instruments, but it was their city and I knew I had to observe their rules. We were all good union men, so we went down to the union hall to find out what the rules were. They said, "First of all, how can a traveling band come in here and take a sit-down job at the Garrick Theater?" I said, "I didn't know we were violating any rules. I thought everything was checked with the union. I thought I was cleared with AFTRA." Howard Miller, who was doing a television show at WBBM and had gone with me to the union hall, said, "This fellow is new in town, but he'll do what's right." By the night of our first show, we had patched everything up.

Jack Soebel was a big help. He flew in every Saturday morning to be there for the rehearsal and the show. He'd tell me what I couldn't do and what I shouldn't do or what I'd done wrong and how I could do it right the next time. He told me, for example, not even to move the microphone because that was the responsibility of the stagehands. He said, "Put all movements of stage property in the script, and they'll take care of it. Whatever you do, don't get the stagehands mad at you!" After I'd learned all the rules, I was on good terms with everyone. On the first Christmas after our show opened, I did something that sealed our good relationship. At that time a partner and I had opened a leather shop on Bardstown Road in Louisville. I got the names and sizes of all the stagehands and the wardrobe girls, and my partner hand-tooled their names on individual belts. On our Christmas Eve show I brought them all up to the microphone and called out each person's name and presented them with their customized Christmas presents. "If it weren't for these people," I said, "we wouldn't have a show. We couldn't put on a show without them."

Everything has an end. After almost six years on the air, I was in the studio one day rehearsing when Mr. Atlas walked in and said he wanted to see me in his office. His son Frankie was with him. He said, "Pee Wee, you've done a great job for us. You've taken the nine to eleven slot of WBBM on Saturday nights and raised the rating from .03 to 9.1. You've got the highest rated show in Chicago. We appreciate the good work. But we want to put on a different kind of programming in that time slot. We've just paid a lot of money for a package of top-rated movies, and that's the only place we can show them. So I'm giving you two months' notice. Frankie will go over the details with you. We want to do right by you. Do you understand what I'm saying?" I said, "Yes, I guess I do." When he left, Frankie asked me if I wanted a couple of shots. I said, "No, one will do. What's going to happen to my show? Will we get another slot?" He said, "No, you're going off the air." That was it. Our show in Chicago closed down. The local musicians union started the rumor that they were responsible for closing the show down, but that was a lie. I don't think, however, that the local musicians ever forgave us for coming in and having such a successful show. We were simply a traveling band from out of town, and they were jealous of our popularity. They said of us, "How those guys ever got anywhere we can't understand." It wasn't our choice to be taken off the air, but I don't think the show could have lasted much longer anyway. Every show has its run, and ours was a good one. The WBBM show gave us a good income for more than five years while we were on the air, and for at least ten more years we never had any trouble getting bookings in the Chicago area. Everybody there knew us, and they turned out in droves to see us at fairs, festivals, concert halls, barn dances, and park concerts.

After we lost the Chicago show, we still had plenty of work to do. I had my Monday show in Cleveland on WEWS, an ABC affiliate. I also had a Wednesday show in Cincinnati and my Thursday show in Louisville. In addition, I had my national radio show on NBC. In 1955, thanks to Jack Soebel, I was the summer replacement for the Sid Caesar-Imogene Coca *Your Show of Shows* for thirteen weeks. It was a half-hour variety show, and we did mostly pop songs from the *Billboard* chart. I had big-name guests like Patti Page, Eddy Arnold, Mahalia Jackson, even the leader of the Ink Spots who had broken out on his own. Then in 1956 I did an hour-and-a-half network show on Monday nights on ABC television from Cleveland. It was called *The Pee Wee King Show* and lasted for almost six years. We started with forty-eight stations and ended with more than seventy and were getting up to five thousand letters a week. Our guest stars included Ernest Tubb, Hank Snow, Porter Wagoner, Audrey Williams, Del Wood, the Everly Brothers, Faron Young, and Rocky Marciano.

I was, of course, trying to do too much during those busy years. It was a hectic schedule. In later years I did a few short television series and occasional guest spots. In 1979 I did thirteen half-hour shows for WKPC-TV, public television in Louisville. It was a sort of historical survey of country music, with guests like Marty Robbins and Minnie Pearl. I was also on national public television several times when I appeared as a guest on *Austin City Limits*. When my big TV shows ended in the late 1950s and early 1960s, so did my main sources of income. I told the band I wouldn't blame them if they struck out on their own. Most of them stayed with me, and we continued to play dates. But the golden days were over. I had proved, however, that television was, indeed, the medium of the future. Even the Grand Ole Opry finally saw the light and caught up with the times. Who can imagine the Opry today without television?

Most of the country and western music business was done in those early days on a shoestring. There was little capital to support it. Country music didn't pull in much money for anybody—the performers, the promoters, or the theater owners. It wasn't easy for Gene Autry to make money with his music even after he made movies and did live shows. It took a lot of hard selling by George Gobel to get a country music show in Madison Square Garden. There was still a lot of prejudice against country music. We made little or nothing from our radio broadcasts, and sometimes we hardly broke even when we took our shows on the road.

We remained the poor cousins of the entertainment business until we began to get recording contracts, and for most of us that didn't come until the mid-1940s or the 1950s. Jimmie Rodgers, Ernest Tubb, Roy Acuff, the Carlisle Brothers, Red Foley, Eddy Arnold, Hank Williams—these were among the first. The big recording studios were in Chicago, New York, and Hollywood; and that's where we had to go to make our records. Hank Williams was first recorded by Sterling Records in 1947 in New York, then later moved over to MGM Records. Columbia started putting out a lot of country records in the 1940s, and early on they had an American Folk Series, with songs by Gene Autry, Bill Monroe and His Blue Grass Boys, Molly O'Day and the Cumberland Mountain Folks, and Bob Wills and His Texas Playboys. Soon they had an impressive roster of country stars. Finally, all the major labels were jumping on the country music bandwagon, and they even began opening recording studios in Nashville.

A lot of new labels were issued, including King Records, which was founded by Syd Nathan in Cincinnati in 1944. He was soon recording some of the top rhythm-and-blues artists, gospel groups, and country stars, like the Delmore Brothers, the Stanley Brothers, Cowboy Copas, Hawkshaw Hawkins, Moon Mullican, Hank Penny, Jimmie Osborne, and Homer and Jethro. One of King's exclusive recording artists was Wayne Raney, a harmonica player from Wolf

Bayou, Arkansas, who wrote dozens of songs and recorded many of them himself, including "Why Don't You Haul Off and Love Me?"

The Golden West Cowboys and I made our recording debut in 1945 when we started our own Nash label. We planned the company to sell not only my records but those of Minnie Pearl, Cowboy Copas, Bradley Kincaid, and other artists who were on the road with us. We would sell our records as a package during our personal appearances. They wouldn't be in record shops. About that time Mr. Frank got a call from Gene Autry, who said, "Joe, have you started your record company yet?" Mr. Frank said, "Started it? We've got everything ready. We're going to press ten thousand records. The labels are printed." Gene said, "Well, I've got bad news for you. In a couple of months we're going to have the damnedest shellac strike you ever saw, and the record companies are going broke." We didn't have any capital to work with, so Mr. Frank went to Jim Bulleit, a bank manager in Nashville, to borrow money to pay for the first batch of records. Mr. Frank said, "I need seven thousand dollars to pay for some records made by my performers. I need to take them on the road and sell them before a music war breaks out between BMI and ASCAP, which will kill the recording business. Give me the money and the company will be yours." BMI and ASCAP are licensing companies that charge fees for the use of copyrighted music and pass part of the royalties on to the owners. Radio stations, for example, have to pay a small fee every time they play a recording of "The Tennessee Waltz" or any other copyrighted song. So Jim said, "Let me think about this for a while. Come back in a couple of days."

When Mr. Frank went back to see him, he said, "Jim, I can't wait any longer. I have to have some money to pay for the records." Jim said, "Will you take five thousand dollars in cash?" Mr. Frank said, "I'll take five thousand dollars now and when you pay me another two thousand dollars, Nash will belong to you." So Mr. Frank got his money and paid his debts, and Jim got the Nash label, which he soon changed to Bullet Records. One of his first recordings featured Francis Craig, who was the nephew of C.A. Craig, the president of National Life and Accident Insurance Company. The younger Craig headed an orchestra that played popular music at the Andrew Jackson Hotel. Jim went to Francis and said, "I'm starting a record label. How would you and your orchestra like to do a recording for me?" They put their heads together and put out a record with "Red Rose" on one side and "Near You" on the other. "Near You" hit the public like a tornado. It made Francis and his orchestra one of the most popular in the country, and Bullet Records went sky-high for a while.

In 1947 I moved over to RCA Victor, which had been the company of country music pioneer Jimmie Rodgers, "America's Blue Yodeler." A record distributor friend of mine, Murray Nash, recommended me to their A & R director, Steve Sholes. My first release with Victor had "Steel Guitar Rag" on one side and "Tennessee Central No. 9" on the other. During our seventeen years with Victor we put out some 157 records and 15 albums and made millions of dollars for the company. For them, we recorded "The Tennessee Waltz," "Kentucky Waltz," "Tennessee Tears," "Alabama Moon," "Bonaparte's Retreat," "Bimbo," "Slow Poke," "Busybody," "You Belong to Me," "Silver and Gold," and many other best-sellers. It's interesting how we happened to record "Silver and Gold." Redd and I were out in Los Angeles appearing on a "Double or Nothing" show, and Bob Crosby, who was substituting for Walter O'Keefe, asked me and Redd to sing a tune that he and Del Sharbit and Henry Pritchard had written. The song was "Silver and Gold." That was its first public performance and the audience loved it. We decided right then and there to record it, and it became a huge seller for us. Indeed, we put out some very good recordings during those years with Victor.

You can't just make a record and expect it to take off. It has to be promoted in a carefully orchestrated way—on TV and radio and in personal appearances. You have to go to trade shows, like the jukebox conventions, which are showcases for all the record companies and their top stars. A lot of us used to perform at the conventions to get the jukebox operators to use our records. I went to the 1959 convention in Chicago along with a lot of pop and country musicians—people like Perry Como, the Fontaine Sisters, Red Foley, as well as the Golden West Cowboys. I got to be good friends with Hirsch D. Levy, who was president of the Jukebox Operators Association. Before I left, he put his arms around me and said, "If I had more entertainers like you, I'd be happy."

I was trying to be a good record promoter when I got into a

bad disagreement with Victor that caused me to leave them. It was 1958, and I had a hot TV show in Cleveland and a hot record called "Bimbo," and I thought it would be clever to give away some albums as a promotion for the show and the record. So I called the Victor office in New York, and asked for twenty-five records to use as a giveaway. This promotion guy said, "I don't give twenty-five records to anybody. We don't give away Elvis Presley records." I said, "Okay. I'll tell you what. You won't hear from me again. I'm finished with RCA Victor." When I told my sponsor in Cleveland what had happened, he said, "Why didn't you ask us to buy the records as a giveaway? We would have done it." I said, "No, that's not what I wanted. I wanted Victor and the Golden West Cowboys to give them away. It would have been a goodwill promotion." The whole matter upset me no end. There I was, Victor's top country and western seller, and they wouldn't provide a couple of dozen copies of my own record for a big promotion. So I left it. It was a matter of principle to me.

Paul Cohen, who was a big recording director working in Nashville for Decca, had a stable of performers that read like a Who's Who in the Record Business. Shortly after my trouble with Victor, he saw me and said, "I hear you've left Steve Sholes. Would you like to do a session for me? I can put you on Decca or on an independent I have called Briar Records." I decided to do a couple of recordings for him and put a collection of polkas called "Old Time Dances" and a recitation called "History Repeats Itself" on his Briar label. We also did several recordings for Todd Records, another of Cohen's labels, but none of them worked out very well. Paul Cohen was a fine man, a great producer, director, and A & R man. Perhaps if I'd met him before I met Steve Sholes, things might have worked out differently. But I have no axes to grind with Steve. He and I worked together very well for a long time and put out some good recordings that were enormously successful.

I did a few sessions with a couple of other small labels, but what I really wanted to do was start my own recording company, which I did. I called it Ridgeway Records. I didn't know it, but my timing was very bad. It was right before the payola scandals, when record companies got a dirty name for paying off disk jockeys to play and plug their records. I'll tell you more about Ridgeway when I talk about my other business ventures, most of them failures.

Country Shows

THE SHOW IS THE THING. It's what the people come to see and hear. It's where all your talent and training and experience and inspiration and determination come together for one purpose—to entertain an audience. Your success or failure is determined by the show. So what have I learned about what makes a good show?

To begin with, you have to develop a stage image or personality, something that sets you off from everybody else. That means not only what you do as an entertainer, what kinds of songs you play and sing, but how you package yourself. You must learn to have a stage presence and a poise while on stage, how to get on and off stage without stumbling and falling, and how to get out of an embarrassing situation—like an open fly or a musical miscue. It means that you must feel at home on the stage.

Mr. Frank shaped my image as Little Pee Wee King with a big accordion. He also helped us shape images for the entire band. The single boys we showed off as eligible bachelors to please the young girls. Four of the boys became the Golden West Quartet, and they were serious and solemn while they were performing religious songs. On the other hand, we took three of the boys and called them the Bardstown Bucklebusters. They did comedy routines and novelty songs and played each other's instruments during a number. One would be playing a mandolin, another the guitar, and another the bass fiddle; and then they'd switch instruments and keep the same tune going. Then I'd walk up and say to the heavyset bass player, "I want to join in too." He'd say, "Pee Wee, you'll never be a bucklebuster." I'd say, "I don't want to be a bucklebuster, and don't call me buster. Them's fightin' words." He'd say, "Well, let's fight." I'd say, "I don't fight except in the ring." So he'd pretend to draw a ring on the stage, and we'd do a little sparring. Our routine wasn't scripted, but we knew what to do because we knew our roles.

Gene Autry taught me a lot about stage conduct. He showed me how to bow with my hat and make an introduction. I was holding my cowboy hat like a boy scout and saying, "Ladies and Gentlemen, here is the star of our show, Mr. Gene Autry." He said, "Pee Wee, if you do that again, I'm going to kick your butt." I said, "Okay, show me." He said, "First take the hat off, then crush it with your hand because it's not going to break. Then go down and sweep the floor with it. If it gets dirty, you can have it cleaned. Then you put it back on and say, 'Ladies and Gentlemen, the singing star of *The National Barn Dance*, star of Republic Pictures, Oklahoma's singing cowboy, Gene Autry.' Then you look and point toward the side I'm coming from." Well, as luck would have it, the first time I tried it his way, I got everything right except I pointed to the wrong side of the stage. Then I turned toward him and said, "Oh, there he is," and everybody laughed, except Gene.

I also learned early that a performer had to do what he does best. I knew I wasn't a very good singer, but I could play the accordion and tell jokes and keep the show moving. So I learned how to be the best emcee I could be. I learned that I controlled the movement and the pacing of the show. It was my fault if it began to drag, and I had to pick it up. I learned that after I had introduced an act, I should stand away from the microphone and give the complete spotlight to the performer. A lot of booking agents had to hire emcees for their shows, except when they hired the Golden West Cowboys. With us, they got an accordionist, a bandleader, and an emcee all in one. My point is this: whatever your role, you build on it, perfect it, then add some little flourishes.

You learn that you can never rest on your laurels. You have to prove yourself at every show. Regardless of how famous you get, you can never get too big for your britches. You have to give the audience its money's worth at every performance. You cannot coast on the reputation you built last week or last year. The audience will know and not forgive you. Several years before he died in 1983, we were booked with Junior Samples, one of the stars of *Hee Haw*, for a show in Washington, Pennsylvania. I loved Junior and the character he created for television. But he began to take his reputation for granted. First, he was late in arriving and missed the one o'clock show. During the break between shows, I went outside and saw a dilapidated car with a trailer hitched to the back of it, with a crude sign that read, "Junior Samples, Star of Hee Haw." I walked over to where several of his boys were standing and said, "Weren't you guys supposed to be here for the first show?" One fellow said, "Yes we were, but we've been having trouble with this car. We just got here, and Junior walked over to the hotel. I don't know whether he plans to do a show this afternoon or not." I said, "What's that? You must be kidding. You go tell him that we have another show in an hour at four o'clock and he'd better get here."

Junior arrived a couple of minutes before the show started, and I said, "Junior, how do you want me to introduce you?" He said, "Well, I don't care how you do it. Any way you want to. All you got to say is 'Junior Samples' and if they don't laugh and clap, I walk off. But I know they will 'cause they always do. But if they don't, I'm gone." I said, "Okay, so if you don't walk off, what will you do?" He said, "Oh, I do about three jokes, and I sing my big song. Then I tell 'em I enjoyed myself being here; then I tell 'em so long. That's my act. That's all of it." I said, "Well, it says on the program that you do twenty minutes. Is the band going to fill out what you have left?" He said, "I don't do but about ten minutes, so I reckon they'll have to do the other ten minutes if they get done. I don't know what they can play 'cause I just hired 'em to back me up for my song. So you can ask them if you want to know."

With an attitude like that, it's no wonder Junior laid an egg. The audience wasn't very amused at his act, and they didn't applaud much when he left the stage. What Junior didn't understand is that a good performer is like a good salesman. You may have a good talent and a famous name, but you've got to sell something to every audience, and that something is yourself. Only the live person on stage can do it. Your name can't do it. Your money can't do it. Your TV show can't do it. Your records can't do it. Every time you perform, you start with a clean slate, and it's up to you to write a good performance on it.

Television can take a person who doesn't have much talent and make him famous as a curiosity. Tiny Tim proved that. But he was a curiosity with a slick gimmick and one song, "Tiptoe Through the Tulips," and that wore thin very soon. Junior Samples was an auto salesman who was made famous by *Hee Haw*. He had one song about going fishing with his brother, plus a few stumbling jokes. The audience that afternoon in Washington, Pennsylvania, liked him on television, but they didn't like him in person. He just didn't have the talent or the push to develop the country bumpkin character for a stage show.

I think Junior was simply lazy. He didn't want to work hard, and show business is hard work. But even if he was sick or tired or if he was having personal or family problems, he should have put on a first-class show as if he didn't have a worry in the world. A good performer leaves his problems and cares in the dressing room. The show has to go on. The people have paid their money and are waiting for their money's worth.

I have gone on stage many a time when I didn't feel like it. But I found that once I was performing, I got a pick-me-up from the audience. It was like a shot of adrenalin, a natural high. I've performed when I was too sick to stand up. I've never collapsed on stage, but I got close one time. In 1953 Colonel Parker got us an important booking at the Shamrock Hotel in Houston, and I came down with the flu. I had it so bad I was sweating in an air-conditioned room. Eddy Arnold was playing nearby at the convention center and offered to substitute for me. He said, "I can run over and take your place for about fifteen minutes." I said, "Don't worry. I'll be all right in fifteen minutes." Well, I wasn't. I drank orange juice and wiped my face during the entire show. I managed to stay on my feet, but it was a close call. When the show was finally over, I went backstage and collapsed. It's hard for a man or woman with show business in his blood to call it quits. A lot of us want to perform right up to the end. Roy Acuff had two of his players die of heart attacks while performing on the Opry. And in November of 1991 Minnie Pearl collapsed and was carried off the stage. The show must go on, and we are vain enough to think that it cannot go on without us.

To please most audiences a show has to have variety. I've been looking at a program for the Philip Morris Parade of Stars during the Kentucky Derby Festival in the early 1970s, when Anne Murray and a local singer, Angie Humphrey, appeared with the Golden West Cowboys. I opened the show and thanked Philip Morris; then Angie sang "Hey Good Lookin'," followed by two of our songs, "Bonaparte's Retreat" and "Slow Poke," followed by our arrangement of "Jambalaya." Other parts of the program included a salute to Duke Ellington; an audience sing-along of "My Old Kentucky Home"; the Marlboro theme music; an introduction of dignitaries; awards for best floats; a medley of songs by the Thoroughbreds, a local male chorus; a couple of songs "to watch girls by," including "Satin Doll"; a salute to Louisville native Lionel Hampton; Anne Murray singing "The Tennessee Waltz"; concluding with our arrangement of "In the Mood." There was something in that show for everybody. Our usual shows were not quite so varied, but we always managed to have love songs, novelty tunes, and one religious song to close out the show—plus, of course, a few jokes scattered here and there throughout the program.

Sometimes our show would be part of a longer bill that might include circus acts, beauty contests, plowing competitions, rodeo acts, high-wire acts, and fishing contests. In 1941 Minnie Pearl and I and the Golden West Cowboys played a picnic and barbecue at Moore's Grove near Clarksville, Tennessee, that also featured two baseball games, a hog calling and husband calling contest, and footraces. I learned very early that show business is unpredictable. One day you're on the same bill with Mahalia Jackson, and the next day you follow a tractor pull.

I also learned that there are some acts you simply can't compete with. You can't upstage a dog, but he can upstage you. Sometimes you have to compete with an animal and the weather at the same show. One time Lassie from Hollywood was booked with me at Buck Lake Ranch near Angola, Indiana. It was bad news from the start. When we arrived at the park, it was raining cats and dogs. The park manager came out and said, "Pee Wee, you're wanted on the phone. It's the booking agent in Chicago, Jack Lindahl." So Jack said, "Pee Wee, Lassie is still here in Chicago, and I hear you have a heavy thunderstorm down there. How am I going to get this dog to you?" I said, "Charter a plane and land it on the long blacktop road right by the park." So Jack rented a single engine job and brought Lassie and her owner to Buck Lake.

Lassie arrived soaking wet. We had just started the show and were dripping wet ourselves. It was hot as the devil in the old dance hall, and we wanted to wash up and dry off and change clothes while Lassie was performing. I asked the owner how long the Lassie act would last. He said, "Well, she's really too wet now to perform at all, but we'll try three or four minutes." There went our cleanup and clothes change, so we stayed in our soggy costumes and watched Lassie perform, such as it was. All they did was play around the stage with Lassie barking and growling and pretending to bite her owner. It lasted maybe three minutes—not a second more.

Then we performed our second act, and the show was finally over. The manager came over to me and said, "We didn't do too good. The storm kept people away. I had to pay for Lassie in advance, but here's your check." I said, "No, I don't want that check. I just want to bathe and change into some dry clothes. Just give my boys their expense money." So he gave each one twenty-five dollars and they were satisfied. His wife came over crying and said, "Pee Wee, Roy Acuff did that for us one time too, and I couldn't believe it. It was a terrible storm when he came, and we didn't have much of a crowd. So he took our check and tore it up. I'll remember both of you long as I live."

I played Buck Lake Ranch many other times when the weather cooperated and the crowds were large. Once I filled in for Gene Autry after he'd been in an accident. He called and said, "I'm booked at Buck Lake. I can't make it and I want you to work for me there. I'll send Pat Buttram to help you." I was free that day and agreed to pinch-hit. Pat flew into Louisville, and we drove up to do the show. Pat drew a big crowd because that's when he was appearing on *Green Acres* with his pig. "That pig," he said, "is more popular than I am. Everybody wants to know about the damn pig!" Later, when I was guest on his *Melody Ranch* TV show, Gene gave me a belt for taking his place.

Audiences like animal acts partly, I think, because they are so unpredictable. I got through more than ten years of my career without an animal in my act. Then one day when I was still a regular on the Opry, Mr. Frank said, "Pee Wee, you're a country music star, and

you grew up at least partly on a farm in Wisconsin. Now, everybody expects a farm boy to ride a horse and know something about
cows. I don't know how you could use a cow in your show, but I do
think it's time you bought a horse to work the fairs and parks and
festivals. I know a guy who's got a trick horse for sale. I want you to
go see him." I said, "Mr. Frank, I don't want a horse. I've already
got too much stuff to lug around. I guess you think I need a horse
because Gene Autry's got one." He said, "Pee Wee, you've got a
good band. You and Minnie Pearl make a good combination. But
you need something to draw kids to your shows. A trick horse will
draw hundreds of kids to matinees. Get a horse." So I got a horse, a
pinto, and a saddle and a horse trailer to haul him around in. I also
got a horse trainer, Bill Carr, who traveled with us. We named the
horse Boots, and later on I got a younger horse, a mare, that we
named Boots, Jr. They were good companions for each other and
ran and frolicked in the pasture behind our house.

Boots came to live with us when we were living in Goodlettsville,
just outside of Nashville. In 1943 I bought five acres and a house
and three-car garage for seven thousand dollars, and I made it into
a regular western-style ranch with a white fence around it. We had
two little creeks with bridges over them. There were three houses
in our compound. Lydia and our family lived in one house. Mr. and
Mrs. Frank bought two acres and a house next door, and one of his
sons lived in the third house. I built a barn for Boots and for the
Tennessee walking horses that Mr. Frank bought. All of us in the
family rode the horses.

So I guess it was inevitable that I would have a horse sometime. After all, my group was called Pee Wee King and the Golden
West Cowboys. We were a cowboy band. And what do cowboys
have? Horses, of course. Even though it was Mr. Frank who un-
loaded the horse on me, I quickly learned to love him, and I missed
him so much after he passed away. Before long, Boots had become
a star in his own right and began to receive fan mail. One of my
songbooks shows me on Boots on the front cover and on Boots, Jr.,
on the back cover. They were so much alike they looked like the
same horse. Inside the songbook there are pictures of Cowboy Copas,
the Golden West Cowboys, and even Lydia all mounted on our horses
in front of the stables at "King's Ranch."

Mr. Frank was right about how much the kids would love Boots. They flocked to the outdoor shows and rodeos to see Boots do his tricks. I'd say, "Boots, how old are you?" And he would tap his hoof on the ground the correct number of times. Boots could also drink out of a bottle. I'd say, "Boots, what did you drink last night?" and hold out a Coke bottle. He'd shake his head, and I'd say, "Is this what you drank last night?" and hold out a bottle of beer. Then he'd nod his head and show his teeth and drink from the bottle. He could also do about twenty other tricks, including several dances.

We also did indoor shows with Boots, and I'd make my entrance on him as the band played "Turkey in the Straw." I stayed mounted as I had him do his tricks. Minnie didn't much like working on the same show with Boots. I'd say, "Now that Boots has done his tricks, Minnie Pearl will do hers." Sometimes she'd whisper to me, "Get that damn horse off the stage and sweep it off before I go out." There was no sanitary problem when he performed at fairs and parks, but sometimes on the stage he would leave little pies behind that smelled up the place. Minnie was always a sport and did her part of the show the way a good trouper should.

I toured with Boots for about two years, but I never took him out in the wintertime—except for once, and it was a mistake. That was in Newark, Ohio. We were trying to unload him next to a coal chute. As he was backing out, he slipped on the ice and almost fell through the chute. If he had fallen, it could have crippled or killed him, and I said, "No more. I'm not taking Boots out until the sun shines hot again."

When we moved back to Louisville in 1947, we brought Boots with us and boarded him outside of town in Fern Creek with a Shrine brother of mine, Buren Bandy, and his wife. I continued to use him in occasional shows, but he was getting older and I didn't want to abuse him. One time I decided to use him on my TV show at WAVE, back when the studio was on the corner of Preston and Broadway. We were having a special show to plug the Masonic Home Picnic and had invited some of the children from the home to come see Boots perform and have their pictures taken with him.

I thought it would be easier if I took Boots to the service entrance on the ground floor and brought him up the service elevator to the studios on the third floor. Buren was helping me take him up. We waited until after office hours, and we thought everybody except the crew for my show was out of the building. I said, "Buren, you go on upstairs and catch us as we get off, and I'll stay and come up with the horse." Buren went on up and I thought, "Well, this is easy. It's going to be a piece of cake." I took Boots and led him into the service elevator, and then I thought, "Hell, it's too crowded with both of us in there. What's the use of me going up with him anyway? I'll just close the door, punch the button, and Buren will be there waiting when the elevator stops to take him out."

As luck would have it, however, Boots had his rubber shoes on and the front one caught in the doorway, and the elevator stalled—or so I found out later. I punched the button and ran like hell up the steps to the third floor to help take him off. When I got there, I was out of breath, and the elevator hadn't arrived. In fact, the light was still on for the ground floor. So I rushed back down, and there was Boots stuck in the elevator kicking and snorting and rearing. I managed to push his hoof back inside and clear the door, and the elevator took off this time with Boots inside. Unfortunately, about that time some idiot on the first floor decided he was going to take the service elevator up to the third floor too. So he punched the button just as Boots was leaving the ground floor, and soon the elevator arrived and the door opened, and there was Boots' rear end sticking out. About that time, I had made it up to the first floor and stopped to see what was going on. I said, "What's the matter, buddy? See an elephant?" He said, "No, but is this your horse in the elevator, Pee Wee?" I said, "Yeah. Is anything wrong?" He said, "No. But I'm glad you came. I had just said I'm gonna quit drinking."

This time I got on the elevator with Boots and we went on up to the third floor studios without any trouble. When we got off, Buren said, "Is everything all right? What have you been doing?" I said, "Oh, we've just had a little performance on the first floor." That was the only time I tried to have Boots on the television show. It was just too much trouble.

Boots was the innocent and indirect cause of a broken friendship with a sergeant at Ft. Knox. I met this guy and we became friends because we both had horses. One day he came to my house and said, "Let's go out to Fern Creek and see your horse." When we got there, we went in and talked a while with Buren, and then I said, "Sarge, if you want to, go on out and saddle up Boots, and see what you think of him. But be careful. He's a trick horse, so you have to watch where you touch him." He said, "Oh, don't worry. I know all about trick horses. I've tried to teach my horse tricks, but he's just an old plow horse."

I stayed behind in the house with Buren and his wife Ruby, who had just made us a cup of coffee and some coffee cake. I watched through the window as the sergeant harnessed Boots and saddled him up. Everything was looking good; then suddenly Boots took off out the gate and ran into the pasture with the sergeant hanging on for dear life. By the time we ran out and got to the fence, the sergeant had him under control and was bringing him back to the stables. He pulled up and said, "Pee Wee, I must have touched him in the wrong place. Now, how do you get him to raise up on his hind legs?" As I gave directions, the sergeant pulled back the reins and took his cowboy hat off. When he did that, Boots went way up and reared over backwards and landed on top of him. We ran over and I could see that one of the man's legs had a bone sticking out. I said, "Sarge, you've got some broken bones. What should we do?" He said, "Damn it. Take me back to Ft. Knox right now to the base hospital." I said, "We got a doctor right here in Fern Creek who can take care of you. Why do you want to go all the way to Ft. Knox?" He said, "Do as I say." So we put him in my car and I drove like crazy to get him back to camp before he passed out. On the way he said, "All right, I'll tell you why I gotta go to the military hospital. I'm gonna tell them I fell down some steps on base and broke my leg. That way it won't cost me anything."

That incident strained our friendship, and another one broke it. The sergeant had a pretty young daughter, who I used to tease about getting married. I said, "I want to see the kind of man you marry, so don't forget to invite me to your wedding." When she got engaged, she said, "Daddy, Pee Wee promised to come to my wedding, so I want to make sure he's invited."

The sergeant called me, and I said, "I hope I can come, but that is my busiest time of the year, and I'm out of town a lot." He said, "By God, Pee Wee, you've got to come. You promised her you would. And be sure to bring your accordion along." I said, "Bring my accordion for what?" He said, "Well, you know, we got to make some noise at the reception." I said, "Well, hell, just get some pots and pans and beat 'em together. In fact, I've just checked my schedule and I can't be there at all." I've not heard a word from him since. I've not called him and he's not called me. He's a master cook and makes excellent burgoo. I saw him a couple of years ago at a Kentucky Colonels picnic and again at one of Bill King's sports shows, where he offered me a bowl of burgoo. I declined because I had to go on stage.

I don't know what happened to the sergeant's horse, but I know that Boots lived to the ripe old age of thirty-one. He was well cared for by Buren and Ruby until the end. On Buren's seventy-fifth birthday, he brought Boots right up into the house for a piece of his birthday cake. When Ruby's mother was a hundred years old, she asked me to dedicate a song to her on the Opry, and I did. It was the least I could do to thank the family that had kept my horse so long and so well. I don't regret that I had a horse, but he was a lot of trouble. A number of country stars had horses at one time, including Ernest Tubb, whose horse was named Pal. Once I asked Garth Brooks, "Why don't you get a horse and become a singing cowboy?" Garth said, "I hate horses." I guess a horse would be a lot more trouble now than when I had mine. Mr. Frank wanted me to get Boots, and it was a challenge I accepted. I did it partly to show him that I could. I had learned to ride on my grandparents' farm in Wisconsin, so I wasn't a stranger to horses. I was never a very good horseman, but I was good enough to handle Boots.

I got Boots for the same reason I wore a cowboy suit and traveled hundreds of thousands of miles and slept in lonely, dreary motel rooms and wrote songs and endured a lifetime of separation from my family. I did all those things because they were necessary if I wanted to put on a good show to entertain my audiences.

Like nobody else in the entertainment business, country musicians go the extra mile for their fans; and that's why I think there is a special bond between us and them. It's like a marriage, and it's a lifetime commitment. That's one reason I could never have considered another career. I have always loved entertaining people who want to be entertained—people who choose to hear your music on radio and television, on recordings, or in person. Every show is a new show, a new challenge, when you walk out on that stage and try to please that audience that's in front of you for the first time. You can always tell when you're in tune with them after you've done a couple of songs and told a few jokes. You can smell it if you're laying an egg. Then you'd better change directions, or the whole show turns bad. Regardless of what you want to do and what you think is good, you've got to make sure you're doing something the audience wants done. What Wayne King told me about dance music fits all forms of entertainment: "You've got to watch the feet and set your beat." If you're not playing their song, they won't be there next time.

Yes, I think country entertainers are the best at pleasing their audiences. We speak to and sing to our fans like the old vaudeville players. Like them, we know how to warm up our audiences. It's like we're all home folks having a good time together. That's why they want to invite you to their homes. It's not unusual for big stars to go home with fans after a show and have supper, or have a picnic lunch with them after a show in the park. Their relationship is a tie that binds.

Certainly, I've always felt close to my fans. I've tried to give them a good show when I'm onstage, and I've been polite and friendly to them offstage. I've never tried to shut them off. I always remember that they're paying my salary. Where would I be without them? I know it's not as common as it used to be, but I've eaten many lunches and dinners with fans all over the country. I have visited them in hospitals and signed arm and leg casts by the dozens. At NCO clubs on military bases, I would go by tables and sign autographs on napkins. Recently, at an old-timers reunion in Illinois, all of us aging country stars sat at a long table and talked and signed autographs for more than a thousand people. We stayed until everybody was gone. If you sneak out the back door and go to your hotel, they know you don't really care about them. But if you say, "I'll be standing right over there, and I'll autograph until we empty the house," they know they're not taken for granted.

Probably the best country star with audiences was Marty Robbins. We'd be doing a show together on the road or at the Opry, and he'd say, "Pee Wee, you don't mind if I do just fifteen minutes more, do you?" Or he would say to a performer scheduled to follow him, "Is it all right if I do just one more song?" He had such charm that no one ever said no to him, even if he ran thirty minutes over. Then he'd go out to the signing desk at the Opry and autograph programs and record jackets until the last fan left. They loved him for that. Country stars, you see, learn early that talent alone is not enough. The minute a guy says, "Sorry folks, I don't do autographs," that's when the fans freeze on you. If you don't have time for the fans, they know your interest stops at the dollar sign. What's more, I've never seen a country star charge for an autograph. I don't know how sports stars get away with charging kids fifty dollars for their signatures. I always considered that a part of my obligation to the people who bought tickets to my shows.

I tried to maintain a personal touch with my fans. If I saw someone in the audience I recognized from an earlier concert, I might say, "It's good to see Mr. and Mrs. Rodgers. Little Jerry was sick the last time we were here, and I'm glad he's out again and looking good." I have always answered my fan mail personally. There's no telling how many thousands of postcards I've mailed to them from hotels and motels and tourist cabins all over the country. Even now, I get birthday and Christmas cards from my old fans.

I've never stayed overnight with fans. It was better on us and our hosts if we stayed at a hotel or motel. If I liked a certain motel, I'd try to stay there each time we played the area. If we were performing near Mattoon, Illinois, for example, our office in Louisville knew we could be contacted at the Holiday Inn. It got to be a custom when we stayed there that the manager would put up a sign on the marquee saying, "Welcome Pee Wee King and the Golden West Cowboys." That was good hospitality—and valuable publicity. It told thousands of people driving by that we were playing a concert somewhere close by. I'd joke with the manager, "With the great work you're doing for us, we don't need to advertise."

I've played everywhere from barrooms to ballrooms, and I've had very little trouble with sharpshooters in the audiences. The few times that I remember were in military installations, and those were exceptions. Sometimes somebody would drink too much and get sullen and belligerent. One time I was playing an NCO club and a drunk came up to the band and said, "You ain't played your hit record yet. Why don't you play it?" I said, "Which one is that?" He said, "Twelfth Street Rag." I said, "Sir, that's not our song. You're thinking of Pee Wee Hunt." He mumbled, "I know you're the one. Don't make no excuses. I want to hear 'Twelfth Street Rag.'" I said, "OK. We'll play it the best we can with our string band. We don't have any horns like Pee Wee Hunt." He then stumbled over to Big Jim, our 300-pound steel guitar player, and said, "Can you play 'Twelfth Street Rag' for me?" Big Jim said, "Yeah, we can play it." The drunk said, "Then why in hell don't you play it? I know this is Pee Wee Hunt's band and you recorded it." Big Jim said, "I'm sorry you're wrong. This is not Pee Wee Hunt's band. It's Pee Wee King's band."

The soldier staggered around some more and argued, but nobody could convince him that we weren't Pee Wee Hunt's band. Finally, he said, "If you guys don't quit lying to me, I'll use my switchblade on you." That's when I called the club manager and said, "Look, there's a guy over there who's got it in his head that I'm Pee Wee Hunt, and I can't convince him that I'm not. I think he's about to start a fight." The manager said, "Don't worry about him. He's more bark than bite. He's always getting drunk and harassing the musicians. If he keeps on, I'll have him thrown out." The manager finally had to have him carried out. After he left, I got to thinking he might be waiting for us outside and ambush us with his switchblade. One of the sergeants said, "Don't worry. I'll give you an escort when you're ready to leave, but I'll bet you won't find him within twenty miles of this place." So that was that. We never saw him again.

Another time we were playing an air force base in North Michigan, and two or three Cajuns in the audience started bugging us to play some Cajun music. One of them went to the manager and complained, "They won't play any Cajun songs for us." The manager came to me and said, "Can't you play some Cajun music for these boys?" I said, "Sure we can, but what they want isn't a dance tune, and these people want to dance." Before long, the Cajuns started a fight, and we had a battle royal until they were taken out by the MPs.

We've been in a few other tense situations, but our closest call came right after Martin Luther King was killed and we were playing at the Great Lakes Naval Base near Chicago. We played our usual numbers for about an hour, but the mood was like a funeral and nobody wanted to dance. One guy asked us to play the national anthem, but I said, "I don't think it's appropriate for dance music, and that's what we're supposed to be playing. We play music you can dance to." We continued to play for a while; then a fight broke out between some black and white soldiers. Finally, the manager came up to me and said, "Everything in town is shut down. It's too dangerous for you to keep on playing. Just sack up and leave. We'll make sure you get back to your motel safely." It had become like a tinderbox in that dance hall, and the least spark could have started a riot. So we shut down quickly and left.

These were all exceptions. We had no trouble at all with most of our military tours. Even after 1948, when President Truman integrated the services and we played to mixed audiences, there were few racial incidents. We tried to play music that would appeal to both whites and blacks and not take sides. Every time we needed a date on the way to Florida, I could depend on the NCO club at Ft. Rucker near Ozark, Alabama. One time the manager of the motel where we stayed handed me a pamphlet and said, "Mr. King, here's your next president." It was a picture of George Wallace. I thanked him and said I thought Governor Wallace had good taste because he used "The Tennessee Waltz" on his campaigns. I didn't say if I would vote for him. I knew that it was best for a country musician to keep away from partisan politics—unless he was being paid to perform.

Like a lot of entertainers, I had a fan club that kept me in close personal touch with many of my fans. It was started by Delores Klaft of Posen, Michigan, in 1945, and at one time we had almost eight thousand members all over the United States. They paid one dollar in annual dues and got a newsletter four times a year called *King of the Golden West*. The members were a group of hard-core fans who supported me and the Golden West Cowboys by buying our records, coming to our concerts, and serving as a kind of lobbying club for us. Members were urged to write radio stations and ask disk jockeys to play our records. After we made the movie, *Flame of the West* with Johnny Mack Brown, my fan club lobbied Monogram Studios in Hollywood to put us in a movie of our own; but the campaign failed. Delores did such a good job with the fan club, I finally got permission from her parents to bring her to Louisville, where she served as my secretary for seven years.

Country music stars still have a good relationship with their fans, by and large, but in this time of megaconcerts and superstars and groupies and random violence, it can be a risky proposition. It's not as easy as it used to be for performers and fans to know each other personally. Beginning in the early 1970s, the Country Music Association and the Grand Ole Opry began sponsoring the International Country Music Fan Fair in Nashville. For seventy-five dollars admission, fans can meet, attend parties given by their favorite performers, and get autographs from such stars as Garth Brooks, Reba McEntire, Johnny Cash, Charley Pride, Clint Black, Ricky Skaggs, old-timers like me, and a host of others. It's an updated way that country musicians can still pay tribute to their faithful fans. I don't know of any other part of the entertainment industry that says thank you in such a personal way to the people in the audience who pay the bills.

Country Ventures

I'VE NEVER BEEN CONTENT to put all my eggs in one basket. As a country and western musician, I've put money into a lot of music-related ventures, guessing that I'd make a big profit on my investments. Unfortunately, I usually guessed wrong. First, let's go to the movies. . . .

I've had good luck and bad luck in my love affair with the movies. I made a movie one time called *Country-Western Hoedown* that cost me a lot of money. But I'll hold the bad news till later. First, the good news about my movies that somebody else paid for. I believe I was the first Opry performer to make a movie, and I made four of them. The first one was Gene Autry's *Gold Mine in the Sky*, which was released by Republic Pictures on July 4, 1938. After Gene went into the service, I made one Western with Johnny Mack Brown and two with the Durango Kid. They were made so long ago and were so forgettable, I have trouble remembering their names.

I guess like most kids of my generation I was movie-struck. It seemed to me to be a glamorous and easy way to make a good living. Before Gene Autry left Louisville in 1934 for Hollywood, he said to me, "By God, if I make it out there, you're going to be with me. We'll make a movie together." I never wanted to live in California, but I thought it would be fun to go out there from time to time to make a movie. Gene had already been in four or five Westerns, but it wasn't until 1938 that he was ready to star as a singing cowboy in his first big movie. By that time, we were hotter than a pistol at the Grand Ole Opry and were attracting big audiences wherever we played.

On Friday, May 13, 1938, the Golden West Cowboys and I were getting ready to start our road show at the high school auditorium in New Hope, Alabama. It was a few minutes before 8 P.M., and the auditorium was already filled. As usual, we were a little anxious, but on this particular evening we were more nervous than ever. We had been waiting all day for a call from Hollywood telling us whether we had been invited to go to California to appear in Gene's movie, *Gold Mine in the Sky.* Just before we went on stage, the telephone switchboard operator burst into the auditorium out of breath, saying, "Mr. King, Gene-Gene-Gene Autry is waiting to talk with you on the telephone. Can you come back with me now?" I said, "I sure can," and asked the band to cover for me until I got back. Fifteen minutes later I returned and announced to the boys and the audience, "Gene Autry wants us to come to Hollywood and make a movie with him, and he wants us there by Wednesday." The audience went wild. The band was so excited and hyped up, I think we gave the best concert of our career that night. At least, it was the loudest. After the show, we hurried back to Nashville to prepare for our trip to California. By the next evening we were packed and ready to leave right after our 11 P.M. Opry broadcast.

We all went in two cars—Milton Estes, Abner Sims, Curley Rhodes, Texas Daisy, Cowboy Jack, in addition to our little daughter, Marietta, Mr. and Mrs. Frank and me, and Elizabeth Stone, who was the wife of the Opry's general manager. We were packed like sardines. We drove straight through in our four-door Chevys, stopping only to eat and gas up and switch drivers. We passed deserts and mountains, cactus and tumbleweed, and narrowly missed a tornado near Amarillo. It was a very long and hot trip, but we had a form of air-conditioning in one of the cars. There was some sort of container up by the front window on the passenger side that we put ice in, and when we pulled a cord, cool air would blow into the car.

We arrived exhausted but safe and excited in Hollywood at 6:30 on Tuesday morning. We didn't have much time to rest because we had to report to the studio right away. The musical director sketched out the songs we were going to play in the movie. Smiley Burnette came in and said, "I'll answer any questions you have when you come over to my house." I said, "Oh, are we coming over to your house?" He said, "Yes, we'll rehearse the songs for the movie, and we're having

a steak and salad cookout tonight to welcome you. I make the best
Caesar salad in Hollywood." And I believe he did. What a place he
had! I'd never seen a house like that—fifteen closets full of clothes.
Smiley was a great comedian and songwriter and had gone to Hollywood with Gene from Illinois. He and his wife Dallas were wonderful to us. After dinner we rehearsed the songs that he and Gene
had written for the movie.

We were in California for about four weeks, and what a thrill
it was. We had rooms in the Padre Hotel, where Lydia, Marietta,
and Mrs. Frank stayed while the rest of us went out to Big Bear
Mountain to film the exterior shots for the movie. We went out in
studio buses and got settled in cabins, which were our quarters while
we were on location. We spent some time rehearsing and some time
in front of the cameras, but mostly we spent time waiting. We were
able to spend a little time climbing and horseback riding in the mountains.

Like all the cowboy Westerns, *Gold Mine in the Sky* had a simple
plot and a lot of comedy provided by Smiley, who was Gene's comic
sidekick in a lot of his movies. There is a scene where a big limousine comes driving by filled with the crooks who are trying to buy
the ranch. Smiley and the ranch hands are whitewashing a building
and turn around and splash the car with whitewash. The story is
about the good guy, Gene Autry, of course, who is mad at his girl
who has spent all her dad's money and is about to lose the family
ranch. The villain with a mustache is the fellow trying to steal the
ranch, and he's in cahoots with the girl. We were in a lot of the
scenes, but we didn't have much to say because we were usually playing
music. One of the main sets was a dance hall where the cowboys
would visit when they came into town. Gene said, "Play something
simple we can dance to," so we spent most of our screen time backing up Gene for a solo or playing the background music for a dance.

Most of the Golden West Cowboys were very inexperienced
with horses, and we needed to improve our riding skills. It was a
skill that came in handy later when I got my own horse for my shows
back east. One time all of us were mounted on our horses, when
the director, Harry Knight, came over and said, "All right, hold it. I
want Pee Wee's band to dismount and stand over there. You are
being paid to act and make music and not to ride horses. If you get
hurt on the horses, it will cost us money." We said, "We want to

ride the horses." He said, "You want to risk getting hurt and delay-
ing production and costing us money?" We said again, "We want
to ride the horses." So we learned to ride horses, some of us better
than others.

In one scene Abner Sims, a tall, lanky guy from Corydon, Indiana, was mounted, and his horse was following Gene's horse because they were stablemates. Abner wasn't supposed to be in the
scene and started pulling his horse to go in another direction when
the horse reared up and Abner fell off. He jumped up and started
running after his horse, and Mr. Knight hollered out, "Cut! Cut!
Cut!" He turned to Abner and said, "Just what do you think you are
doing?" Abner said, "I was just trying to catch him so I could get
back on." The director said, "I warned you fellows about getting
hurt. It's not your job to get thrown off horses. We got stunt men
to do that." Everybody was laughing at Abner. Mr. Knight said, "Now,
we have to reshoot the whole scene, and Abner, you're going to have
to decide which you're going to be, a musician or a stuntman." Abner
decided he'd better be a musician for the duration of the movie.

Only two horses got hurt, and that was the fault of the cowboy riders. In one place the horses reared back and threw the riders
when they balked at a rattlesnake nest. The horses ran on through
the bushes and got skinned up a bit. We sometimes saw scorpions
fighting each other, but nobody in the cast or crew got snake or
scorpion bit.

Gene wanted to do his own stunts, but he knew what he was
doing. He was an excellent horseman. He did his own riding and
took his own falls and did his own fighting. He loved the fight scenes
and got a big kick out of all the action. Gene did have one accident
while we were shooting the movie. It was part of a fight scene. He
was supposed to jump off his horse onto another guy and they would
tumble down a hill. Mr. Knight wanted the stuntman to take the
fall, but Gene insisted he wanted to do it himself. When he was
jumping out of his stirrups, he got his legs crossed and fell to the
ground on his knees. He had to be taken to the hospital in Hollywood and didn't get back for two days. While he was gone, we shot
around his scenes, which was hard to do, since he was in most of
the movie.

All the guys that worked for Gene just loved him. They worshipped him. Smiley told me that once he was working with Gene on a movie right before Christmas, and the producer decided to stop production for a couple of weeks. It bothered Gene that the actors and crew wouldn't have paychecks just before Christmas, so he turned a piece of his bad luck into their good fortune. Gene got his knees injured in a fight scene and had to spend a week recovering, but he made sure everyone got paid for the time he was laid up. That's the kind of guy he was.

I've always tried to learn from people who know more than I do about things. For example, Smiley had been in a number of movies already and he knew the ropes. He taught me how to make sure I got included in the scenes and wound up on the screen. "Stay close to Gene," he advised me. By George, I was out there in Hollywood to make a movie, and I wanted to make sure my face was on the screen and not on the cutting room floor. Every time I saw a camera come on, I put on my best stage smile and edged toward Gene. While we were shooting the first scene inside the dance hall, Gene walked on the set and saw me standing there with my white cowboy suit on. He said, "Kid, who told you to wear a white suit?" I said, "Nobody. This is all I brought. We came here directly from the Opry, and it's what I wear down there." He said, "I know you wear it on the stage at the Opry, but I'm the only one who wears a white suit in my movies. Now you get on up to the costume wagon and get another suit." I said, "But Gene, that's way up the hill, and I'll never make it back in time to shoot this scene. Anyway, I'll bet they don't have a suit in my size." Gene said, "Okay, we'll figure out something. You go over there to the piano and make believe you're playing." So I went over that way, but I watched where Gene and the leading lady would be coming to, and I shifted toward that spot. It took some fancy footwork and twisting around, but I did it. Later, when I led the band, I got Gene to come over to where we were. I said, "Gene, with all this noise I can't hear you from over there. Come over here so I can hear your cues." That's what he did. And that's why I'm in so many of the scenes in my first movie.

When I was playing with Gene back in Illinois, I was using my sister's accordion, which was pink. Gene took one look at it and said, "You mean you're going to play that?" I said, "Sure, why not? It's the only one I got." The accordion I took to Hollywood, however, was a new thousand-dollar instrument with rhinestones all over it that spelled out my name. In one scene where I'm supposed to be riding on the stagecoach, Smiley said, "Kid, you want to be seen, so we'll put you up there on top next to the driver." The driver was Joe Yourogoin, who was also one of Gene's doubles. As I was climbing up, the director saw me and said, "No, we can't let you get up there. It's too dangerous. You might fall off." I pleaded with him and finally Smiley said, "Oh, once we get him up there, he won't fall off. We can boost him up there, then haul up his accordion and put it in his lap, then strap him to the seat. He'll bounce around, but he won't fall off." So with the help of a young extra named George Montgomery, they hoisted me up and strapped me in with my accordion.

But I wasn't home free yet. Just as I got to the top and had the accordion settled in my lap, Mr. Knight came by and said, "Pee Wee, come down from up there." I said, "I can't, Mr. Knight. I'm strapped in with my accordion." He said, "It's too dangerous. You're bound to fall off. Have you ever ridden on a stagecoach before?" I said, "Well, no sir, but I'm willing to try anything for this movie." He sighed and said, "All right, go ahead and try it. But hang on, especially when the stagecoach turns those curves." I was a little nervous, not because I might fall off but because I thought the stagecoach might tip over. Joe said, "Don't worry, Pee Wee. I've lived and worked with horses all my life. I know how to control them. They know what to expect from me, and I know what to expect from them. I will say, however, that you'll be the first accordion player that ever rode up here next to me in the driver's seat."

The scene went off without a hitch. It comes early in the movie, and there I am on top of the stagecoach as it's coming around a hill, playing "She'll be Coming 'Round the Mountain" on my accordion. Actually, I'm pretending to play the song because, of course, we recorded the actual music for the sound track later in the studio. Afterwards, Mr. Knight said, "Pee Wee, I don't know how the hell you managed it, but you stayed on. You've got nerve." Mr. Frank wiped his brow and said, "I was worried about that accordion. If it had fallen off and broken, you could never have scraped together enough money to buy a new one." What really surprised me was that they let me use my accordion with the sparkling rhinestones.

The girls weren't allowed to wear wristwatches, rings, or any kind of jewelry, and there I am on top of the stagecoach with my rhinestone accordion glittering in the sun. It was a lot of fun, but I'm sure no real westerner ever had an accordion like that.

We had to be up and ready for makeup by five o'clock every morning. Then we'd sit around and wait for our scenes to come up. Sometimes they'd ring the dinner bell and we hadn't done one thing. We'd get off under a tree or tent and talk or play cards. It was our luck to be in the middle of a good card or dice game or in the middle of our dinner when somebody would holler, "Pee Wee King and the Golden West Cowboys, you're needed on the set now." We'd break up our game or gobble down our food and run to the tavern where the cowboys were shooting each other, and Mr. Knight would look over and see us coming and say, "Pee Wee, what in the hell are you doing on the set?" I'd say, "The call girl said for us to come." He'd say, "Well, she's wrong again. Get the hell off the set and go back where you were."

Frankie Marvin, who was Gene's steel guitar player and right-hand man, was also a prankster. One day our cook, a big, heavyset black fellow, called out, "Come and get it." At the same time Frankie came running down to the chow wagon holding up something long and snakelike, hollering, "There's a snake over there by the chuckwagon." The cook lit out running, then saw that Frankie was holding a rubber hose, and said, "Don't you ever do that trick again. If I had stumbled into that hot tub of water over there, I'd be boiled by now." The food was usually good and always plentiful. On location, we generally had sandwiches for lunch, but for dinner we'd have steaks or pork chops or chicken and delicious hot homemade bread. When we filmed at the Republic Studios in Hollywood, we ate at the studio commissary and could pick what we wanted.

Gold Mine in the Sky was Gene's first movie to be shown on Broadway, and it went on to be popular all over the country. When it opened in Nashville at a first-run theater, we played a concert in connection with it. Gene was a smart businessman and knew how to squeeze the most money from a movie. He chose popular bands like ours from large cities to be in his movies, and he named movies after popular songs—such as "Gold Mine in the Sky" and "South of the Border." But his best formula for success was this, as he said:

"Surround yourself with good, talented, hard-working people; and you're bound to be successful." Gene loved to make money, but he loved the work he did to make it.

It took us about fifteen days to shoot the movie, but we were in California for about four weeks. For our entire band Mr. Frank got about $7,500. My share amounted to several hundred, and it seemed like a huge amount back then. Our other compensation was being in California and seeing the sights and meeting some of the movie stars. I met Eddie Cantor, who invited us to appear with Gene on his radio show while we were in Hollywood. I also met Leo Gorcey, who was staying at our hotel while making a movie with the Dead End Kids. One day he and some of the Bowery Boys were in the lobby playing with a hand sweeper when Marietta, who was just starting to walk, toddled over and grabbed hold. Leo said, "Hang on, little girl. We're going to walk up and down, up and down the hall." So Marietta wore herself out holding on and laughing with Leo Gorcey as he pushed the sweeper back and forth. She finally got so tired Lydia had to put her to bed for a nap. After that, we always claimed that Leo Gorcey taught Marietta how to walk.

When we finished the movie, we had time to do some sightseeing— the Rose Bowl, the Brown Derby, the Pacific Ocean. It was all great fun, but I learned that moviemaking was not all glamour. I learned it was a lot of hurry up and wait. It was long hours. It was regimentation. But I was still movie-struck. I got a kick out of knowing that thousands and thousands of people all over the world would see our movie. I left Hollywood knowing, however, that I didn't want to stay in California and make movies my main career. I preferred playing the Grand Ole Opry and doing road shows. Of course, I was always available for another movie offer, should one come along. . . .

Actually three more came along, one with Johnny Mack Brown and two with Charles Starrett, the Durango Kid. In 1945 we made *Flame of the West* with Johnny Mack, which was set in the Old West. Mr. Frank went to Hollywood to try to work out a deal with Gene Autry to appear in a film with Roy Acuff about the Grand Ole Opry. Gene was tied to commitments to Republic and couldn't get loose. He did suggest to Mr. Frank that I might be interested in doing a film at Monogram Studios with Johnny Mack Brown. Mr. Frank arranged the deal and called me. "Be out here in two weeks," he

said. "I'm sending you the script. You'll get feature billing with Johnny
Mack Brown." Becky Barfield and the boys in the band drove out,
and I took a plane. It was right after the war and air traffic was heavy,
so they arrived before I did. I had to change planes twice and was
on standby both times.

Our movie with Gene was set in the present, and we had cars
and telephones. Johnny Mack's Brown's movie was set in the past,
and we played ourselves as members of the Golden West Cowboys.
There were eight of us in the band: Shorty Boyd on fiddle, Redd
Stewart on fiddle, Terry Tichy on guitar, Sticks McDonald on drums,
Gene Stewart on bass, Chuck Wiggins on guitar, Gene Engle on
piano, and I was on accordion. I also had a young lady from Alabama named Becky Barfield, who was Texas Daisy's replacement.
Spade Cooley later hired her from me, and she moved to Hollywood and married one of his guitar players. I even had a little dialogue in the movie, but the only line I can now remember is when
someone says, "Have you got anything you can play?" and I say,
"I've got some humdingers." We were even able to get one of the
songs Mr. Frank and I wrote used in the movie. It was called "You'll
See the Day," and was sung by Lynn Carter, the leading lady. We
got paid an extra hundred dollars for it.

I had not met Johnny Mack before, but I found him to be a
good man. He was from Dothan, Alabama, and was an All-Ameri-
can halfback at the University of Alabama, where he'd played in the
Rose Bowl in 1926. He had made his movie reputation in B Westerns, but in our movie he played a doctor who also knew how to
handle a gun. He looked old and haggard in a business suit, but he
was courteous and kind to me and the band. One day he took me
and the band to a barbecue at the home of Richard Barthelmas, who
lived next door to him. There were a lot of other movie stars there
that we recognized, but I told the boys not to talk to them too much
or call them by name. We just smiled and spoke when they spoke
to us. When you talk too much to people you don't really know,
you sometimes say the wrong things. You can even call people by
the wrong names, and that can be embarrassing. You feel you know
movie stars because you see them so many times on the screen, but
you can get them confused in person. So we just played it safe.

We had a fifty-day contract for the movie, but we only worked about twelve days. Like Gene's movie, it told a simple story of good guys and bad guys and was set mostly in an old-fashioned saloon with call girls upstairs. You can see Lynn Carter going upstairs with the cowboys, but you're never told what they do up there. It was a bit suggestive but a lot tamer than what Dolly Parton did in *Best Little Whorehouse in Texas!*

We made both movies with Charles Starrett in 1952. Just before he died, Mr. Frank had made all the arrangements so that we could make the movies while we were playing the Riverside Rancho in Riverside, California. We worked at Riverside on Tuesdays, Thursdays, and Saturdays, and worked Mondays, Wednesdays, and Fridays on the movies. When we made *Rough, Tough West,* the National Ballroom Association had just selected us as the number one western swing band in the nation, and the boys were up on cloud nine. They had worked hard to make us number one, and now they were excited about making a movie. This one was an ordinary shoot-'em-up cowboy picture and was made at Columbia.

I was moving up the studio pecking order and getting a little more for each movie. I had a few speaking lines in *Rough, Tough West,* and the band played two sets of roles. In the daytime we were the fire department and spent most of the time looking for Smiley Burnette, the fire chief. At night, we were musicians and played in the local dance hall under our real names. Smiley thought up a lot of the funny situations. In one scene the hotel was on fire, and some girls and cowboys were trapped and trying to get out. The weather was hot and dry, and the building burned quickly. Smiley hollered out, "Hurry up firemen, we got to put this fire out before it burns up those people and destroys the whole town!" So we backed up the fire engine to the hotel, pulled out a long hose, and started toward the fire. The director called cut, and we took a lunch break. We'd been doing our part of the scene, so there was no actual fire yet. During the break Smiley and the director agreed that the episode was getting too long and that it could be reduced by shortening the hose and redoing the scene. Well, nobody told us about the change, so we went back to finish up what we started. We were all lined up ready to pull the hose to the fire. I said, "All right boys, let's run like the devil and get this fire out." I assumed that we'd run to the earlier stopping place. We all started running, and suddenly we ran out of hose. It slipped through our arms, and the guys started piling up on one another. We were wearing plastic helmets, but a couple of fellows got cut in the pileup and were taken to the first aid station so their nicks and scratches could be covered with makeup. We finished the scene, and the mix-up was so funny, the director decided to leave it in.

Like Johnny Mack Brown, Starrett had played football in college and had come to Hollywood and made his early reputation playing romantic leads, then switched to cowboy roles in the mid-1930s. He and I hit it off right away. He didn't have to make movies for a living since his father owned the Starrett Tools Company in Massachusetts. The second movie we made with him was called *Riding the Outlaw Trail* and also costarred Smiley Burnette as his sidekick. That was the last movie I made in Hollywood. After Mr. Frank died, I never got invited to do another one. But I must have still been movie-struck because in 1963 I produced my own movie in Kentucky. Now comes the bad news!

In 1963 Bill King, our lawyer Chris Duvall, and I formed the TeleKing Corporation and made a movie called *Country-Western Hoedown*. We couldn't release it until 1967 because it took that long to get all the legal tangles and copyrights cleared up. Even then we couldn't give it away! I thought we had hit on a surefire formula for a popular movie, but boy! was I wrong.

The idea for the movie came from Art Standisch and Jim Sullivan, who had a production company called Jam Art Pictures. Art was a distributor for United Artists, and Jim was a photographer and had a camera shop on Broadway in Louisville. They had made a successful movie about Renfro Valley that had made them some money. So they approached me about making a movie with them. In fact, they hunted me down and talked me into it! I was so gung ho on the project, I wouldn't listen to anybody's advice. Bill King, who was my manager at the time, said, "Now Pee Wee, look at it this way. You don't need this movie. You've got money in this hand that you earn from your TV shows and personal appearances and recordings. You've got your living expenses and a big payroll, but you're making good money and you don't have to worry about finances. So what in the hell do you need with a movie? You're taking money out of this hand and putting it into the other hand, and it's just not worth the risk. You could lose a lot of money." I said, "I know it's a risk, but I believe it's a good investment." Lydia agreed with Bill. Time proved both Lydia and Bill right.

I talked some more with Chris Duvall about the movie, and the more we talked, the more excited I got. It seemed like a surefire hit. Finally, we talked Bill King into going along with us. In the back of my mind were two pieces of advice that Joe Frank and Marty Robbins had given me. Mr. Frank had said years before: "No one makes it alone. You must have help." Marty said, "Pee Wee, why don't you make your own movie?" I said, "When did you make a movie, Marty?" He said, "I wrote a song about it called 'Every Man's Got a Mountain to Climb.'" Well, I put those two pieces of advice together and it seemed to me that I should do it. A lot of people were interested in the project and wanted to help. I also knew that any new venture is risky. I soon learned that it was riskier than I dreamed. I knew that several country music stars had made movies and most of them were flops. Paramount had made a movie called *Country Music Holiday* with Ferlin Husky, Faron Young, Rod Brasfield, and June Carter, which had a pretty good run. Probably the most successful one was *Country Music on Broadway*, which featured every star the producers could fly into New York. I convinced myself that I could build on the successes and would learn from the mistakes.

So we began putting all the parts together—the script, the music, the musicians, the singers, the actors, the director—all the thousands of details that go into a movie. We shot the indoor scenes in a Louisville studio and the outdoor scenes down at Renfro Valley. It was a simple story set in a western hotel where people would come from all over the United States and stay and be entertained by country music stars. We had seven barn dances represented from all over the country, from Chicago and Renfro Valley to Hollywood and Nashville. My secretary, Delores, wrote the script, though we didn't really need one because we made most of it up as we went along.

I depended on my friends to let me use their songs, but I found out too late that they couldn't give me the rights to the songs they wrote. Only the publishers can do that, and I didn't know that until the film was finished. Then we got involved in a slew of lawsuits. As I started adding up how much we would have to pay in permis-

sions and penalties, I almost went out of my skull. I spent a lot of
sleepless nights worrying about it. The actual making of the film
was an exciting time. The low point came right afterwards when I
discovered how much it would cost to settle with everybody.

When we were finally able to release it, the film was dead. We
did the best we could and advertised in all the trade publications,
calling it "The happiest wildest country-western rip-snortin' shing-
dig to come your way, with 33 hit songs, 15 top stars direct from
the stages of 7 national barn dances." We had all the Golden West
Cowboys, plus the Collins Sisters, Bonnie Sloan, Ginger Callahan,
Jack Leonard, Red Murphy, Eller Long, Redd Stewart, and many
others. It was directed by William R. Johnson and filmed in Eastman
Color. It was filled with a riot of songs: "Anytime," "Slow Poke,"
"Petticoat Junction," "San Antonio Rose," "Bonaparte's Retreat,"
"You Belong to Me," "Bimbo," and many more. Our stars were from
barn dances, and we made believe that each act was a guest for a
week, during which they would entertain. We brought the stars to
Louisville all expenses paid, plus their fees, which were usually union
scale. It cost so much money I lost track. Delores would say, "Pee
Wee, you're spending too much on these acts. We're going way over
our budget."

Art Standisch and Jim Sullivan were supposed to promote and
distribute the movie, but they didn't know diddly-squat about it.
We had to distribute it ourselves, and we didn't know what we were
doing. We finally managed to place it with regional distributors in
a few cities like Cincinnati, New Orleans, Washington, and Atlanta.
The film did very well in some theaters, especially at summer drive-
ins. But we didn't make any money. In fact, we took a beating. We
published a souvenir album to sell at theaters where the film was
playing, and it was more popular than the movie. At that time my
office was in the Vaughn Building at Third and Main in downtown
Louisville. I had a chance to buy the building, and with the money
I lost on the movie, I could have!

I tried everything to make the movie turn a profit. I even took
it out to Hollywood and showed it to Gene Autry and his film director. Gene laughed and said, "Pee Wee, with all your experience
and know-how about show business you learned from Joe Frank,
you should have known better." His director said, "Well, you did a

good job considering what you had to work with. But we make movies for a living out here in Hollywood. If you're going to spend this kind of money on a picture, you need to make it with people who know what they're doing. Louisville ain't Hollywood." I said, "Don't worry. I'm never gonna make another movie."

So I learned from my movie experience. I was like the boxer who thinks he's ready for the championship but gets knocked out in the first round and says, "Well, I guess I wasn't quite ready." I was knocked out in the first round, but I did get moviemaking out of my system. Most of my life I can honestly say I would live over without any changes—with this exception. I would never again invest time and money in a movie. No, I don't even have a copy of it. I gave the only copy I had to the Country Music Museum in Nashville. I've tried to find another copy. I wrote to the Washington distributor, but even he didn't have one. He must have thrown them all away. If he had a copy, it would have been in mint condition because he didn't book any of them. I know *Country-Western Hoedown* wasn't a good movie, but today it would be a collector's item if anybody could locate a copy.

Like a lot of Americans, I think I just wanted to strike it rich by investing in something. You know, put down a dollar and get back a hundred. Well, not many investments pay off like that, as I found out. Through the years, I have put money in a variety of ventures, ranging from a leather shop in Louisville to a café in Goodlettsville, Tennessee. In 1945 Mr. Frank and I were having a beer at a little motel and tavern on Highway 31 north of Nashville where we usually stopped on our way home. The owners were looking for a buyer. I said, "Dad, you know this is a pretty nice little place. We could do a little remodeling and fixing up and put a kitchen in the back and sell barbecue, beer, and pretzels. Why don't we try it?" He said, "No, I don't want *us* to try it. I want *you* to try it." So we started right then drawing up plans for parking and renovations. Mr. Frank said, "I've got the perfect name for it—Pee Wee King's Hitchin' Post." That was it. I bought the place, fixed it up, and before long we had a good business, especially on Saturday nights when the country people came to town for the Opry.

A woman named Bessie Carnahan was running the place, but I got a fellow who was doing tent shows with us to take it over. His wife had got pregnant and wanted him to stay home with her. I soon found out it was a mistake. He was skimming off the top. Mrs. Carnahan said, "Pee Wee, you're too trusting of people. That man's not worth the powder to blow him up with." So when he came in that day, I said I didn't need him any longer. I gave him a week's notice and went on a road tour. When I got back, I discovered he'd left and taken half the café with him. Mrs. Carnahan said just before he left she noticed his trailer parked next to the cafe. When she went to the trailer, he told her not to come in; but she could see through the door that it was crammed with pickles and cases of beer and cans of vegetables. He had just about cleaned out the storage room. I said, "That's all right. If that's what it took to get rid of that rubbish, then it's money well spent." I was trying to do him a favor by letting him be manager, and that was the way he repaid me.

I didn't keep the place much longer. It got to be such a chore to supervise when I was on the road that I finally sold it. Within a few weeks, a short in the wiring system burned it all down. I just about broke even because I sold it for what I paid, about $1,500. Of course, that's not counting what I spent to fix it up and what I lost while I was running it. After Mrs. Carnahan took it back over, it could have made a little money, but I had too many friends from the Opry who were down on their luck and needed a free meal. They always knew they could get it from Mrs. Carnahan.

I know that I am sometimes a pushover. One time a fellow I knew from Nashville drove by a service station where I do business in Louisville in his big Cadillac, had it filled up with gas and the oil changed, then said, "Pee Wee King and I are good friends. We are working together tonight, and he'll pay for this." I hadn't given him permission to charge anything to me, but I went ahead and paid the bill anyway.

Maybe I got my poor business judgment honestly from my parents. They always taught me to be frugal with what I had, but they never showed me how to make money. In fact, they were usually showing me by example how to lose money. In the late 1920s a friend of theirs married and went to Canada to work for the railroad. When he came back to Wisconsin to visit, he talked my parents into buying some railroad stock. Dad went whole-hog-wild. He said, "Kid, we'll buy this stock, and when it gets high enough, we'll sell it and buy a couple of lots and build a grocery store and restaurant." In the crash of 1929 he lost it all. We never had any return on that investment. In fact, not even the investment was returned!

I've had some better luck with my stocks, though I've only invested modestly over the years in such stocks as Russell Stover Candy and the Waltham Watch Company. On long road trips I had plenty of time to read, and I'd take the *Wall Street Journal* and pick a few stocks that looked like they had a future. I had a booking agent one time who was also a stock broker, an organist, and a Mormon. He was apparently a better organist and Mormon than a stockbroker and booking agent. Once he booked me at a place in Blackwell, North Dakota, and the night I played there they had the biggest tornado in history. Of course, that wasn't his fault, but he made other bookings and a few stock investments for me that didn't pay off. I decided he ought to give up stockbrokering and booking and go back to church and play the damn organ!

I've never made or lost much money in stocks because I've never dumped much money in them. I bought chemical stocks one time at $34 and they went up to $41, so I sold them and made $5,500 in eight months. That's about my only big success story. Investing in stocks is like gambling, and it's like entertainment. Timing is everything. And if you gamble long enough you're going to lose, whether it's the stock market or a crap game. I'm not a lottery bug either. And I got cured of horses many years ago. I had a jockey friend back in the 1940s named Steve Brooks. We'd meet for an afternoon martini at the Henry Clay Hotel bar in downtown Louisville. He taught me a lot about horses and betting. He said, "Pee Wee, consider this. If you bet on the favorite and he wins, you haven't won anything. If you bet on a longshot and he loses, as he usually does, then you've lost all you bet. It's a no-win situation. Over time, you can make more money in a savings account."

I do love horses, however, and I've always enjoyed going to the Kentucky Derby, where we've had a box every year since 1947. The box is for eight people, and every year part of my family goes on Friday to the Kentucky Oaks and the other part on Saturday for the Derby. We go mainly because it's a social occasion. We do place a few bets. I always get Lydia to do the betting because she has better luck than I do. As my jockey friend said, we've never won any-

thing big. But that's been the story of all my other investments too—
even the successful ones!

Early in my career, I found out that one way to increase my
income was to publish and sell songbooks and sheet music to our
audiences. We would sell them on the road, and people could also
order them through our radio programs. Just about every popular
country and western musician had a souvenir songbook with personal and family pictures. Some of them featured songs by the performers themselves, and some of them were filled with traditional
classics. From the 1930s through the 1950s, hundreds of thousands
of songbooks were hawked by country stars for a quarter or fifty
cents. In 1939 the American Music Company of Portland, Oregon,
published the *Golden West Cowboys' Folio of Songs of the Golden West*.
Most of the songs were traditional westerns like "Old Paint and I,"
"Under the Western Sky," and "I'll Never Be a Saddle Tramp Again."
There were a few songs that could be loosely called country or mountain:
"It's Swingtime in the Valley," "When It's Apple Blossom Time,"
and "I'm Lookin' for the Man Who Sings Those Hill-Billy Songs."
I'm pictured on the cover with my accordion, and inside there is a
picture of Mr. Frank. There is also an untrue promotional blurb:
"During the fall of 1936, Frank toured the western states corraling
the finest cowboy singers and instrumentalists he could find." At
that time I don't think a single one of us had ever seen the west
bank of the Mississippi River.

The American Music Company specialized in western and in
what they called "Hill Country" songs. They published songbooks
by popular folk musicians like the Sons of the Pioneers, Don White
and the Carolina Boys, Al Clauser and His Oklahoma Outlaws, with
titles like *Bob Nolan's Folio of Original Cowboy Classics* and *The Drifting Pioneers Song Folio*. There were a few other publishers who would
issue country and western songs, such as Ralph Peer in New York
and the M.M. Cole Company in Chicago, which published songs
by popular folk musicians like the Carter Family and Jimmie Rodgers.
But most of us country musicians had to publish our own songs.
There were very few country music publishers in the South before
the early 1940s, and practically none in Nashville, even though it
was already becoming the capital of the country music business. It
wasn't really until 1942 when Fred Rose and Roy Acuff started Acuff-

Rose Publications that Nashville began to become a center for country music publishing. Most of their first songs were written by Rose and Acuff, and they sold a lot of music. But it was "The Tennessee Waltz," which they copyrighted and published in 1948, that put them on the map in a big way. Soon they were publishing and protecting songs by many country music composers, including Hank Williams and, later, the Everly Brothers.

In 1943 Mr. Frank started his own publishing company and put out a songbook featuring Pee Wee King and the Golden West Cowboys, which we promoted as "25 Songs for 25¢." Almost all of the songs were written by Mr. Frank and me in collaboration. We sold them during intermission and after the show in school auditoriums and theaters—anywhere we played. Of course, the twenty-five-cent cost included an autograph if the fan wanted one.

In the early 1950s Redd Stewart, Mr. Frank, Charlie Adams, and I formed our own publishing house, which was affiliated with BMI, called Ridgeway Music. I wanted to call it Gateway to honor Louisville as the Gateway City to the South, but there was already a Gateway publisher. So we chose Ridgeway instead because ridges suggest the folk and country music we were intending to publish. We also started another publishing house called Longview, which was connected with ASCAP. That way, we were covered by both licensing agencies that protected and enforced our copyrights. ASCAP was the older company and had guys like Irving Berlin as clients. BMI opened an office in Nashville with Frances Williams Preston at the helm and signed up a lot of country music composers. We worked with both agencies because some composers wanted to be ASCAP songwriters, and some wanted to be licensed by BMI.

We got in the publishing business because we were writing songs like crazy and giving them to Acuff-Rose. We thought we could eliminate the middleman and publish our own songs as well as other composers'. Charlie Adams was running a publishing business for the actor Fred MacMurray, so we wound up buying MacMurray's business and combining it with our own. MacMurray's company published songs from motion pictures. It was a sideline, and he got tired of it. It didn't take me long to get tired of the business too. Before long, I realized it was taking too much of my time, and I wanted to get out. Mr. Frank died right after we started the companies, and Redd

soon sold us his interest. Charlie was supposed to be choosing the
songs we published, but he started taking a lot of junk, and we weren't
making any money. I was beginning to see that I was in too many
enterprises and not overseeing any of them very well.

Steve Sholes, my Victor A & R man said, "Pee Wee, why don't
you forget about being a publisher and stick with what you do best,
being an entertainer?" I could already see that we would never be
able to compete with the Irving Berlins and the Goodman Brothers. I thought about moving the companies to Kentucky, where I
could be close to their operations, but I finally decided that the best
action was to sell them. A fellow who was close to both me and
Gene Autry said to me one day, "Gene is a friend of yours, and I
will be meeting with him on a business deal in a few days. Do you
want me to tell him your publishing company is for sale?" I said,
"It's all right with me, but I don't think Gene will be interested.
Anyway, I've already offered the company to Lawrence Welk." He
said, "Well, don't expect to hear from Welk. He's awfully tight with
money. He won't pay you what the company is worth." So he went
ahead and talked with Gene, and Gene called me on Thanksgiving
night and said, "Why in the hell didn't you ask me to buy your publishing company?" I said, "Well, I didn't think you'd want it." He
said, "What does it say on my stationery letterhead? 'Gene Autry
Music Group.'" Gene went ahead and made a deal with Charlie and
bought both of our companies, Ridgeway and Longview, and both
the BMI and ASCAP song rights. He got the rights to our entire
catalog of 470 songs, including "You Belong to Me" and "Slowpoke."
Gene started a new record company called Republic Records and
hired Charlie to run his recording studio until Charlie's death in
1982. Charlie had made a mess of our companies because he couldn't
say no to people. When he went to work for Gene, he became Gene's
yes man, but that's what Gene wanted. So that's the story of my
adventure in music publishing.

One of my most successful ventures was King's Record Shop,
a business that disproves the old saying that you should never go
into business with a member of your own family. My partner was
my brother Gene. He was my kid brother and still living with my
parents on the farm when I left Wisconsin to come south. Gene
hated the farm, and he hated school. When he was still in his teens,

he joined the army and became an MP, but he didn't care much for army life either. When he was discharged, he came to Louisville to visit Lydia and me, and I said, "Well, Gene, what are you going to do now?" He said he had no definite plans, but he'd probably go to Milwaukee and look for a job. I said, "Why don't you stay here and work for me? We can put another chair and desk in my office and you can work with my secretary Delores."

After a couple of weeks in the office, he said, "You don't need me in the office. Delores has got everything under control. I'd rather go on the road as your road manager." So that's what he did for a year or so. He would go to a town where we were going to do a show a day or two early and distribute flyers and check on the stage and other arrangements and make sure the radio stations got our records to play. Soon he met a girl from Bowling Green, Kentucky, and a couple of weeks later they got married. Then, as so often happens, she began to complain about him being gone so much.

Then Dame Fortune came our way. Pat Patton, who had an orchestra and played at nightclubs on Seventh Street Road in Louisville's South End, asked me to play in his band at Stone's Dance Hall over at Georgetown, Kentucky. While we were en route to the dance, Pat suddenly said, "Pee Wee, I've got a deal for you. My mother has a little record shop downtown on Jefferson Street that I bought a couple of years ago to keep her busy. She was wilting and going downhill at home, so I put her in the shop peddling records." Pat was also working with Southern Distributing Company in Louisville and helped distribute records in their territory. He furnished record shops and loaded jukeboxes. "But just a few days ago," he said, "she slipped on the ice and broke her hip and can't work in the shop. I had to close it, and it's costing me money. Mother will never be able to stand on her feet and take over the shop again, so I need to sell it. How would you like to own a record shop?" I said, "No. . . . Well, how much do you want for it?" He said, "Right now, I'd take $1,700 for everything—the shelving, the cash register, the inventory, the whole shebang." I said, "I don't know for sure, but let me think about it. I have an idea. Don't sell it until you hear from me."

The next day I went to see Gene. I said, "Your wife doesn't like for you to be away from home so much. You like the music business. Well, I think I've got something in music that you can do here in Louisville. I can fix you up with a record shop." He liked the idea, talked it over with his wife, and I bought the shop. When we took over in 1960, the shop had an inventory of only six hundred LPs and singles. I quickly loaded him up with hundreds of new albums, mostly country but a lot of pop too, and taught him how to read *Billboard* and other trade publications. When he started out, he thought Shapiro-Bernstein, one of the biggest music publishers in the country at the time, was a fish market in Brooklyn. Soon I sold him my interest in the business. He loved it so much he would often stay open until nine at night. No one could ask him for a record that he couldn't find somewhere, and he soon developed an international clientele. He decorated the shop with autographed photos of country stars like George Jones, Waylon Jennings, Dolly Parton, and Randy Travis.

His big break came in 1987, when Rosanne Cash used a photograph of the shop for a new album of her songs and called it "King's Record Shop," a collection of honky-tonk songs. Her husband at the time, Rodney Crowell, happened to see a photo of the shop in Nashville that one of his band members had taken, and he came up to look it over for a cover idea. He walked around the shop and came inside and said, "Gene, your shop front would make a good album cover for Rosanne's new song collection. It's a perfect building for a record shop in a honky-tonk part of town." Gene said, "That sounds good to me. Do whatever you want." So Rosanne came up here from Nashville and posed in front of the shop, which became famous all over the world. Gene did an autograph party for Rosanne at the shop, and he began to ship the album and T-shirts everywhere. Rosanne Cash fans came and posed for snapshots leaning against the store's doorway like she did on the album cover. For about two years he did the best business of his career. He didn't get rich, but he made enough money with the shop to live comfortably and raise four daughters. More important, he spent more than thirty years in a business he enjoyed—and was still enjoying when he died in January of 1993. Gene's record shop was one of the best investments I ever made.

Joe L. Frank and Other Country Gentlemen

I HAVE TRIED TO THANK Mr. Joe Frank on every page of these memories, but now I want to be more direct. Meeting him made everything good happen to me. From him I got the two best things in my life, my career and my wife. He had a more natural right to being in country music than I did. He was born in 1900 on the Alabama-Tennessee border at a little place called Sand Springs, near Ardmore, Alabama, and raised on a cotton farm. One time I went down to his home community and met several of his relatives, and I could tell that he was from a very poor family. The land looked so poor you couldn't raise a potato on it.

When he was a young man, he left home and went to Birmingham to work in the steel mills. After working there for several years, he somehow made it to Chicago and worked as a bellhop in the Edgewater Beach Hotel. That's where he met Lydia's mother, a widow with five children, who later became Mrs. Frank. She was a private investigator for several Chicago department stores, and it was through her that he got into the music business. He didn't know anything about music and had never played an instrument. But a lot of her friends were performers, and she introduced him to local radio personalities like Fibber McGee and Molly, and Mike and Herman. It

211

was through her contacts that Mr. Frank got to know the show people that he began to book around Chicago. Most of the movie theaters in the 1920s had live entertainment like music and vaudeville acts, and that's where he booked most of his clients.

After a while, he started booking acts for the "National Barn Dance" on WLS. That's when he met Gene Autry, who had come to WLS for an audition. Gene was already a radio and recording star, but he didn't have a manager. He and Mr. Frank liked each other, and Mr. Frank became Gene's manager and booking agent from about 1932 until he left WHAS in Louisville to go to Hollywood in 1934. Gene had already formed his image as a singing cowboy, but Mr. Frank helped him refine and polish it for the movies that Gene wanted to make. Gene asked Mr. Frank to go with him to Hollywood, but he said, "Gene, I don't see how I can help you out there. You already know what you want and how to get it. I'll just stay in Louisville and get Freddie and Frankie to take your place." They were the Log Cabin Boys and had been performing in Chicago.

The history of country music can be told with the last twenty or so years of Mr. Frank's life, from about 1930 to his death in 1952. He professionalized county music. He took the hick out of hillbilly music. He took country stars out of schoolhouses and honky-tonks and put them in big city auditoriums and concert halls and vaudeville theaters. He managed many of the legends of county music, including Eddy Arnold, Minnie Pearl, Roy Acuff, Ernest Tubb, Cowboy Copus, Grandpa Jones, and Archie Campbell. He took performers when they were young and raw, and groomed and shaped them for the big time. He placed acts on the biggest barn dances and country shows. He was a man of honor who knew the art of the deal. He was the Billy Rose of country music who believed in quality work. "Things done by half," he said, "are never done right." His motto at J.L. Frank Attractions was "J.L. Frank Attractions Don't Cost—They Pay!"

Indeed, the story of my career—and that of many others—could not be written accurately without mentioning Joe Frank on every page. And when we lost him in 1952, it was almost my death blow as well. It was in early May, around Derbytime, and he was in Detroit arranging a booking for me and the Golden West Cowboys at the Orpheum Theatre, where Eddy Arnold and Louis Armstrong had just played. He was staying at the Wolverine Hotel with an act from Nashville, Dot and Smokey. He called me on Derby Eve and said, "Well kid, you've got the booking at the Orpheum. I'm sorry I can't be there in Louisville with you for the Derby, but I know you all will have tickets near the finish line, and I'll be watching on television to see you and Lydia."

The next day he and Dot and Smokey were up in his room watching the race and trying to see us on the screen. Finally, he said, "Well, I don't see Pee Wee and Lydia anywhere, and he's supposed to be there." Smokey told me later that he kept looking for us. Indeed, we were there in our usual box until all the races were over. We got home about eight o'clock that night. We had a big party, with the jukebox blaring here in this basement and the people eating and drinking and dancing and having a great time. Finally, everyone went home, and Lydia and I went to bed.

Early the next morning, while we were still in bed, the phone rang and a voice said, "Is this Pee Wee King?" I said, "Yes, it is." He said, "I'm sorry to have to inform you that your father-in-law has just died." I said, "Who in the hell is this? Is this some bad joke?" He said, "I'm the manager of the Wolverine Hotel where he was staying." I was still sure it was a gag. I thought maybe one of the people with Mr. Frank had too much to drink and decided to pull a practical joke. So I hung up. Lydia said, "Who was that?" I said, "Oh nobody. Just some dope." She said, "What did he want?" I began stammering because I didn't want to repeat what he said. Then the phone rang again and the same voice said, "If you're Pee Wee King, you should know that your father-in-law has just died. You have to come up here and make arrangements." Lydia was close to the phone and said, "Oh Pee Wee, I heard what he said. I heard." I went over to hug her and we both broke down. Now we knew it was no gag.

I had to call Mrs. Frank at her home in Nashville, and that I dreaded more than anything I'd ever done. I first called my pilot, Art Greenamyer, who said, "Come on, Pee Wee. I'll fly you up." Then I called Mrs. Frank and made arrangements to meet her in Evansville, Indiana. Later that morning we took off, picked her up, and flew on up to Detroit. It was the saddest trip I've ever made.

When we arrived we went to the hotel and saw the room where he had died. As we walked into the room, Lydia noticed a window slowly closing by itself. She turned to me and said, "I feel like Dad has just told us goodbye." From there we went to the morgue, and the coroner showed us the body. He asked Mrs. Frank, "Is that your husband?" She said, "Yes, it is," and began to cry. Soon we were all crying.

Mr. Frank's sudden death was a great shock for everyone who knew and loved him—his family, his friends, the performers whose careers he had boosted, the fans whose lives he had enriched behind the scenes. At the funeral in Nashville, Roy, Eddy, and I stood by the casket. I put my hand on it and said, "Dad, nobody will ever take your place." Then I said from the bottom of my heart, "But right now, if I could, I would." It was almost more than I could bear. Eddy said, "Pee Wee, why don't you stay home a few days and let me take your place in Detroit with the Golden West Cowboys. We can put some spots on the radio announcing the change. I can do a couple of numbers, then the band can do the main show, and I can close it out." I said, "Eddy, you were just up there, and I can't let you do it. No, I'll pull myself together and go. If Mr. Frank were standing here, he'd say, 'Let the show go on.'" Eddy said, "Well, all right. But I could have announced that I was brought back so soon by popular demand. That would look good on my résumé." Somehow that tickled our funny bone, and there we were—Eddy Arnold, Roy Acuff, and Pee Wee King—three men to whom Mr. Frank had meant so much, laughing our heads off right beside Mr. Frank's casket in the Nashville funeral home. Roy said, "Such damn silly asses. We shouldn't be here laughing." But somehow we knew that Mr. Frank would understand and say well done.

The more I thought about Mr. Frank's death the more questions I raised in my mind. The coroner said he died of a heart attack, but he had no history of heart disease. He did have emphysema, and he coughed all the time. It's possible he choked to death. I had an argument with the insurance company about that. Dot and Smokey told me he ordered a steak sandwich and a six-pack brought up to his room about 2 A.M., and he asked them to join him. They said they weren't hungry and left him in his room in good spirits. Smokey said, "He looked tired, and we wanted to let him eat and go on to bed because he had to be up early the next morning. I wished to God we had stayed until he ate his sandwich." I said, "Smokey, I wish to God you had too." But they didn't, and he died. My theory is that he was eating his sandwich when a piece of it got lodged in his throat. We found evidence in the wastebasket that he had thrown up some of the food he had eaten. That's what I told the insurance company, but they wouldn't pay off for accidental death. Lydia believes he had an allergy reaction to a penicillin shot for a strep throat and cough, but his death was officially listed as a massive heart attack. I'm still not convinced.

Mr. Frank's death was not only a terrible personal loss but a huge loss to country music. Although he had accomplished a lot in the country music business, in many ways he was at the height of his career. He was preparing a number of performers for stardom. His years of experiences had taught him how to make the right contacts and book the right places for his clients. He knew what audiences wanted and how they would turn out for an act. In 1945, for example, he booked the Golden West Cowboys in the Kiel Auditorium in St. Louis. That auditorium has two sections, one with a capacity of three thousand and the other with a capacity of five thousand. Mr. Frank told the manager he wanted to book both sections. The manager said, "Are you sure you can fill all those seats? We don't fill that many seats with some of the biggest shows that come to St. Louis." Mr. Frank said, "I'm going to pay the rent on both sections. You wait and see." People were lining up for our three o'clock show at noon. The manager said, "Joe, you son of a gun. I never would have believed it. I've never seen people line up for a show this early. You've made a believer out of me." The manager became a true believer when all the seats were filled. That's what made Mr. Frank so successful. He knew what the people wanted. He gave it to them. And he got them to come see it.

Soon after his death I began to work hard to get him inducted into the Country Music Hall of Fame. In 1967, some fifteen years later, Mr. J.L. Frank became the first nonperformer to be so honored. On his plaque in the Hall of Fame he is called "a pioneer promoter of country and western shows," an "unselfish, compassionate man" who helped "develop the careers of Roy Acuff, Gene Autry, Eddy Arnold, Pee Wee King, Minnie Pearl, Ernest Tubb and many more." It was an honor he so much deserved, but it was no easy task. You can't buy your niche in the Hall of Fame, and election is the result of a lot of influence and politicking. It's like the Academy Awards in Hollywood. You've got to politick to get nominated and you've got to politick to get elected. No man was prouder of Mr. Frank's election than I was.

His placement in the Hall of Fame was not only a tribute to him but to all the other managers and booking agents, those hard-working, unseen men and women who put the "business" and pro-fessionalism in the country music business. Mr. Frank was the best of them all. But there were—and are—many other fine examples around the country. Nobody sings their praises, but it deserves to be shouted from the housetops. Old-timers like Hap Peebles and Ward Beam got us work and made it possible for us to make a liv-ing. It was Lucky Moeller who put together a package show for Minnie Pearl and me after she got hot on *Hee Haw*. I have been blessed with having the best agents in the business. I found out how impor-tant they are when for a couple of years after Mr. Frank's death I tried to be my own manager and almost worked myself to death. Then in 1954 I was lucky to get William H. King. Earlier, he had worked out of Hollywood and was booking people like Rex Allen, Tennessee Ernie Ford, and Judy Canova. Soon after he returned to Kentucky, he began to manage me and continued for twenty years. At that time I had four television shows and numerous road shows and needed someone to take care of my bookings and paperwork. Next to Mr. Frank, he was the best.

One of the most legendary of all managers and booking agents is Colonel Tom Parker. A performer who finds someone like him is exceptionally fortunate, and he'd better cling to him. A Colonel Parker is the man who represents you better than you could represent yourself. He worries about you and makes sure you get the best deals, whether you're making public appearances or doing radio and TV shows or making recordings and movies. When Colonel Parker took Eddy Arnold over, Eddy was all he worried about. When he took over Elvis, Elvis was his main concern. When he represented me and the Golden West Cowboys, he did his best for us.

I knew Colonel Parker before he was a "colonel" and before he handled Elvis. He was just plain Tom Parker. Mr. Frank hired him down in Florida, when he lived near Tampa and headed a humane society. He had dozens of animals at his little place—cats, dogs, cows, deer, and other animals that were abandoned or hurt or sick. It was in 1945, and I was still living in Nashville. Mr. Frank was down in Florida and met Parker. He called me and said, "I'm setting you up to play theaters down here for about three weeks. It's going to be a bicycle arrangement, where you'll play two theaters the same evening and run back and forth between the two, with a movie in between." I said, "That sounds fine. Who's handling the local arrangements?" Mr. Frank said, "Tom Parker." I said, "Who's he?" He said, "He's a guy I just hired. I like his style and we're going to start booking together." So we went down to Tampa, and the first date we had was in a hotel for a show and a dance, and the house was packed. Mr. Frank said, "See? Tom Parker has potential." Indeed, he did, especially after he started handling Elvis a few years later. That was a match made in heaven.

When Parker was working with us, he was a jolly good fellow. He would play cards and shoot dice with us in our spare time backstage. He talked with a kind of foreign sound or maybe a lisp, and he always had a hundred-dollar bill in his wallet. He said, "Now, don't tell nobody about that hundred dollars. I don't want nobody to know I got it. That's my secret kitty and I'll spend it when I need to." We called it his hidden bank, but one night I saw him lose it. It was in Norfolk, Virginia, where we'd gone to dedicate a new USO auditorium. The mayor and other dignitaries were there, and I introduced them; then we did half of our show and went backstage for the intermission. There were six or seven of us, and while we were waiting, we all started shooting dice and got carried away.

Tom said, "There's about a hundred dollars in the pot, and I'll tell you what I'm gonna do. Let me roll the dice and I'll cover all of it if you let it stay in the pot. I feel lucky tonight." We all looked at each other and said, "Well, why not? He wants to get his feet wet, so we'll just let him jump in the river." We gave him the dice, and he started shaking them in his hand and talking to them: "Honey, hear me now. Roll out 7 or 11, but don't give me no snake eyes." Then he hauled back and threw them on the floor and he got a deuce—snake eyes—and lost his hundred-dollar bill. In one roll of the dice he had lost his secret kitty, his hidden bank, but I'll bet it didn't take him long to replace it.

Colonel Parker wasn't the only performer I've known to carry hidden money for emergencies. I once had a fiddle player who always carried a five-dollar bill in his boots. When I started out, I'd put a twenty-dollar bill in my cowboy slippers. I knew that if I got stuck somewhere, I would at least have enough money to get me a place to stay and something to eat.

But to get back to the prince of managers. With Mr. Frank managing us, I never had to worry about getting stranded anywhere without money. He was the best of the best. One time during a lean, dry period, I was working a theater up in Pennsylvania with my trick horse, Boots. Mr. Frank sized up the situation and said, "Now Pee Wee, you're going to have to put rubber boots on your horse to work that stage. If it works out and you do a good job, I can line up a dozen or more theaters on the Schine Circuit for the same show." The horse and I did a good show. The audience loved it. The rubber boots protected the stage. Suddenly we were on easy street again. After the show the theater manager came to me and said, "What a great show! Mr. Frank is the best booking agent I've ever worked with. He's a jewel. He's amazing. Here's this hillbilly from Alabama, and he's managed people like Fibber McGee and Molly, the Hoosier Hot Shots, Gene Autry, Ernest Tubb, Roy Acuff, and you. That man is sharp as a pencil. Hell, he's sharp as two pencils. What do you think of your father-in-law and manager?" I said, "He's the greatest guy in the world."

Yes, I admired him so much. I envied his knowledge of show business. I respected his tact and ability to work with people. I revered his honesty. He never cheated anybody. He wasn't greedy. All he wanted was enough to feed and take care of his family and provide them with a few comforts. I've tried to live the model he set.

The Country Hearth

I COULD NOT HAVE HAD MY CAREER without Joe Frank's stepdaughter, Lydia, who became my wife on December 23, 1936. Since then, she has been my wife, the mother of our four children, my friend, my partner, and my biggest booster. She was in show business long before I met her, and she knew what it meant to marry a professional musician. She knew of the strains on relationships and how hard it is for marriages to last. Show business is unstable, and so are the marriages of show business people. If the guy doesn't make it, the marriage is in trouble. If he does make it, he succeeds during long absences from home; and that puts a marriage in jeopardy. If the entertainer is the wife, the stress may be even greater. Small wonder, especially during our unsettled times, that so many country music marriages don't last. You don't find many that last as long as mine and Lydia's.

When we were first married, Lydia traveled with our band, even after our daughter, Marietta, was born. As the family grew, she decided to stay at home and devote all her time to them. I was away on the road when the first two were born, but I happened to be between tours when Lydia went to the hospital for the third time. When the nurse came out of the delivery room and told me I was the father of twin sons, I said, "Well, I'll be damned," and passed out.

Lydia is very talented and could have made a good career in

music. She has a perfect ear and can sing any part harmony you give her. For a while, when her sister Marie visited us from Chicago, we would try to reunite them under their old stage names as the Sunshine Girls or the Little Hoosier Maids. But they wouldn't do it. Sometimes they'd do a little show for the family, and they sounded as good as when they were performing professionally. I even persuaded them to sing on my Opry show once. But if she ever regretted giving up her career, she never said so. She loved her kids. They were a lot more important to her than show business.

I think Lydia modeled herself after her mother, who supported her husband in his career. Mrs. Frank raised her family and took an interest in the people he was managing, whether it was Gene Autry or Fibber McGee and Molly. She was always ready to help any way she could. Once when Gene was about to go on stage and discovered his trousers were too big for him, she cut them down on the spot. Like Lydia, she was never starstruck. They both enjoyed knowing famous and talented people, but they were never as much in awe of them as I was.

Lydia has done an outstanding job with our children—Marietta, Frankie, Jr., and the twins, Gene and Larry. She made sure they had a stable home life and went to school and church. Lydia was a German Lutheran, and I converted to her church after I married her. We're old-time members of St. John Lutheran Church in Louisville, and all our children were baptized and raised in the church.

After the children were grown and married, Lydia started traveling again with me. We still keep in close touch with all the children and grandchildren. We're proud of all of them. None of the children chose a career in show business. I think Lydia was glad, though she never said so. All she said was, "One star in the family is enough." She never tried to lead them toward or away from any career. "Do what you want to do," she'd say. "Do it right, and you'll make a good living and enjoy it." All our children could have gone into entertainment if they'd wanted to because they all took lessons in music and the arts. Gene studied the trumpet, Larry the piano, Frank the accordion, and Marietta dance. None of them chose show business, but they're all doing what they want to do and doing well at it.

Unlike some show business parents, I never tried to influence my children to follow in my footsteps. Justin Tubb used to come over to our house to see Marietta, and he said to me one time that his dad was pressuring him to take up a music career. As it happened, Justin did go into show business and made a success of it. There are a few others who followed successfully in their fathers' or mothers' musical footsteps—Johnny Cash's daughter Rosanne and the sons of Marty Robbins, Faron Young, and Hank Williams. But even they are still in their parents' shadow.

All Lydia and I have ever wanted for our children is for them to be healthy and happy. It has pleased us to see them start families of their own, even when they get a late start like Harriet and Frankie. They were married for twenty-one years and desperately wanted children but couldn't have them. Doctors couldn't do anything to help. Then when he was forty-six and she was forty-four, it happened. She called me one day and said breathlessly, "Pee Wee, you won't believe it, but I'm going to have a baby." When the baby was about to be born, all the family gathered in her hospital room as excited and expectant as the mother. Afterwards, we were kidding her about having a baby so late in life. Suddenly, I went over to the dresser and picked up a towel and wrapped it around my head. She said, "Grandpa, what are you doing?" I said, "The last time a miracle like this happened there were Three Wise Men that came from the East, and I'm going to make sure I get to the manger on time."

As you can see, we have a close family. At my seventy-eighth birthday party about two years ago, we had twenty-eight members of the family present. It started at 5:30 in the evening and lasted until 1:00 the next morning. All of my family was here except for my son and his family in Michigan—and they called during the party. My three children that live in Louisville were here. Our four children so far have given us six grandchildren and five great-grandchildren. I'm so very proud of all of them.

One of my granddaughters came over recently with a little friend, and they brought some submarine sandwiches to eat with Lydia and me. Lydia made some iced tea, and we sat around the table and talked. She told me about her new job at the Outback Restaurant that she loves. She asked me if I'd ever eaten a submarine sandwich before. I said, "Jackie, when I was a boy of about fifteen, one of my best friends was an Italian boy named Angelo Giardino. He'd come by my house and eat Polish sausage, and I'd go by his house and eat

Italian sausage. We'd make them into a long sandwich that we called hero sandwiches. They looked very much like your subs. Yes, we were doing things sixty-five years ago that you are just now discovering." She smiled and said, "You did?" Moments like that connect the generations of my family.

Of course, my little grandchildren are growing up in a world very different from mine. They can use computers by the age of six, and I don't even know how to turn one on. I can't even operate a photocopier. None of my grandchildren so far seem inclined toward show business either, though I have a grandson who likes to pound on the piano. Who knows? Maybe we have a Floyd Cramer in the making!

Lydia and I have had our ups and downs, but we've never had a problem we couldn't solve by ourselves. My dad used to say to me, "Frankie, don't you ever strike your wife. If you do, your arm will fall off." I said, "Pop, how do you know?" He said, "Just don't ever try to see. It'll be too late then." Neither of us ever tested his rule. He never hit my mother, and I've never hit Lydia. Lydia and I have never been to a marriage counselor. She's never left me, and I've never left her. That's another rule I was taught, and I believe it still: When you're married, you're married for life.

I'm getting to be an old man now, and I'm not as active as I used to be. I've had to slow down a lot since my stroke in 1978. It was a wake-up call for me, and I heard it. Redd Stewart and the Collins Sisters and I left Louisville on July 1 early in the morning in my station wagon to go to Indianapolis to do a show at Bobby Helms Music Park. Bobby was a popular rock 'n' roll singer, and had hired us to do a nostalgia 1940s show for a four-day run. Ernest Tubb and Jeanne Pruett were also scheduled to be on the show. It was misting when we got to Indianapolis. As I was checking into the Holiday Inn, I noticed something peculiar. I tried to sign the register and couldn't hold the pen. I started scrawling in big letters, and they got smaller and smaller. I said, "I think something is wrong." The clerk said, "Can I do anything for you, Mr. King?" I said, "I don't know what's going on. I'm feeling funny." He said, "Sit down. It'll probably pass. Do you want someone to take you to your room?" I said, "No, I don't have time. We've got to get out to Bobby Helms park for a matinee show." He said, "You'd better hurry or you'll get wet. A heavy rain is moving in."

We rushed on out to the park, and by the time we got there, we were in the middle of a rainstorm. I went to my dressing room in a trailer, and Bobby came by and said, "I was going to open with Jeanne Pruett and her new hit, 'Satin Sheets and Satin Pillows,' followed by Ernest Tubb, but neither one of them is here yet. So it looks like you'll have to open and emcee the show." I said, "No problem," and went out, introduced Redd and the others. Then I said, "Now I'll do 'Deck of Cards,'" which was my popular recitation number. I leaned over to pick up my accordion and couldn't lift it. Then my mind went fuzzy. I turned to Redd and said, "You'd better take over. I'm not feeling good." I stumbled down the stage steps like a drunk and bumped into a tree.

About that time Ernest Tubb's bus pulled up right in front of me, and Ernest jumped out and said, "Pee Wee, what's wrong? Let's get you out of this rain. Come on in my bus and sit down in the driver's chair." I said, "I don't feel too good, but I think I can make it to my dressing room. It's up at the end of the row." Somehow I staggered on up to my trailer and got inside. That's the last I remember until after the show, when Redd roused me and said, "Pee Wee, I think you've had a stroke, and we're taking you back to Louisville right now." I said, "What are we going to do about the other three days we're supposed to work?" He said, "Don't worry. We'll take care of it. Let's go to the car and get your home."

When we got to Louisville, Lydia put me to bed and called Dr. Mier Bizer, my doctor who lives across the street. He came over, examined me quickly, and said, "Pee Wee, we've got to get you to a hospital immediately." At the hospital they made all kinds of tests and found a little plaque about the size of a pencil point that had broken loose and lodged close to my brain. The doctor put me on medication and said he thought it would dissolve itself in a few days. I arranged to have Redd and Johnny Russell play some dates for me in New England, and I stayed in the hospital for observation for about ten days. I was champing at the bit, wanting to go home, but the doctors wanted to do more tests and have me close in case of emergency.

Finally, they let me come home to recuperate. I felt like I'd been freed from prison. Just before Labor Day one of my booking agents called and said, "Pee Wee, remember you've got a date to play a furniture convention at the Chicago Convention Center." I said, "Okay, I think I can make it. I've been recovering from a stroke." He said, "You what? You've had a stroke?" I said, "Yes, but I didn't die and wasn't paralyzed. I'm sure I can come." I called Dr. Bizer, and he said I could go up if someone drove me and if I limited my performance to five or ten minutes. I was booked to do two shows, so I did ten minutes for each show. Everything went fine. When I returned home, I checked in with my doctor and said, "See, I got by easy. I did ten minutes. I talked and told a couple of jokes. I didn't even lift my accordion. The first show was a piece of cake, though I did have to scramble a little for the second one." He said, "Second one? What do you mean? You did two shows? You dog! You lied to me!"

I knew I was taking a slight risk to push myself that much, but I'd only had a mild stroke—nothing like the one that cost Minnie Pearl her speech and physical coordination and put her in a wheelchair. Just recently, in June 1994, I had another mild stroke, but I'm doing all right now. I have angina, which I take as a warning to slow down. The tightness in my chest is similar to a heart attack, but I can control it pretty well with the nitrate pills. I take them when I get overexcited or overworked and overtired. Then I say, "Okay, Pee Wee. Take it easy. Go slow to wherever you're going— or you won't get there at all."

I've had to change the way I live my life. I don't rush and strain myself any more. Used to, when we'd finish a road show at, say, ten o'clock on a summer evening, I'd say, "Well boys, it's still early. You'll get an extra ten dollars if we drive straight home now. We can save that hotel bill and get home early too." When I had my first stroke I weighed about 170, and for me that's too much. I now keep my weight down to about 140. I don't eat much except on big occasions like Christmas or Easter or family dinners. I do very few public appearances, restricting myself to reunions and big events at the Opry. Lydia and I did drive down to Gene Autry, Oklahoma, to help celebrate Gene's eighty-seventh birthday on September 29, 1994, for the annual festival there. Lydia does most of the driving now on our trips. Bless her soul! I don't know what I'd do without her. She looks after me at home and away. She's in pretty good health, thank God! She's got some hypertension and high blood pressure, but she's controlling it with diet and pills.

That stroke really scared me. I didn't feel that I was going to die, but I didn't know what to expect. I knew that strokes sometimes come with old age, but it was new territory for me, and I didn't know what it meant. For a while I tried to joke it away. An old golf partner would say, "Pee Wee, I hear you've given up golf. Play me, and I'll give you three strokes aside." I'd say, "Thanks, but I've had one already." I feel lucky to still be here. I'm not afraid to die when my time comes. I just don't won't to rush it.

On the farm in Wisconsin we learned about death in a natural way. We saw animals being born and some of them slaughtered and some of them dying a natural death. Death was not hidden from us, whether it was an animal or a loved one. Of course, nothing can prepare you for the death of a loved one. Mom died in 1967 and Pop passed away about five years later. We were expecting Pop to die, but Mom's death was unexpected and shocking. She died on their farm, which was close to my Uncle Tony's farm near Abrams. Late in the summer of 1967 Uncle Tony asked Pop if he could put six of his heifers in Pop's pasture at the back end of his farm. Pop said, "Sure, go ahead and move them on across the river." The Pensaukee River ran through their farm and close by their house and eventually emptied into Green Bay. So Pop and Uncle Tony moved the heifers across the river and into the pasture. In the summer the river normally got down to about knee-deep, but they had a very wet season that year. For about six weeks the rain poured down in torrents, and the river was very deep, well over a man's head.

Soon after they moved the cows, Mom said, "John, in the butcher shop this morning in town, I heard talk of cattle rustlers being back in here." The area where they lived was like a big game preserve and had wolves and deer and other kinds of animals in the woods. It was remote and hard to get to—just the place where rustlers might strike. Pop said, "Well, Helen, what do you want me to do about it?" Mom said, "I think we should check on Tony's heifers. Go get the tractor, and let's ride over in the back pasture and see what's going on. I'm a little worried because I can't hear Bessie's bell. They could be dead, and the rustlers could be skinning them for their hides." Pop said, "Helen, you're crazy. The cows are all right. Anyway, that river's too deep to cross now." But Mom kept nagging him until finally he agreed to try.

Mom put on Pop's raincoat and the hip boots he went fishing in, got on the tractor with him, and they started out. Pop remembered a crossing that was usually shallow, so they forded the swollen river without any trouble, except for one thing. The tractor hit a large rock, so Mom said, "Now coming back, move over about six inches and you won't hit that rock again." They went on and found the cows safe and sound. Mom hadn't been able to hear Bessie's bell because it had come off. They started back home and got into the river crossing about the time a big wave came along. It threw Pop off balance and he hit the same rock, only harder, and it knocked Mom off backwards into the river. Pop didn't know she was gone until it was too late. When he saw her floundering and being dragged downriver, he jumped off the tractor into the water. He was too late to reach her. He pulled himself up on the riverbank and ran down the river to where it curved at Uncle Tony's. He got there just as her body was floating by. He and a neighbor who had heard his shouts managed to reach in and pull her out. They gave her artificial respiration, but it was too late. She was already gone. There was nothing more to do. She was dead at seventy-one. Pop walked back to the house alone. He never went back to that damn tractor. He left it standing in the water, and Uncle Walter, who lived nearby, finally moved it.

Pop died five years later at eighty-one. He was lonely after Mom's death, and I think he grieved to the point he didn't care whether he lived or not. He fell off from 197 pounds to 110. He couldn't bear to live in their old house, so he moved to Milwaukee to live with my sister Irene. Another factor in his death was diabetes, but I believe he could have lived longer except for his religious convictions. We were all born Catholics, and in Milwaukee we went as a family to St. Cyril's Church. When they moved to Abrams, there wasn't a Catholic church close to their farm, and they began going to meetings of the Jehovah's Witnesses. Finally, they joined. I didn't know much about their new religion; but when I began to question some of their beliefs, we'd get into arguments. I could see that it meant a lot to them, and I stopped talking about it. Jehovah's Witnesses use door-to-door solicitations to get converts, and I know that Mom and Pop used my name as a door-opener. Mom, especially, never met a stranger. She would knock on a door and say, "You may have heard my son, Pee Wee King, on the radio"; or "Did you see Pee Wee King on television last night? That's our son." I didn't mind having my name used. They were firm believers until they died.

Their religion became a problem for the family just before Mom's death. He had just been diagnosed as a diabetic and developed a serious infection in one of his legs. The leg began to swell up. His doctor called me from Milwaukee. "Pee Wee," he said, "I want you to come up here. Your dad's very sick. I need to amputate a leg, and he won't let me. He knows that if he wants to live his infected leg has to come off. He's a stubborn man, as you know, and he said there was no way he'd let me take it off. Your mother is right by his side, and she won't give me permission either. So I'm calling you out of desperation. Will you get the family's permission to amputate his leg?" I said, "I'm sorry, doctor, he's a Jehovah's Witness, and they don't believe in amputations and transfusions. I can't go against his wishes and his beliefs. But I will come up and talk to him about it."

So I flew up to the hospital. First, I asked the doctor if there was anything that could be done short of an amputation, and he said, "I can give him some insulin, which might help for a while, but eventually that leg has to come off or he will die." I then talked to Pop, but he wouldn't budge an inch. I talked to Mom. "If Pop dies," I said, "you'll be the one people will blame because you wouldn't give permission. Will you let the doctor operate on him?" She said, "No, son, I don't think so. I can't go against our beliefs." Then she looked over at Pop and turned to me and said, "If the doctor promises not to use a blood transfusion, I'll let him do it later if the insulin doesn't work." So the doctor started giving him insulin. When Pop saw the insulin bag hanging up in front of him, he threw a fit. "Frankie," he said, "what's in that bag? It's blood, isn't it?" I said, "No, Pop, I won't lie to you. It's not blood. It's insulin." He said, "Is that going to make me well?" I said, "For a while, we hope. But it won't last long." He said, "Now Frankie, you listen to me, and I'll tell you what I told the doctor. I came into the world with two legs, and I'll leave with two legs. I don't want my leg cut off, with or without blood."

Pop left this world with both legs. He never had the operation. Soon after he left the hospital, Mom drowned. He lived on for several years, but he kept getting worse, and then he died. I've dreamed about this many times. If the doctor had taken the leg off, it might have prolonged both their lives. Maybe Mom wouldn't have drowned, and they would have lived on a few more years together. I hope in the long run we made the right decision. We'll never know. All I know for sure is that they were devout believers, and we felt we had to let them do what they thought was right with their own lives. Nobody else in the family became Jehovah's Witnesses, just Mom and Pop. It gave a lot of meaning to their lives, and I think they both died happy in their faith. After they were both dead, we sold the farm. In many ways, it is still home to me. I still have relatives living around Abrams. But more important is that it's where my parents lived so long and where they now rest in peace.

A man of my age has been close to death many times, and he begins to feel his own mortality. Not only do I try to take better care of myself—with Lydia's help—but I've even given up some of my bad habits. I used to smoke Old Gold cigarettes, which I kept on the bandstand all the time. I started smoking and growing a mustache at about the same time, which was when I was in my early twenties. I must have thought smoking through a mustache was stylish. My sister Irene said, "Frankie, you look like Bruno Hauptmann, that German guy that kidnapped the Lindbergh baby." I was too busy to smoke very much in the daytime, but the boys and I could easily go through a whole pack in one evening. I smoked about five years, and I quit after Lydia and I got married and she got pregnant. One day she said, "Pee Wee, do you have to smoke?" I said, "No." She said, "Well, it's beginning to bother me, and carrying this baby is making it worse." I said, "Okay, I'll stop." So I took my unfinished pack of Old Golds to the bathroom, flushed them down the toilet, and I've never smoked a cigarette since then.

Of course, during most of my career, if you were in the music business, you couldn't help but smoke, even if you didn't smoke. All the places we played, especially the NCO clubs and dance halls, were filled with smokers. A lot of my band members smoked. I told Redd

Stewart just the other day, "I believe you're about two tones down from what you were when I first met you." Then he had a high pitched voice, but now he sounds like he's down low in a bucket. It was all those cigars he used to smoke that lowered his voice.

The other habit that could have become a problem was drinking. I've always been a social drinker, but fortunately I never got addicted to alcohol. And that's a miracle! When I played military clubs, drinking was almost universal, and during intermission, I was always invited to stop by the tables. They'd ask for my autograph and then want me to join them for a drink. They would have considered it rude if I hadn't had something with them. Until I moved to Tennessee, my drink of choice was Scotch; then I switched to Jack Daniels whiskey. For my money, that's the best. After my stroke I gave up bourbon and switched to vodka, which is smoother and has a better taste. I used to drink too much beer, and I've had to cut that out. I don't drink much of anything now. At parties I've learned the art of nursing one drink all evening. At home Lydia allows me one or two vodkas with lemon and lime before dinner. That's all.

Lydia says I have another bad habit that could affect my health—and that's my chronic tardiness. When I'm away from home, people recognize me on the street or in a store and want to talk and introduce me to a dozen other people. Since there are few things I'd rather do than talk, I arrive home late for dinner.

I've never had any serious injuries, despite the hundreds of thousands of miles I've traveled over my career. I've never had any broken bones. One time I fell and injured my shoulder in Charlotte. I went down to my car in the parking lot of the hotel to get my sunglasses, and I tripped over a chain and hit the pavement. The nurse on duty at the hotel examined my injured left arm and shoulder. She twisted my arm around and around, and I could hear it grinding. She said, "Well, it's not broken because a break doesn't make a noise like that." I said, "Oh my God! Here I am dying in pain and you're twisting my arm and telling me I don't have a broken arm. It certainly feels like it." I was only black and blue for a few days.

When my stroke came, it came like a bolt of lightning; and it seemed that the good Lord was saying, "Pee Wee, I love you but I'm not ready to take you home yet. You've still got some life to live. So take it easy. You've worked hard. You've accomplished a lot.

Now relax a little and enjoy yourself from here on in." Do you know the first thing I did after I recovered from the stroke? I formed a little band of five of the best players I know in country music. Music was in my blood, and I couldn't do anything about it.

Once you're in the music business, you can never get out of it. Of course, I'm not as active as I used to be, and I don't practice every day. It's not easy for me to play the accordion now. My fingers are not as nimble any more; and by the time they remember how to play, the song is over. But I stay fit enough to do a couple of numbers when I need to.

Since I turned seventy-five, however, I have played in dozens of special shows, including the Country Music Hall of Fame package show, "living legends" shows, Opry anniversary shows, and the annual reunion of the Hall of Fame members. A few years ago we did a television show called "The Silver Anniversary of the Country Music Hall of Fame Members." The oldest member present was Jimmie Davis, the former governor of Louisiana, who was ninety-three. But the reunion shows get sadder every year, as the old-timers die off. We started with several dozen older members, and we're now down to a handful. But it's good to be around the new stars and to be recognized for our contributions. Kenny Rogers, who was the emcee, said, "I started out recording other people's songs, but I thought if performers like Pee Wee King could write their own songs, so could I."

Kathy Mattea came to see me in the dressing room and said, "Mr. King, I've been asked to sing 'The Tennessee Waltz,' and I want you to know how proud I am to do it." When she introduced the song, she said, "When I came to Nashville, I got a job as a tour guide at the Country Music Museum. One day a man with a happy smile came up to me and said, 'What's your name, young lady?' When I told him, he said, 'And are you going to be a singer?' I said, 'I am a singer.' He said, 'That's the spirit! But right now you've got an important job showing people the history of country music. Let me know if you ever need any help.' I didn't know who he was then, and he didn't tell me his name. I found that out later, and now I want to thank him for being kind to me and for the song I'm about to sing, 'The Tennessee Waltz.' I want to dedicate this song to him and his wife Lydia, who are in the audience." I was so honored to be recognized that way by one of the finest of the younger Opry stars.

There were other stars of the new generation there. Mel Tillis's daughter Pam sang the song that Patsy Cline made famous, "Walkin' After Midnight," and showed herself to be her father's daughter. She and Alan Jackson, Clint Black, Randy Travis, and others made me feel confident about the future of country music.

I think now so fondly of the Opry's sixty-fifth anniversary show because it featured a skit with Minnie and Roy. They had a script, and Minnie said her lines without a hitch. But Roy couldn't see his script and ad-libbed his part. The floor manager suddenly stopped the taping to call Roy's attention to the correct words. "Can you read that?" he said. "Hell no," Roy said. "I can't see it. Not only can't I see the script, I can't even see you!"

The package show we take to state fairs, theaters, and other places on the road. Several years ago I was with the show that played the Swiss Valla Amphitheatre in Lampe, Missouri, which is near Branson. The package included Redd Stewart, Little Jimmy Dickens, Jean Shepard, the Collins Sisters, Kitty Wells, with Barefoot Bob Kinney as emcee. I've also played the shows in more than a dozen states. It's fun to get together again with the people I performed with when we were all young. Right after Minnie's stroke, I played one of those shows, and we all felt her absence so much. Sometimes Ralph Emery is our emcee. At a show near Philadelphia I was working with Bill Monroe and Kitty Wells, and Ralph said to me, "Pee Wee, I'm going to tell you the honest truth. You've been a role model for me since I was a boy. You came to my hometown theater with the Golden West Cowboys, and when you stepped on that stage in your white cowboy suit, white cowboy hat, blue boots, and colored satin shirt, I said to my dad, 'Pee Wee King is my kind of star.'" Redd Stewart and I usually did some of our own songs and such popular favorites as "Orange Blossom Special," which we had fun with, imitating the train and whistle on the fiddle and accordion. Our audiences ranged in age from eighteen to eighty, but most were in their fifties and sixties. They were old enough to remember us when we were in our prime.

An old-timer's show I remember very well was at the Rialto Theater in Joliet, Illinois, when Hank Williams's daughter Jett and his old band, the Drifting Cowboys, played with us performers who had known and loved her father. Her mother was a girl that Hank knew but never married. When she comes on stage, she tells the audience right off that she's proud to be Hank's daughter and she's sorry she never got to know her dad. "He must have been a wonderful person," she said, "to write the songs he did. Now I'm going to sing some of his favorites and mine too." Then she sang "Jambalaya," "Lovesick Blues," and "Mansion on the Hill" and closed with "I Saw the Light." By that time the audience was in her hands. After the shows the people lined up to get our autographs and to buy souvenir programs and T-shirts. To these people we were living legends, or so they called us, but we didn't feel like legends at all. We felt alive and grateful to be having such a good time.

Now that I don't go on the road much, I stay close to home most of the time. This is the house we've lived in for more than forty years. It's comfortable and convenient and plenty big for Lydia and me. I've lived in two cities most of my adult life, Louisville and Nashville. I used to think I might like to retire up in Abrams or Green Bay to be closer to the people I come from. But Lydia would have been removed from her family, and, after all, our children are Kentuckians. I realize also that as I've gotten older, it's much better to live down here. I remember how hard the winters were in Wisconsin when I was a boy, how snowbound and iced-in we would be. We had to shovel a path to the barn to milk the cows. Sixteen is the right age for that kind of climate. After you're eighty, you need a different world.

I can be as active as I want to around my house. I do a lot of my own yard work, and Lydia and I have one of the best-kept yards in the neighborhood. She does all the close work in the yard and knows all her shrubs and flowers. I don't know the difference between a lily and a lungadumdum. My mother used to say, "Lydia has a green thumb like me. She can grow anything." And so she does. That's why we always like to be home in the spring when everything begins to bloom, though we love the yard in all seasons.

I still love sports, but since my stroke I can't participate very much. I used to play golf to unwind and relax. I've never been really good, but I was good enough to enjoy the game. I used to play in charity events like the Foster Brooks celebrity tournaments in

Louisville, and Paul Hornung and I were cochairmen of the Pro-Am Golf Tournament one year. When I was a better player, I'd sometimes risk a few dollars on a game. One day Eddy Arnold and I were playing at the Belle Meade Country Club in Nashville, and I won a dime from him. Eddy hates to lose, and he especially hates to lose money. He threw two nickels at me, and they landed at my feet. "Pick 'em up, Pee Wee, damn it," he said, "they're yours."

When I was a boy in Wisconsin I loved to fish and hunt. On the farm near Abrams we could practically sit on the back porch and cast a line out into the river. We would sometimes catch muskie as long as your arm. In Nashville I pitched softball one summer for the National Life and Accident Insurance Company. I was pretty good with my underarm fast pitch, and we won a lot of games. One time I almost got thrown off the team for wearing cowboy slippers. The umpires called a big meeting out on the pitcher's mound, then said to me, "The other team objects to you wearing cowboy boots instead of cleats. They say it gives you the advantage of a two-inch heel and that's where you get your speed." I said, "I don't see that my footwear is anybody's business. I love cowboy shoes, and I wear them all the time. I would wear them to bed if I could. Anyway, these are not cowboy boots. They're cowboy slippers. They come up just below the ankle. The other team doesn't know cowboy shoes any better than they know baseball." I went ahead and wore my cowboy slippers the rest of the summer, and we won the championship.

Since my stroke I've continued to be active in a number of civic, charitable, and professional groups and projects. I've been active in the Country Music Foundation from its beginning and served as its president in 1978. I'm now a life member. The foundation is doing wonderful work. It publishes books, guides, and the *Journal of Country Music* and has charge of the Country Music Hall of Fame and Museum in Nashville. The museum has thousands of items that tell the history of country music, including one of my accordions.

I've always tried to make myself available for charity work. During World War II I played military hospitals and sold war bonds. I've worked in soup kitchens, done a telethon for the Arthritis Foundation and one for the Community Chest, performed in crippled children's hospitals, and done benefits for the homeless. I've played for the WHAS Crusade for Children, and I've served on the board of the

Salvation Army. I've helped raise money for the Cerebral Palsy Fund, and once I even led the Louisville Orchestra for a charity performance. For years I worked with the Fillies Ball during the Kentucky Derby Festival. One year Ed McMahon and I were grand marshals for the St. Patrick's Day Parade in Louisville. Ed is, of course, a real Irishman, but I was an Irishman for a day. (You remember that I'm actually three-fourths Polish and one-fourth Austrian.) In all these civic and charity works, I've simply tried to give back a little of what the public has so generously given me.

How can I add up the good life I've been blessed to live? I had the good fortune to be in the only profession I ever wanted. I was lucky to be rewarded by it beyond measure. I had a father-in-law who was my manager and taught me the business. I never wished I had married anybody but Lydia. I have been rewarded with a loving family. I have had friends beyond compare. What more could any man want?

I came along at the right time for composing and performing the kind of music I like. Music has changed, and my time has passed. If I tried to record my kind of songs today, I couldn't do it. I hope that my music will become a part of America's music history, but my era is over with. Our music has been done, and we did it. It's time to go on to something else.

I've never had to get up every morning and go to the same job at the same time doing the same thing day after day after day. I don't think I could have survived the nine-to-five routine. I remember the kind of life my uncle up in Wisconsin presented to me when he said, "Frankie, you come to my office after school every day and clean up, wipe the pens, and empty the wastebaskets, and I'll pay you five dollars at the end of the week." That wasn't the life I was looking for. I knew even then that I could play a wedding or a dance or a festival and make more money and have more fun and get more satisfaction. I also knew my choice was a calculated risk. I knew I could get a guaranteed five dollars week from Uncle Lawrence if I cleaned his floors and emptied his wastebaskets. It was a risk I gladly took. Despite some ups and downs in my career, it's paid off handsomely. If the Lord had me start over again, I'd do the same. I've never made a lot of money—nothing like the young stars of today. Uncle Dave Macon, Hank Williams, Ernest Tubb, Jimmie Rodgers—

we were the ones that started the country music business and paved the way for the Nashville superstars and multimillionaires of today. I hope we will be remembered as the pioneers of the business. Whose career today will last as long as a Gene Autry's or Roy Acuff's or Eddy Arnold's? I wonder who will last as long as we did.

Entertainment has not only been my livelihood, it's been my life. It's been hard for me to slow down and stop. I've worked hard for my career and my reputation, and I worry that people will forget our music. There are syndicates going around buying up radio stations and playing just the most popular music. I've worried they won't be playing the old songs any more. I'm afraid that after the people are gone who knew Ernest Tubb and Roy Rogers and Eddy Arnold and Minnie Pearl and Redd Stewart and Pee Wee King, we'll all be forgotten too. I pray that history will be kind to us.

I'm now an old man, and I know I won't be around much longer. I've been a practicing Christian most of my life, first as a Catholic and now as a Lutheran. On the road, I couldn't be active in church work. Now I try to be a more faithful church member. I try to listen carefully to the sermons and think about my own personal faith. I have always accepted the virgin birth of Jesus, His death, and His resurrection; but for a long time it was just something I was taught, along with the fact that George Washington was the father of our country.

Now I believe these doctrines deeply in my heart. I believe that Jesus is the way, the truth, and the life. I don't know of any other belief that's any better. I don't see any other place to turn. I believe that after I die, I will continue to exist in some fashion in some kind of hereafter. If there isn't a continuation of some kind, then this life and all that we've done with it isn't worth much. I believe that this life is important. I believe that it's important to be a good carpenter, a good bookkeeper, a good lawyer, a good country musician. It's important that we use the talents that God gave us, whatever they are. It doesn't matter so much what we do, but we must give it our best licks. We must do our best for ourselves, for our families, and we must help other people along the way. I believe that good works are everlasting. I'd also like to believe that I'll see and know my parents again and Lydia's parents and all our special relatives and friends. Of course, there's no way now to know that we will. It's all a matter of faith.

Not only have I been fortunate in my career and personal life, but I've been recognized and honored by people and organizations I respect. That's been icing on the cake. One of the earliest honors I received was to be on *We the People* on January 4, 1948. I've been performing professionally since the early 1930s, but it was not until the 1950s that my career reached its peak. It was at that time that I began to win recognition and awards, including Best Country and Western Artist from *Cashbox* and the Number One Western Band Leader from *Orchestra World* and *Billboard*. In 1951 I was on the cover of *Country Song Roundup*, and in 1954 I was the cover for *Hoedown*. One of my biggest years was 1952. The band was doing well with public appearances. Our records were selling like crazy. We made two Western movies with the Durango Kid. And I got my star on the Hollywood Boulevard Walkway of Stars. My star is right in front of the Merv Griffin Theatre near a big corner drugstore. If you stand on my star, you can see the Capitol Record Company Building. There are more than two thousand people honored with stars, but it's a real distinction to be selected.

In the 1970s and 1980s I began to slow down professionally, but the honors have continued to come. In 1970 Redd Stewart and I were named to the Songwriters Hall of Fame. In 1971 Governor Louie B. Nunn proclaimed October 23 Pee Wee King Day in Kentucky. In 1980 I was inducted into John Hobbs's Music Valley Museum of the Stars, which is right across the street from the entrance to Opryland in Nashville. Mr. Hobbs, who was president of the Music Valley Merchants Association, said to me one day, "We're going to put your likeness in our new museum." I said, "Oh, is that so? How much is it going to cost me?" He said, "Nothing, except for a suit of your clothes. But I am worried that it might give you the big head." Well, it didn't give me a big head, but the artist gave me a torso that is six inches taller than I am. When I saw it, I said, "John, I can't take that. That guy's so big my suit won't fit him. Why, it makes me look taller than Roy Acuff and Eddy Arnold and Johnny Cash and Bill Monroe and most of the other fifty people in the exhibit. When they see this, they'll laugh me out of town." The museum had taken the Nudie suit I gave them and put it on the statue, and it didn't look natural at all. The only way to make the suit fit was to cut the figure off above his ankles and stick the legs in the boots. Now he's only about an inch taller than I am, but at least the suit fits. There's also a Walk of Fame in front of the museum, where they place the hand and foot prints of the honorees in concrete just the way they do in front of the Chinese Theater in Hollywood. Unfortunately, when I inscribed the concrete in my section on October 9, 1984, I misspelled the first word in the title of my most famous song. I spelled it "Tennesee."

In April of 1981 Redd and I were invited to play in the American Music Series at the National Museum of American History of the Smithsonian Institution. We did a regular show with Patsy Montana and the Collins Sisters. I was the emcee. Just before the show, a fight broke out in the nearby cafeteria, and one of the cooks ran out of the kitchen with a knife, chasing a waiter all around the lobby. Finally, someone called the police, and both of them were arrested. When the show started, I said, "Ladies and Gentlemen, there's no charge for the floor show you just saw downstairs. I do hate, however, to follow an act that's already upstaged us before we start. But we'll do our best to entertain you." During the show we performed our best-known songs, such as "The Tennessee Waltz," "Slow Poke," and "You Belong to Me." Patsy did several of her standards. It was a good mixture, and the audience liked it. It was good to be recognized this way in our nation's capital.

I suppose, however, the best kind of recognition comes from your own folks—the people who know you best, your faults and your virtues. In 1981 I was the honored guest at the annual Abrams, Wisconsin, Family Day Celebration. I led a parade and did a concert and then unveiled a plaque honoring me as a hometown boy. I got to see a lot of old friends and relatives and people who used to know my mother and father. Our old home is sold and gone from the family, but the town still feels like home even though I've been away for almost sixty years. It's a warm feeling to be welcomed home.

Of all the professional honors that I have gained, there is one that stands above the others. That was my election to the Country Music Hall of Fame in 1974. It is not easy to get in. I was nominated three times before I made it—in 1971, in 1973, and in 1974. For me, the third time was the charm indeed. The election process guarantees that only people who have made important contributions to country and western music get in. The top twenty-five nominees each year are evaluated by a twelve-member board from the Country Music Association. The board picks five finalists and then votes by secret ballot for the winner. The finalists are notified, but they don't know the winner until the night of the award. The announcement is usually around the first of October and is made from the stage of the Grand Ole Opry. All the nominees used to sit in the front row, but that's been changed since it was so embarrassing to the losers. I heard Minnie Pearl's husband say to her one year after she'd just lost again, "Honey, we're not going to come to this ceremony any more. You've been nominated three times, and we've come here three times, and you've lost three times." Fortunately, they did come back the next year, and she won.

The year I won was also the year Owen Bradley won. I was pleased to be chosen with him because he is one of Nashville's top musical geniuses. As much as anybody, he invented the Nashville sound. He is a band leader, a songwriter, a publisher, a fine musician, an A & R man for Decca Records—and my dear friend. He has meant a lot to the careers of many of Nashville's legendary performers. I was the twenty-third and he was the twenty-fourth member of the Hall of Fame. The year we won we had stiff competition— Kitty Wells, Minnie Pearl, Merle Travis, and the late Vernon Dalhart, who has been called the father of country music. He and Jimmie Rodgers were two of the earliest country singers to make recordings. He was trained as an opera star, but his Texas accent made him a natural to sing such classics as "Wreck of the Old 97," "Mollie Darlin,'" and "Bury Me Not on the Lone Prairie."

My Hall of Fame election couldn't have come at a better time. I was becoming depressed over some health problems. All summer I played rodeos and fairs and had acquired a lingering hoarseness. Then I began to develop cataracts on my eyes. I got so I was afraid to drive, and Lydia or a band member had to do my driving. One night in Fargo, North Dakota, I got so desperate I called my doctor in Louisville and told him to set up a cataract operation for me— but to wait until after the Country Music Awards. So I went to Nashville, and for the third time I expected to be an also-ran. I sat on the front row. My vision was so cloudy I could hardly see the people on the stage.

As Kitty Wells was singing a song, I whispered to Merle Travis sitting next to me, "Well, Kitty is up there for a reason. I think she's won it." Merle said, "No, I think Minnie will win." Then I heard the announcement that Owen Bradley had won, and I thought, "Well, so much for this year. I'll go back to Louisville and have my eye operation." Then I heard Johnny Cash, who was master of ceremonies, say something about Wisconsin, accordion, and "Tennessee Waltz," and I said, "Oh my God, he's talking about me! I've also won!" Suddenly, I got cry-happy as I tried to compose myself walking to the stage, my eyes filling with tears. Johnny saw my condition and said, "Go ahead and cry, Pee Wee." And I bawled like a kid. All I can remember of what I said was, "God, it's been fun." Loretta Lynn sent me the sweetest telegram I received. It read: "Nice guys do finish first."

I truly regretted that I had won over Minnie Pearl, but at the same time I was happy and gratified that at last I was in the Hall of Fame. It was a wonderful occasion, even though Owen suggested that we go on the road as "the Elderly Brothers." The only ugly part of the awards event that year was that a group of disgruntled performers gathered at George Jones's home to complain about the awards given to Olivia Newton-John and Ronnie Millsap. The protesters felt that Olivia and Ronnie weren't true country stars and hadn't paid their dues. Indeed, I was surprised when Olivia won her award, and I'll bet she was too. But "true" country music—whatever that is—has been changing for a long, long time, and she was on the cutting edge of the country and pop crossover. It reminded me that at one time I was considered an outsider to country music.

Nothing could have dampened the excitement and joy I experienced that night. When I entered the Hall of Fame I joined the group of country music immortals, and the thought humbled me. At the same time, it was like a family reunion where I was meeting and greeting people I already knew and loved. Now, when I visit the Country Music Hall of Fame and Museum and read my plaque with its summary of my career, and when I walk through the exhibits and see the whole story of country music unfold, I feel part of a long and continuing tradition of American music that has given joy and hope to millions of people.

Index